THE WORD *IRONY* AND ITS CONTEXT, 1500-1755

THE WORD IRONY

AND ITS CONTEXT, 1500-1755

NORMAN KNOX

DUKE UNIVERSITY PRESS   DURHAM, NORTH CAROLINA   1961

© 1961, DUKE UNIVERSITY PRESS

Library of Congress Catalog Card Number 60-13606

Cambridge University Press, London, N.W. 1, England

Printed in the United States of America
by the Seeman Printery, Durham, N. C.

To HELEN DAVIS KNOX

The publication of this book was
assisted by grants to the author
by the Graduate School of Duke University and the Carnegie Institute
of Technology and by funds from
the grant to Duke University Press
by the Ford Foundation.

PREFACE

In the last century and a half the word *irony* has become one of the most complex, ambiguous, and fascinating terms in the whole arsenal of literary criticism and analysis, to say nothing of its popularity in day-to-day speech. Cosmic irony, the popular irony of Fate, dramatic irony, Socratic and Romantic irony, the ironies of tension and paradox promulgated by the New Critics—we have only to try cataloging these and the rest to realize how complex are the meanings now available in this protean word; behind the recent notoriety is a long, involved, and sometimes important career which began in the age of Socrates. It is of some interest to have the history of such a word. G. G. Sedgewick wrote the first part of that history in a doctoral thesis presented at Harvard in 1913 when he traced the word from its first appearance in Aristophanes through Classical and medieval Latin; in the present study I attempt to continue his history by following the fortunes of the English word from the early sixteenth through the middle of the eighteenth century.

I have had a second point of view in mind. Since it is not always easy to know what Renaissance and Augustan writers meant when they used such terms as *irony,* a close study of them sharpens our tools for understanding these periods. Consequently I have pursued the uses of *irony* somewhat further than was necessary to a general history of the word and have in addition explored the meanings of *banter* and *raillery,* two other crucial words neither of which has been carefully studied before and both of which were intimately connected with *irony*. I had also hoped to survey two other subjects: English classical criticism of the art of ironic writing; the social and moral attitudes of the Augustans and their forerunners toward that whole range of discourse variously called satire, ridicule, raillery, humor, irony, and banter. In the long history of *irony* moral and social judgments have played an unusually large role, and this was especially true in the English classical period. However, only the first subject plays a part in this book. Although I have collected materials for a study of the second, that will have to wait upon another span of free time.

It may seem to the reader that I have cited evidence and quoted it at inordinate length. I heartily sympathize, but determined on such extensive documentation for several reasons. The materials this study is based on are widely scattered in books and periodicals of all sorts, many to be found only in certain of the great research libraries; however, once found the bits of evidence are usually brief enough to be quoted rather fully. Simply as a convenience to scholars, then, full quotation and citation of sources seemed advisable. Other considerations also demanded extensive quotation. Although the central meanings of *irony* are not hard to substantiate, there is some question as to whether *irony* really did convey certain peripheral meanings during the English classical period. Here the evidence needs to be displayed in all its ambiguity and scantiness. It is helpful, moreover, to see a number of passages illustrating each meaning, for, as we all know, even within defined limits the sense of a word adjusts itself, perceptibly but evasively, to a variety of contexts. I have tried to allow the reader to sample for himself the varieties of context to which each sense of *irony* adjusted itself. And I have frequently supplied a generous portion of context: anyone who has consulted the *New English Dictionary* knows how unsatisfying many of the illustrative quotations there are because of their brevity. Deprived of a covering definition, they would permit various interpretations of the word at issue.

It is in Chapter II that I have assembled the mass of bibliographical evidence on the meaning of *irony* and have attempted to distinguish as precisely as I can among different senses of the word. As in a dictionary, ten basic meanings and a number of subordinate ones are numbered i through x with the subordinate meanings listed i.a.i. and so on. In cross-references I indicate a section of the Dictionary so: "Dict. i.a.i." Under each heading in the Dictionary certain materials follow in invariable order: a general definition and discussion; a list of Classical precedents, if any (arrived at through G. G. Sedgewick's studies, which should be consulted for more comprehensive listings, both Classical and medieval); a list of references to English texts. References to ambiguous passages are followed by a question mark in brackets. The English list is broken at chronological intervals by quotations, sometimes followed by explanatory comments if they seem useful. When the list is taken up again it is preceded by the word "Also."

For the meaning of such a term as *irony* there are of course two types of evidence: the abstract definitions given by the period itself, to be found in rhetorics, dictionaries, and casual explanations; and the actual use of the word in contexts sufficiently concrete to define its immediate meaning. The Dictionary relies heavily on actual use of the word: abstract definitions are notoriously ambiguous and in the average rhetoric and dictionary unthinkingly derivative. For this reason, and also because the stock definitions of the age were themselves a factor which influenced the development of meaning, I have chosen to consider them separately in a note preceding the Dictionary.

Probably very few readers will want to pursue the meaning of *irony* through so detailed and interrupted a discussion as the Dictionary offers; even those who do may be grateful for a summary. This Chapter I supplies, as well as a concentrated history of the word's meaning in Greek and in Classical and medieval Latin, and a discussion of the variety of meanings current in our own day. Chapter I, then, opens the book with a brief view of the whole history of *irony* which for some readers will be enough of that, for others will be a helpful springboard into the Dictionary.

In the first two chapters it becomes evident that for the English classical age the central and dominant referent of *irony* was the rhetorical device of attacking someone or something from behind—or through—a mask of ostensible praise. In Chapter III I have isolated a large number of such ironies, each of which was actually called *irony* by someone writing during the period, and have attempted to analyze the varieties of technique associated with the word. In doing this I have tried not to read back into the eighteenth century our twentieth-century ironies developed in the atmosphere of subjective and individual psychology which began to permeate our world not long after the Augustans passed off the stage; nor have I made any attempt to use the elaborate tools of stylistic analysis which sometimes lead us now to say rather different things about a literary work than the Augustans would have said. What I have tried to do in disentangling the scheme of techniques associated with the word is to work from roughly the same point of view that critics of the English classical age would have taken if one had tackled the job, though none did. My purpose here is twofold: to catalog these techniques; and to fill out the central meaning of *irony* by analyzing the sorts of thing that were most likely to rise to the top of people's brains when the word was presented to them.

However, granting that certain techniques were evident in writing called irony, to what degree did the sense of the word really involve the technique? We should be very cautious in answering this question. For instance, the "grave irony" of Cervantes and Richard Owen Cambridge in presenting their burlesques was often noticed by the Augustans. Both authors made conscious use of what nowadays we would call *dramatic irony*. Are we to conclude, therefore, that our sense of dramatic irony had already attached itself to the word? Chapter IV is a discussion of English classical criticism, both theoretical and practical, of the art of ironic writing and it proceeds after the usual fashion of such essays; then, at the end of the chapter, after reviewing certain developments detailed in Chapters III and IV, I have tried to answer this question about the meaning of the word. In Chapter V the meanings of *raillery* and *banter* are explored and their relationships to *irony* suggested.

Errors of transcription have undoubtedly slipped unnoticed into some quotations and references. I have tried to keep these to a minimum and can only beg the reader's tolerance of whatever errors of this sort have stowed away successfully. The staff of the Duke Press has been most helpful, and I am especially obliged to

Ashbel Brice, William Owens, and John Menapace for their expert handling of a difficult manuscript.

My thanks are due a number of libraries for their courteous
generosity in opening their collections to me and helping me use
them. The chief of these are the Houghton and Widener libraries
at Harvard, the Bodleian at Oxford and the British Museum, the
New York Public Library and the Columbia University Library,
the University of Pennsylvania Library, and the custodians of the
N.E.D. files at the University of Michigan. To Professors James
L. Clifford, E. L. McAdam, and Paull F. Baum I am indebted for
their kind help in getting me started on this study; to Professor
Clifford I am also indebted for the initial impetus towards publication. Generous grants to the author from the Graduate School of
Duke University and from the Carnegie Institute of Technology,
and funds from the grant to the Duke University Press by the Ford
Foundation, have helped to make publication possible. Professor
Benjamin Boyce has, at considerable sacrifice of time and trouble,
read the manuscript at each of its stages and counseled me on its
revision, and Professor George Sherburn has also offered a number
of useful criticisms. That I either began or finished this work, however, is in large measure due to the unfailing aid and encouragement
of Professor W. H. Irving, to whom as teacher and friend, I am
above all deeply grateful.

Bibliographical Note. In the notes to the body of this study I
have given abbreviated references consisting of author's name, short
title, and in parentheses either the date of the edition used if I
used an early edition, or the name of the editor, translator, or
series if I used a modern edition, translation, or reprint. Full data
can be found in the Bibliography.

CONTENTS

THE WORD *IRONY* AND ITS CONTEXT, 1500-1755

ONE

THE MEANING OF *IRONY*: INTRODUCTION AND SUMMARY

i. *The Classical background*[1]

The ultimate force of Greek εἴρων may have been either "saying" or "asking," but when it first appears in Aristophanes and Plato it seems to be "a sort of vulgar expression of reproach"— Billingsgate—meaning "sly, mocking pretence and deception." In both Old (Aristophanes) and New (Philemon) Comedy the fox is the symbol of the ironist. "Sly, smooth deceiver—that is his character." The word is not found in Greek before the Peloponnesian War and is never found in tragedy or the more serious poetry.

The central fact about the history of *irony* in Greek use is its inseparability from Socrates' personality and influence. But it is essential to remember that neither Socrates nor his friends ever used the word in a serious way to describe the Socratic method, and that the idealizations of Socratic dialectic which modern writers have embodied in "Socratic irony" were never attached to the word *irony* in classical Greek and Latin. The dominant sense of εἰρωνεία in Plato as well as Aristophanes was "mocking pretence and deception." Nevertheless, since the modes of deception practiced by Socrates were sarcastic praise and disingenuous self-depreciation, the

---

[1] What follows, including the quoted passages for which no references are given, is taken from G. G. Sedgewick's "Dramatic Irony" (1913). The only available copy of this dissertation is not permitted to leave the Harvard College Library, but Mr. Sedgewick presented the main thread of the story, with the chief references to Classical and medieval texts, in the first of his Alexander Lectures for 1934-35 (*Of Irony*, 1948). Although I have examined in translation many of the major passages to which he refers, I am entirely indebted to Mr. Sedgewick's work for the generalizations here offered.

word was in Plato especially linked with these.   Although there is some possibility that even before its use by Plato εἰρωνεία had emphasized the self-depreciating mode of deception, it was Aristotle in the *Ethics* who hardened this sense into shape by his distinctions between the mean of Truth, the one extreme of Alazony or boastful exaggeration, and the other of Eirony or self-depreciating concealment of one's possessions and powers.   Here for the first time *irony* attains some semblance of dignity, perhaps through its use by Socrates, insofar as Aristotle comments that if a man cannot tell the precise truth, he exhibits better taste in depreciating than in exaggerating his virtues.   But this is faint praise and the dominant connotation of the word remains reproachful.   In Demosthenes and Theophrastus *irony* as deceptive self-depreciation takes another turn. Here it is "a vicious dissimulation of one's political and social powers" for the purpose of escaping responsibility and shirking one's duty.   Theophrastus' character of the Ironist describes a man who "never can be got to *do* anything, or to commit himself in speech so that he is forced to take sides in an active discussion.   This is irony which has become a social vice."

In his *Rhetoric* Aristotle had recommended irony as a rhetorical weapon, although with some distaste, and the word had apparently long been discussed by the rhetoricians before its meaning in this context was defined, for the first time in extant literature, by the *Rhetoric to Alexander*, now credited to Anaximenes of Lampsacus, an historian of the fourth century B.C.   To blame-by-praise and to praise-by-blame—that is the essence of rhetorical irony.   Socrates' way of exalting his opponent while depreciating himself was, as Ariston explained, a mode of it.   By the second century B.C. *irony* had probably passed into common currency both in writing and in speech.   It was no longer a colloquialism or necessarily a term of reproach.   To the concept of irony the late Greeks and the Romans added little.   Although Socrates was constantly in mind as they used the word and although they still felt in it overtones of pretense, mockery, and self-depreciation, all of these were absorbed into the rhetorical strategy of "saying one and gyving to understand the contrarye." This definition was a constant attendant upon later uses of the word.

It was in Cicero that *irony* first attained to a complete and positive dignity; he was flattered to be thought an ironist worthy of Socrates' company.[2] And it was also Cicero who, for the first time in extant literature, distinguished between irony as a mere figure of speech and as a pervasive habit of discourse. The word "discourse" should be emphasized here, for Cicero does not imply a habit of thought or anything approaching a philosophic view, as is clear in a passage often translated during the English Renaissance: "Among the Greeks, history tells us, Socrates was fascinating and witty, a genial conversationalist; he was what the Greeks call εἴρων in every conversation, pretending to need information and professing admiration for the wisdom of his companion."[3] This distinction was made more exact by Quintilian, who, although he names only two categories, the "trope" and the "schema," in effect distinguishes three categories of irony: (1) a brief figure of speech embedded in a straightforward context ("trope"); (2) an entire speech or case presented in language and a tone of voice which conflict with the true situation ("schema"); (3) a man's whole life ("schema"): "a man's whole life may be coloured with *irony*, as was the case with Socrates, who was called an *ironist* because he assumed the rôle of an ignorant man lost in wonder at the wisdom of others."[4] Moreover, irony for Quintilian may act as an indication and expression of that *ethos* "which is commended to our approval by goodness more than aught else and is not merely calm and mild, but in most cases ingratiating and courteous. . . ."[5] Thus Quintilian comes very near to describing irony as "a habit of genuine thought and conversation," though it would be possible to avoid this implication.[6]

[2] The charm which Socratic irony had for Cicero and other Romans is discussed in G. C. Fiske, "Plain Style in the Scipionic Circle" (1919) and Mary A. Grant, *Ancient Theories of the Laughable* (1924).

[3] Cicero *De officiis* I. 30.

[4] Quintilian *Institutio* IX. ii. 44-53.

[5] *Ibid.*, VI. ii. 9-16.

[6] Although I am not at all qualified to speak on the subject, it does seem to me that Mr. Sedgewick pushes Quintilian's conception of irony as an admirable habit of *thought* a little too far.

In the fifteen centuries between Quintilian's death and the first appearance of *irony* in English little that was new happened to the word. The rhetorical definition of it as saying one thing and meaning the contrary—blame-through-praise or vice versa—was passed on from one rhetorician to another: Alexander Numenius (second century), Aquila Romanus (third century), Julius Rufinianus (probably third century), Phoebammon (*ca.* 400), Tiberius Rhetor, Martinanus Capella (fifth century), Zonatus (fifth century), Isidorus (600-636), Bede, Gregorius the Corinthian (*ca.* 1150). These rhetoricians often occupied themselves with distinguishing the minor varieties of rhetorical irony. *Chleuasmus* "is a speech which makes an attack under cover of a smile." *Mykterismus* "is a mocking speech accompanied by a breathing through the nostrils." *Sarcasm* "is to show the teeth." Bede noted seven species of irony out of many. Several of the rhetoricians classified irony under allegory, which can of course be defined abstractly in terms almost identical with those used for irony. Quintilian had so classified it, Cocondrius named two sorts of allegory, irony and enigma, and Bede stated the connection.

The Aristotelian concept of irony as genuinely deceptive self-depreciation did "not often exist in 'a pure state' outside of Aristotle and his school: its presence is usually as vaguely felt in later literature as it was in Greek literature before Aristotle." However, it seems to play a part in certain uses of the word by Cicero, Plutarch, Lucian, Philostratus, Justin Martyr, Themistius (the Byzantine rhetorician of the fourth century), Suidas, and a rhetorician quoted in Bekker's *Anecdota Graeca.* That irony of political and social self-depreciation noted by Demosthenes and Theophrastus apparently disappeared.

The early Greek sense of "cunning deceit," "vulgar, mocking pretence" clung to the word in that it sometimes expressed a greater disapprobation than we feel in it today. Aristotle's praise was half-hearted at best, Themistius thought irony evil, Cicero "knew perfectly well that an εἴρων was generally a person whom one shouldn't know," in Quintilian "irony seemed to carry with it grave and reasonable cause of offence," Plutarch used the word to express disapproval, the general attitude of Dionysius of Halicarnassus toward ironists was hostile, Stobaeus (fifth century) thought irony vulgar, Pollux (*fl.* 180 A.D.) called the ironist a "babbler," and Hesychius of Alexandria (fifth century), Photius, and Suidas expressed similar attitudes. But such disapprobation was not the dominant attitude. "Not late in ancient times men began to look upon irony as we look on it today: as a name and a method that carry no reproach save in being misused."

ii. *The English classical age*

At the beginning of the sixteenth century an educated Englishman could encounter Latin *ironia* in Quintilian and the medieval rhetoricians and lexicographers. The Latin word was, so far as we now know, first translated into English as "yronye" in *Thordynary of Crysten men,* 1502. But throughout the century the Latin or French form of the word was as likely to turn up in an English context as the English form, and although an occasional author ostentatiously aired the word, it is fair to say that it remained esoteric and technical. As the first half of the seventeenth century progressed *irony* became a more readily available English word. In 1615, for instance, appeared a book entitled *Essayes and Characters Ironicall, and Instructive.* But the word, though now available, continued to be a bit of "refined and elegant speech" rather than commonly current. During the Restoration it might have achieved wider currency than it did had not *raillery* been imported from the Continent, for *raillery* became the popular and easy word for referring to the spate of controversial mockery that flowed from the printing presses[7] while *irony* remained relatively technical. It was perhaps Defoe's specific defense of his *Shortest Way with the Dissenters* as "ironic" that began the process which was to bring the word down from its pedestal, for this "irony" of his became a football for the various answerers to his explanation. But it was not until the decade of the 1720's, after the clear-cut ironies of Defoe and Swift and the constant, obtrusive ironies of controversial pam-

[7] See pp. 189-208 below.

phlets and periodicals, that *irony* became common in the literary and general discourse of the day. During this decade Thomas Gordon, the "Essay on Gibing," the *Craftsman,* Orator Henley, the *Dunciad,* and Anthony Collins all paid emphatic attention to irony by name and thus made the word familiar to readers of popular literature.[8]

In view of the relative unimportance of the word *irony* during most of our period, it need not surprise us that there were no major developments comparable to those Sedgewick has traced through Plato, Aristotle, Theophrastus, Demosthenes, and the *Rhetoric to Alexander,* or those which remain to be traced in the nineteenth and twentieth centuries. The contribution of the English classical period was to introduce certain Classical concepts of *irony* into the main stream of English literary culture and to develop these older concepts in small ways. As it happened, the great achievements in the use of irony by English ironists of the Restoration and Augustan periods were precisely in that mode encompassed by the traditional concept of *irony* as a verbal device of blame-through-praise. This fact stimulated the elaboration of that concept but it did not stimulate anyone to extend *irony* into startlingly new realms.

Nor were the developments that did occur primarily the work of "great" authors, as Mr. Sedgewick seems to say they were in the Classical ages or as to some extent they have been in the last 170 years. So far as the English classical period is concerned, developments grew out of the circumstances and spirit of the age, and they were often defined by little men voicing common thoughts. Thus in the history of *irony*'s meaning John Hoskins was more important than Ben Jonson; in criticism of the art of irony Thomas Gordon was more important than John Dryden.[9] This is not to say that no major authors of the period contributed at all to the history of the concept of irony. Gabriel Harvey seems to have had a wide acquaintance with the tradition of ironic writing from Aristophanes to Sir Thomas More and a real admiration for the fine art of the thing.[10] Francis Bacon had some interesting things to say about

---

[8] For a more detailed discussion of the currency of *irony*, see pp. 24-30 below.

[9] See pp. 24-30 below for evidence indicative of the relatively minor rôle played by most of this period's "great" authors in developing the meaning of *irony*.

[10] Dict. I.A, III.B.i, III.B.ii.

the philosophical method and the irony of Plato and his master, Socrates, comments which indicate the limits of the concept of Socratic irony in Bacon's time.[11]   Shaftesbury, inspired by his theories of good taste and good humor and by an abiding esteem for Socrates, may well have been one of the few men during our period to view irony so named with independent originality.[12]   More than any other English author Jonathan Swift elaborated and gave importance to the concept of irony as praise through seeming blame, and he also focused attention on the grave manner which came to be closely associated with *irony*.[13]   Although both Pope and Swift used *irony* primarily to mean blame-by-praise and praise-by-blame, their lively perceptions led them to extend the word to other devices as well, devices not strictly definable as blame-by-praise.[14]   Although Fielding's contributions as a critic of the art of irony were considerable, his use of the word itself was conventional.   It is evident, then, that the history of *irony* during our period was not a dialogue among great authors.

Formal definitions, however, were important during our period because the word was not, until late, in frequent and easy use.   Not being sure of it, people went to the definitions of the rhetorics and dictionaries for instruction.   When these were misapplied, as they easily could be, *irony* found itself being used in strange ways.   Nevertheless, in spite of a considerable loss of interest in rhetoric after the Restoration, these stock definitions were by and large the starting points for thought about *irony* until well into the eighteenth century.   After all, what else was there?   It was only in the early eighteenth century, when ironic writing had become a popular and clear-cut mode, that people were impelled by such writing to pursue the concept of irony somewhat further than its conventional formulations.

There were four of these.   By far the most popular was the formula that *irony* is "saying the contrary of what one means." Derived from Cicero, Quintilian, and the medieval rhetoricians,

[11] Dict. III.B.i, III.B.ii.
[12] Dict. II.B, III.A, III.B.ii.
[13] Dict. III.B.i.
[14] Dict. III.B.ii, IV.B, V.B, VII.

this definition appeared regularly from *Thordynary of Crysten men* to Dr. Johnson. A much less popular formulation, although it turned up occasionally from Miles Coverdale to John Lawson, was that *irony* is "saying something other than one means." Cicero had distinguished this irony as different from the first, because it does not say "the exact reverse of what you mean" but only something "different." Although this distinction was noted in one or two English versions of the formula, it was more often ignored. The third stock definition, less stereotyped in phrasing and more useful than the first two, had been stated by Quintilian as "to censure with counterfeited praise and praise under a pretence of blame." Though not stated as frequently as the first formula, this definition was used by a number of writers from Thomas Wilson to the Earl of Chesterfield. Finally, the English defined the word as meaning any kind of "mocking or scoffing," regardless of the rhetorical structure. Although Cicero and Quintilian had described irony as one type of jest, they had not extended the word's reference in this wholesale way. But the definition seems to have reflected actual usage, as we shall see.[15]

In the rhetorics of the Renaissance especially, three words were closely related to *irony*. *Antiphrasis* was used as a synonym, with no distinguishing difference. *Sarcasm* was also considered to be very near in meaning to *irony*, with the difference that it referred less definitely to a specific rhetorical method. The emphasis of *sarcasm* was felt to be on the "bitterness" of feeling displayed by a verbal attack, and generally speaking, this distinction continued in actual use into the eighteenth century. As we saw above, Quintilian and some of the medieval rhetoricians classified irony as a type of *allegory*. This connection continued in three Renaissance rhetorics—Sherry's, Fraunce's, and Puttenham's. The association was based on the observation that both irony and allegory say something different from what they mean. In the seventeenth century the connection fell into disuse. However in the Augustan age a number of writers—Thomas Gordon, Pope, the *Publick Register*, Allan Ramsay—pointed out the allegorical methods involved in certain treatises that were also ironical, and the irony involved in certain

[15] For a more detailed discussion of stock definitions, see pp. 30-37 below.

allegories. But none of these men identified irony and allegory as variations of the same method, and Ephraim Chambers' *Cyclopaedia* for 1778-88 pointed out the all-important difference: "*allegory* imports a similitude between the thing spoken and intended; *irony* a contrariety between them."[16]

When we turn to actual use of the word *irony* in contexts sufficiently explicit to limit its meaning, we find that the situation was somewhat more complicated than the abstract formulas indicated, and that certain developments, relatively minor in nature, did occur during these 250 years.

Although it was certainly not common or conventional, the sense of deception which had been attached to the word in Aristophanes, Plato, Aristotle, Demosthenes, and Theophrastus and which continued as an overtone in some medieval writers, also cropped up during the English classical period. The instances of such use before 1640 can all be explained as Classical reminiscences of the kind we might expect to find during this period of self-conscious recovery of the Classical heritage. Thus *Thordynary of Crysten men,* which contains the earliest appearance of *irony* as an English word, translates into Christian terms the Aristotelian doctrine of the two extremes which depart from the mean of truth: the lies of boasting, called "jactaunce," and the lies of self-depreciation, called "yronye."[17] Near the end of the century there is in several of Gabriel Harvey's uses of *irony* the distinct sense of genuinely deceptive speech and action, clearly derived from his acquaintance with Classical usage.[18] In his *Christian Morals* Sir Thomas Browne uses *irony* to mean "constant dissimulation," and one suspects that he chose the word to display his erudition, for in his day *dissimulation* was the natural and common word to use here.[19]

The relationship of *irony* and *dissimulation* was actually rather complicated. When Greek *irony* had been adopted into Latin it had not always been transferred as *ironia;* it had frequently, as in Cicero, been called *dissimulatio.* Consequently several Renaissance

---

[16] For a more detailed discussion of words related to *irony* see pp. 35-37, 135n. below.

[17] Dict. I.B.

[18] Dict. I.A.

[19] Dict. I.A.

handbooks, notably Thomas Wilson's *Rhetorique* and Hoby's *Courtier*, discussed the various devices of rhetorical irony under the term *dissimulation*—without any notion of conveying the sense of actual and complete deception. At the same time, since English *irony* did not customarily retain the Classical sense of deception, English translators often preferred other words to translate Greek εἰρωνεία when it was meant to convey this sense, and *dissimulation* was a natural English synonym which they often chose to use. This rather confusing situation cleared up after the early seventeenth century. Thereafter *dissimulation* was rarely used to name the ironic devices of verbal attack but continued to be an available substitute for *irony* as real deception.[20]

The sense of deception in *irony* did not, however, totally disappear with the Renaissance. Two uses of *irony* as at least limited deception, dated 1640 and 1696, can probably be dismissed as obtuse or disingenuous misapplications of a stock definition to suit an argument.[21] But in the Augustan age there was a very real sense of the trickiness involved in much of the controversy and pamphlet warfare of the time. It seemed to some people that the rigor of battle and the rigor of the laws led a few ironists to use less than honest irony; that is, the insincere praise of the ironists was not really meant to be seen through at all, or not, at least, by those who could harm the ironist. Thus *irony* once more attached to itself upon occasion the overtone of actual deception, though this usage was not frequent.[22]

By far the most frequently used meaning of *irony* was, during the English classical period as during the preceding eighteen or nineteen centuries, "censure through counterfeited praise." This meaning was attached to the word upon its first appearance in English, and thereafter, according to my sampling, two out of every three appearances of *irony* utilized it. So dominant was this sense that people sometimes assumed that if a device was referred to as irony it must necessarily be blame-by-praise, although it might in actuality be something else.[23] The stock definitions always linked

[20] Dict. I.
[21] Dict. II.A and II.B.
[22] Dict. I.C and II.B.
[23] Dict. III.B.ii.

blame-by-praise with "praise through counterfeited blame," but this sense was much less frequently invoked in actual use of the word. Only after Swift and his group had made praise-through-blame a pervasive and delightful mode of letter-writing and conversation did this sense gain importance, and it is worth adding that only in this sense did *irony* achieve a positively warm and agreeable connotation.[24]

To blame-by-praise, then, was the central and dominant meaning of *irony*. But it was not the only meaning. No doubt there are a number of ways by which a word can widen its area of reference, but two of them were especially important to the history of *irony*. First of all, the irony of blame-by-praise has a feeling, an atmosphere, which is characteristic. It sometimes happened that people felt this effect and called the device which elicited it *irony*, although analysis shows that the device was not blame-by-praise. Second, we have seen that the most popular definitions of *irony* were not "blame by praise" and "praise by blame" but were more abstract: "saying the contrary" or "saying something different." Such definitions could lead a writer to call a thing *irony* which was not blame-through-praise. These factors came into play especially when the rhetoricians, beginning with Cicero and Quintilian, set out to illustrate and classify various rhetorical devices.

Thus the device sometimes called *praeteritio* or *negatio* was called *irony* in the rhetorics of Quintilian, Abraham Fraunce, John Smith, Hobbes, and Anthony Blackwall. By *negatio* we refuse to say what in fact we are saying: "I will not call him a thief, I will not name all the safes he has cracked." And of course this refusal is the "contrary" of what we mean. Moreover, Quintilian and at least a few writers of the seventeenth and eighteenth centuries used *irony* to refer to certain other logical contraries than this, as when Pope commented on Swift's setting out "to praise the Court, or magnify Mankind." It is only fair to add that a number of the uses of *irony* to name such contrary speech which is not blame-by-praise do have a tenuous connection with blame-by-praise. Pope was attributing to Swift an attitude of approbation rather than one

[24] Dict. III.B.i.

of disapprobation, and *negatio* sometimes refuses to blame. But since not all the instances I have collected can produce even a tenuous relationship to blame-through-praise, it seems reasonable to consider this sense of *irony*, i.e., the employment of contraries other than those of praise and blame in saying the opposite of what one means, an established, though minor, meaning of the word.[25]

Cicero and Quintilian both exercised a good deal of ingenuity in discussing and classifying jests. One of the obvious characteristics of many jests is indirection, which produces surprise; indirection is also an invariable characteristic of the irony of blame-by-praise. It may have been this likeness of effect, this working by implication rather than by direct statement, which led Cicero and Quintilian to connect two types of jest with *irony*. One is the statement of a corollary of one's criticism without statement of the criticism itself. Thus Afer replied to Didius Gallus, who after making great effort to secure an appointment complained on getting it that he had been forced into accepting, "Well, then, do something for your country's sake."[26] The second type is the meaningful reply to a submerged meaning of some remark. For instance, when a witness asserted that the accused had attempted to wound him in the thighs, Gaius Caesar replied, "What else could he have done, when you had a helmet and breastplate?"[27] Like the irony of blame-by-praise, these tactics are indirect attack, but they are not blame-by-praise. Although English rhetoricians did not use general terms with any great consistency in referring to jests, some did classify such indirect verbal attack under *irony*, and there are one or two instances in casual writing during our period of the same extension of meaning.[28]

With the exception of the irony of manner, which we will return to shortly, we have now surveyed the fortunes during the English classical period of the various meanings that first appeared in the Classical use of our word. But the English were not unoriginal during this period, although their first contribution may be

[25] Dict. IV.
[26] Quintilian *Institutio* VI. iii. 68.
[27] *Ibid.*, VI. iii. 89-92.
[28] Dict. VI.

considered somewhat unfortunate.   We have already observed that one of the stock definitions for *irony* throughout the English classical period was "mockery, derision,"[29] and this definition seems to have reflected actual usage.   It is not difficult to understand how, in the Renaissance at least, the name of a particular kind of derision could be used loosely to refer to any kind of derision, especially since *irony* was not a very familiar term and the period had a cavalier attitude toward words.   Perhaps this usage would have died out in the Restoration and Augustan periods had it not been for the tremendous quantity of blame-by-praise irony that was published.   Much of this was very complicated stuff and no one could be blamed for not trying to distinguish in every case between blame-by-praise derision and other kinds, especially since blame-by-praise probably was the dominant mode.   Consequently one occasionally encounters in the early eighteenth century as well as in the sixteenth and seventeenth the general use of *irony* to mean simply derision, mockery, ridicule of any sort.[30]

The second innovation made by the English was to use *irony* for the sort of understatement we are familiar with in Anglo-Saxon literature.   In the rhetorics of the English classical period such understatement was discussed regularly under the names *litotes* and *meiosis*.   However, at the end of the sixteenth century John Hoskins, apparently for the first time, called it *irony*, and in this development we see once more the feeling of the thing together with the ambiguity of stock definitions leading to an extension of meaning.   Just as all blame-by-praise irony works by indirection and implication, so too can understatement work by "*Intimation*" and "dissembling," as Hoskins comments.   It says something different from what it means and leaves the intended meaning "to our understanding."   Moreover, understatement often has somewhat the effect of blame-by-praise or praise-by-blame.   Thus, to say of a man that he is "no notorious malefactor," meaning he is just short of being that, has the surface effect of defending him.   Or to say of an Atlas "Milo had but a slender strength" has the surface effect of minimizing his strength when in actuality we go on to praise it.

[29] See p. 34 below.
[30] Dict. IX.

Some such factors as these led Hoskins on to illustrate under *irony* the kind of understatement which in fact uses a method quite different from blame-by-praise, for to say "Titormus had a reasonable good arm" when we mean that he had a remarkably strong one is not to blame him but to understate his capacity. Thomas Blount and John Smith, as we know, copied from Hoskins, and thereafter understatement seems to have been an available meaning of *irony*, as it is today.[31]

The chief contributions of the early eighteenth century seem to have grown out of the nature of its satiric literature. We have already noted that a great deal of this satire was blame-by-praise irony, much of it employing very complicated techniques. We have only to think of the *Tale of a Tub*, the *History of John Bull*, the Scriblerus papers, *Gulliver's Travels*, and *Jonathan Wild* to realize how prominent was the technique of using a fictional structure of some sort to elaborate, or to serve as the vehicle of, an irony. Such fictions were not meant to be taken seriously even as fiction, and readers of the Augustan age became quite sophisticated about such things. They were exceedingly conscious that almost any pamphlet or periodical they happened to pick up might proceed very gravely to pull their leg, usually with the intention of satirizing someone or something and often by means of a simulated approbation of it. Considering the vague and cavalier way in which such terms as *irony*, *ridicule*, *raillery*, and *banter* were popularly used under the impact of such literature, we need not be surprised that the Augustans sometimes extended *irony* to mean any kind of discourse not meant to be taken seriously, or any gravely elaborated fiction the purpose of which was to mystify or satirize—whether through blame-by-praise or some more direct method.[32]

iii. *Groundwork for the modern ironies*

But what of those ironies which have become catchwords in the last 170 years? During the English classical period did no one

---

[31] Dict. v.
[32] Dict. VII and VIII.

use *irony* to mean the irony of Fate? dramatic irony? the irony of philosophic detachment? Before we can settle this point it is crucial to arrive at working definitions of these modern ironies. David Worcester's dissection of contemporary meanings is a good starting point. He arrives at a definition of the *irony of manner* through analysis of the individual manners exhibited by the *eiron* of Greek comedy, Socrates, Chaucer, *ingénu* satire of the eighteenth century, and of the twentieth.[33] The *eiron* of Greek comedy "is the close-mouthed Yankee who has no objection to being thought a fool. He will even encourage his detractors by speaking in a thick dialect, tugging his forelock obsequiously, or otherwise depreciating himself."[34]

The whole personality of Socrates is a complex and sophisticated analogy to this rather simple character-type of comedy. In argument and philosophical inquiry that personality expresses itself by feigning ignorance and asking disingenuous questions under a mask of sympathetic approval. "As in jiujitsu, the expert presses gently and the victim ties himself into knots."[35] But more than this, Socrates was able to encompass the most diverse contradictions without faltering. He could take both philosophers and street-corner loafers seriously; he was at home in aristocratic society or in the marketplace. He hid mystical ideas beneath ugliness and buffoonery; he claimed to be the most ignorant and was declared by the oracle to be the wisest man in Greece. He could treat the most serious and the most comic matters in the same breath.

Chaucer exploited the manner in his own way. In his poems he appears "bashful and a little weak in the head" and is "all anxiety to please,"[36] with ready sympathy for another man's point of view. Literary powers he makes no claim at all to—he is merely the stenographer, the translator, the harmless drudge. Too, he is a somewhat lonely figure in the band of pilgrims, "in the company but not quite of it, observant of every nuance despite his downcast eyes . . . he preserves his own detachment instead of wooing the

[33] David Worcester, *Art of Satire* (1940), pp. 90-108.
[34] *Ibid.*, p. 92.
[35] *Ibid.*, p. 94.
[36] *Ibid.*, p. 95.

regard of anyone." This, says Worcester, "is the very bearing of the ironical observer";[37] Chaucer's "ironical manner ... diffuses an air of genial skepticism and penetrating humor through his major writings."[38]

In the *voyages imaginaires* of the eighteenth century the irony of manner received a new incarnation in the "simple soul" who relates his adventures, "a plain, matter-of-fact sort of man, a close observer of detail, but no critic of higher principles and no philosopher."[39] The twentieth century has given the manner a further twist:

> Theodore Gumbril in *Antic Hay*, Walter Bidlake in *Point Counter Point*, by Aldous Huxley; Paul Pennyfeather in *Decline and Fall*, Adam Fenwick-Symes in *Vile Bodies*, by Evelyn Waugh—all follow a common pattern. They are gray, subdued observers in a world of startling events and startling people. . . . Through their wondering eyes we have a kaleidoscopic vision of a violent, chaotic, and purposeless civilization.

> There is something new and striking in this development of the *ingénu* theme. Older writers used irony as a means of lending force to their creative beliefs. The Socratic irony takes wing into the Platonic myth. Swift's writings constitute an inverted evangel of reason. Behind Voltaire's icy grin is the burning resolve, *"Ecrasez l'infame!"* But the irony of the modern hero serves no ulterior purpose and reveals no creative thought. It is irony for its own sake; a manner worn as a protective garment by a dissociated and neurotic personality.

> . . . this sort of irony turned back on itself is the natural vehicle for the writer who wishes to jar our civilization into the realization of its own frustration and spiritual chaos.[40]

Our guide now turns to *dramatic irony* and the *irony of Fate*. Relying on their "knowledge of life," their assumption that in a particular situation certain facts and principles are dependable guides, men proceed to act on them in the expectation that foreseeable and desirable results will follow. Regrettably, what follows is often exactly the consequence they did not foresee and least desire. They can perhaps then look back to see that certain facts would have forewarned them if they had not been blind, oblivious of the preg-

---

[37] *Ibid.*, p. 98.
[38] *Ibid.*, p. 101.
[39] *Ibid.*, p. 103.
[40] *Ibid.*, pp. 106-8.

nant omens. Now, their eyes open, they see that they were deceived—by Fate? Just as a conceited fop may after being deceived by ironical encomiums on his beauty see through the disingenuous praise, just as an innocent reader may after being deceived by Socrates' self-depreciation and mock sympathy penetrate his real intention, so in everyday life a man may feel that some omniscient Fate has been cleverly misleading him toward an unexpected event. He calls this "the irony of Fate."

When the irony of Fate occurs in a piece of literary art two other factors are usually part of it. First, the omens of the final event can be controlled by the author. He may, if he likes, use soothsayers, prodigies, and portents; he may use the equivocations of oracles; he may use double-edged language of any sort. Although the characters in the play are blind to any underlying significance in these omens, the audience understands it—as the characters too will eventually understand it. Thus, just as in the *Modest Proposal* we follow Swift's real meaning as he says one thing and means another, so we follow the omens of a play which mean one thing to the characters caught up in it and mean another to us, the audience. Here we have *dramatic irony*, also sometimes called *tragic* and *Sophoclean irony*.

In dramatic irony, the ringmaster disappears. There is no signpost, not even a misleading one, to inform the spectators that irony is present. All the work of detection and interpretation is left to them. There is no obligation to explore beneath the surface level of the narrative. As a result, everyone who does so is translated into a ringmaster on his own account. To detect for oneself the freakish operations of chance in human life, the opportunities missed by a hair, the warnings ignored, the prayers that, granted, bring destruction, is to be the omniscient author, to look down from a great height, and to feel a complete detachment from human affairs.[41]

Such detachment is what produces the highly complex irony of, for instance, Aldous Huxley as he juxtaposes human passion and biological determinism, the emotional content of music and the mechanics of sound, sentimentalism and behaviorism, rationality and irrationality.

[41] *Ibid.*, pp. 119-20.

Romantic irony, says Mr. Worcester, is simply a vague historical term which can be reduced to the two meanings already distinguished:

What Schlegel admired was dramatic irony, in which the author suppresses his own personality and arranges his materials in such a way that every spectator is his own ironic observer. Although the author is inscrutable, he is revealed in the choice and juxtaposition of materials. What Tieck practised was irony of manner, bolstered up by the traditional tricks of burlesque. . . . Tieck's fictitious personality, constantly intruding in his work, is reminiscent of Sterne, Cervantes, Fielding, and Byron, though less finished than any of these.[42]

Mr. Worcester, then, would like to reduce the terms for modern concepts of irony to two, or possibly three: *irony of manner; dramatic irony;* and the *irony of Fate* where *dramatic irony* is inappropriate. It is only fair to warn the reader that Mr. Sedgewick breaks down this complex of ideas in a somewhat different way and uses different names. Thus he limits *Socratic irony* to Socrates' dialectical method.[43] Isolating that element of detached observation which plays a part in Worcester's *irony of manner* and *dramatic irony,* Sedgewick calls it the *irony of detachment* or spiritual freedom. "By this we mean the attitude of mind held by a philosophic observer when he abstracts himself from the contradictions of life and views them all impartially, himself perhaps included in the ironic vision."[44] Romantic irony, Mr. Sedgewick goes on to say, is a form of this irony of detachment.[45] *Dramatic irony* he defines in much the same way as does Worcester, except that he does not include under it the concept of spiritual detachment. There is no disagreement over the *irony of Fate.* For further observations on the meanings of *irony* as they have developed over the past 170 years the reader may turn to A. R. Thompson, J. A. K. Thomson, F. McD. C. Turner, and the commentators listed by Haakon Chevalier.[46]

---

[42] *Ibid.,* pp. 125-26.
[43] G. G. Sedgewick, *Of Irony* (1948), pp. 12-13.
[44] *Ibid.,* p. 13.
[45] *Ibid.,* pp. 14-18.
[46] A. R. Thompson, *The Dry Mock* (1948); J. A. K. Thomson, *Irony* (1927); F. McD. C. Turner, *Irony in English Literature* (1926); H. M. Chevalier, *The Ironic Temper* (1932).

"I am confident," says Mr. Sedgewick, "that Socratic irony contains the germs of all the newer ironies which have so afflicted the literature of the last century."[47]   It is certainly true that modern minds have found at least four distinct ironies in the life of Socrates. There was first of all his repeated use of the limited figure of speech which we have called blame-by-praise and praise-by-blame.   There was, second, Socrates' elaboration of this figure into his dialectical method, a novel and fruitful technique for puncturing sham and pursuing truth.   It is this dialectical method which Mr. Sedgewick means by Socratic irony.   Third, there was Socrates' whole way of life, his deepening of self-depreciation and mocking sympathy into a pervasive manner of action toward people and ideas and events. This Mr. Worcester calls the irony of manner.   And finally, there was Socrates' genius at encompassing the most diverse elements in harmonious thought.   In this Mr. Worcester finds what Sedgewick calls the irony of detachment.

So far as I have been able to discover, no one during the English classical period used the word *irony* to refer to a dialectical method, either Socrates' or anyone else's,[48] and no one found in Socrates the irony of detachment.   It is, I think, fair to say that most people during this period thought of Socrates' irony as simply a famous example of mixing blame-by-praise and praise-by-blame in an extraordinarily effective figure of speech.   We have already noted that Ariston and Cicero and Quintilian had so described it, so that from the beginning of the English classical period people would have been familiar with the idea.[49]

But we observed above, in our survey of Classical notions of irony, that Cicero and especially Quintilian had also distinguished between *irony* as a figure of speech and *irony* as a pervasive manner, a manner which in the life of Socrates permeated all his actions and words.   Quintilian's observations were of course available to English thought from the beginning of our period, and it is certainly true that the English were aware not only that Socrates used irony as a figure of speech but also that he used this figure con-

[47] G. G. Sedgewick, *Of Irony* (1948), p. 13.
[48] Dict. III.B.ii n. 5.
[49] Dict. III.B.i and III.B.ii.

stantly. But there is a difference between the repeated use of a verbal device and the extension of the principle of that device through the creation of a whole personality, and in English classical references to Socrates' constant use of irony it is usually impossible to discern whether the irony of manner is implied or not: certain references and translations during the Renaissance and later *may* imply it. In Shaftesbury, however, I think we do find the word *irony* used to name a manner, inspired by Socrates, that is very near our own conception. So far, then, Sedgewick is right; whatever notion of our irony of manner there was in the English classical period stemmed from Socrates. There is, however, the startling exception of Fulke Greville, who used "*Ironia*" to name the irony of manner which an author may assume throughout the whole of one of his works. Greville's use of *irony* does not seem to be directly inspired by Socrates, although it is reminiscent of the Classical notions of self-depreciation.[50]

The case of dramatic irony is even more ambiguous. In Thomas Nashe I have unearthed two contexts and in Robert Burton one context in which *irony* appears, seemingly, to mean dramatic irony as Worcester defines it. Whether this meaning was consciously intended or was accidental, whether as Nashe and Burton were playing with words in their exuberant Renaissance way the word *irony* accidentally exploded, I have no way of determining.[51] What does seem clear is that people did not notice the explosions, for I have found no later uses of *irony* which invoke this sense of the word in a clear-cut fashion. On the other hand, certain mid-eighteenth-century developments in the methods and criticism of blame-by-praise irony do seem to indicate how a sense of dramatic irony evolved. These developments are discussed in Chapters IV and V below, where we find that in the second quarter of the eighteenth century *irony* began to be used rather frequently to name the ironic approval of an author in presenting fictitious characters and situations, characters and situations which an audience discovers to be ridiculous through interpretation of the dramatic situation it-

[50] Dict. III.A.
[51] Dict. X.

self rather than through ironic comments made by the author in his own person.   Although I do not myself think that mid-century writers used the word *irony* to mean any more than the ironic approval of the authors of such fictions, it is not hard to see how frequent association of the word with such dramatic constructs might lead to the extension of meaning we are looking for.[52]

[52] See pp. 185-86 below.

TWO

THE MEANING OF *IRONY*:
THE DICTIONARY

i. *The currency of* irony *during the English classical period*

By the mid-eighteenth century *irony* as an English word had passed through three stages. (1) During the sixteenth century the term was seldom used except in technical works and by an occasional author airing his erudition. The English classical rhetorics and dictionaries sometimes specify the French *ironie* as mediator in bringing the Latin *ironia* into English[1]—as does Skeat[2]—but in the linguistic travail of sixteenth-century England it was often doubtful that *irony* was naturalized; the Latin or another form was as likely to turn up in an English context as the English. (2) In the seventeenth century the English form was customary and capable of natural use in an erudite context, but it was by no means a part of popular speech or even of general literary discourse. (3) In the first decades of the eighteenth century *irony* began to appear, though not widely, in general literary discourse; then between 1720 and 1730 it settled into literary discussion and general speech as one of the conventional terms of literary reference. The reason for this final development is evident. The clear-cut ironies of Defoe and later of Swift and the constant, obtrusive ironies in controversial pamphlets and periodicals were matters of daily talk from

[1] John Smith, *Rhetorique* (1657), p. 45; "IRONICAL, *Ironique*, F. of *Ironicus*, L. of 'Ειρωνιυὸς, *Gr.*"—Bailey, *Universal Etymological English Dictionary* (1724); "IRONY (of *ironia*, L. of ειρωυ, G. a dissembler)"—Benjamin Martin, *Lingua Britannica Reformata* (1749); "IRONY. *n.s. ironie,* Fr. ἱερωνεία"—Johnson, *Dictionary* (1755-56); "IRONY *ironie,* F. of *ironia,* L. of εἱρωνεία, Gr."—Bailey, *Universal Etymological English Dictionary* (1766).

[2] W. W. Skeat, *Concise Etymological Dictionary* (1882).

the City through Covent Garden, St. James's, Westminster and out to Twickenham; the word had to be taken off its pedestal to deal with this pervasive thing.

But at the beginning of the sixteenth century only the best educated were acquainted with it. J. A. K. Thomson remarks that "the word was hardly in use in Latin, and in English not in use at all."[3] It was, however, available in the medieval rhetoricians and lexicographers,[4] and in Quintilian, whose influence dominated educational circles.[5] The English form "yronye" appeared, so far as we know at present, for the first time in *Thordynary of Crysten men*, 1502.[6] In Whytinton's 1534 translation of Cicero's *De officiis* I.30, Socrates was "a symuler whom the grekes call *irona.*"[7] In Wylkinson's 1547 translation of Aristotle's *Ethics* the word is not used at all: in II. vii the opposite of the boaster is "called humble";[8] in IV. iii the ironical self-depreciation which the magnanimous man may use in speaking to common people becomes simply "thynges of mirthe";[9] and in IV. vii. 1-17 the opposite of the boaster "dispraiseth himself": "the humble mã dispraiseth himself to fly strife & busines as did *Socrates* to have quiete life."[10] Wylkinson evidently does not understand Aristotle's notion of the ironical man nor does the English word occur to him as an equivalent. In 1548 John Hooper categorizes one of Moses' remarks as "*ironice*"[11] and in his 1553 translation of *De officiis* I.30, Grimalde uses the Greek word but not the English equivalent.[12] Huloet's *Dictionarie* of 1572 does not list *irony*.[13] Not once in his translation of Plutarch does Thomas North see fit to use *irony* in a context in which

[3] J. A. K. Thomson, "Erasmus in England" (1930-31), pp. 73-74.
[4] G. G. Sedgewick, "Dramatic Irony" (1913), pp. 172-89, 192-94.
[5] J. W. H. Atkins, *Renascence Criticism* (1947), p. 40.
[6] *Thordynary of Crysten men* (1506), Part IV, sec. xxii.
[7] Roberte Whytinton, *Tullyes Offyces* (1534), sig. G1r.
[8] John Wylkinson, *Ethiques of Aristotle* (1547), sig. C2rsv.
[9] *Ibid.*, sig. E2v-E3r.
[10] *Ibid.*, sig. E5v-E6v.
[11] John Hooper, *Early Writings* (Parker Soc.), p. 420.
[12] Nicolas Grimalde, *Ciceroes duties* (1558), fol. 47v.
[13] Richard Huloet, *Dictionarie* (1572). Cooper's Latin-English dictionary lists *Ironia*, illustrating it with five allusions to Cicero and one to Terence. Thomas Cooper, *Thesaurus* (1578).

Plutarch had used the Greek word.[14]   Baret's *Alvearie* of 1580 translates Cicero's *ironia* with "mocking, or dissimuling" but not with
irony.[15]   In the English rhetorics of the second half of the century
this figure of speech was usually listed as *ironia*.[16]   "Ironicè" appears
again in Danett's *Comines*, 1596.[17]   Perceval's *Dictionarie* neither
in 1599 nor in 1623 gives *irony* in the English-Spanish section,
although *ironia* appears in the Spanish-English section.[18]

This negative evidence illustrates the degree to which in the
sixteenth century *ironia* was not yet at home in the English language, but the English word was used at times, though almost
always with some tentativeness or ostentation.   This is not entirely
gone in Jonson's *Cynthia's Revels* (1601):

> "... the whole Court shall take it selfe abusde
> By our *ironicall* confederacie."[19]

In 1615, however, John Stephens felt safe in calling the second
edition of his book *Essayes and Characters Ironicall, and Instructive*,[20] and Brinsley's 1616 translation of *De officiis* I. 30 makes an
indicative advance over earlier versions: Socrates was "an Eironist
in al his speech, whom the Grecians named εἰρῶνα...."[21]   The
status of our word at this time is nicely settled by Henry Cockeram.
His *The English Dictionarie: or, An Interpreter of hard English
Words...*, 1623, includes both "*Ironically*" and "*Ironie*."[22]   In the
1626 edition he explains the two parts of the lexicon:

The first book hath the choisest words themselves now in use, where-
with our Language is inriched & become so copious, to which words the
common sense is annexed.   The second Booke contains the vulgar words,
which whensoever any desirous of a more curious explanation by a more
refined and elegant speech shall look into, he shall there receive the
exact & ample word to express the same....[23]

---

[14] North, *Plutarch* (1595), pp. 197, 290, 461, 559-60, 688, 849, 948, 1019.
[15] John Baret, *Alvearie* (1580).
[16] Warren Taylor, *Tudor Rhetoric* (1937), pp. 35-36.   It is of course true
that most of the figures were given their Latin names in the rhetorics of this time.
[17] Thomas Danett, *Comines* (Whibley), p. 200.
[18] Richard Perceval, *Dictionarie* (1599) and (1623).
[19] Jonson, *Works* (Herford-Simpson), IV, 130-32.
[20] John Stephens, *Essayes and Characters Ironicall* (1615), title page.
[21] John Brinsley, *Tullies Offices* (1631), p. 221.
[22] Henry Cockeram, *English Dictionarie* (Tinker).
[23] *Ibid.* (1626), "A Premonition from the Author to the Reader."   Robert

"Ironie" and *"Ironically"* are honored with a place in the first book, and in the second, *"Ironically"* is offered as the elegant equivalent of *"Mockingly."* There is no change in the 1639 edition.[24] Neither Francis Hickes in translating Lucian's *True History* II. 17[25] nor Thomas Heywood in translating Lucian's *Dialogues of the Dead* XX. 5[26] chose to use *irony* where Lucian had used the Greek word, but in translating Lucian's *Literary Prometheus* I[27] Jasper Mayne did. John Bulwer's *Chirologia* (1644) and *Pathomyotomia* (1649),[28] two rather pretentious discourses on the gestures which should accompany effective speech, use "ironie" and "ironicall" to describe the various gestures of this type. John Smith's *Rhetorique* of 1657 uses both *ironia* and *irony*, but the English form appears far more often.[29] In his 1680 edition of *De officiis* L'Estrange translates I. 30 not with *irony* but with *"Innocent Raillery,"*[30] an example of how *raillery* became at this time the popular word while *irony* remained esoteric. The same preference for *raillery* is evident throughout Ferrand Spence's translation of Lucian (1684-85)[31] but in the *Fisher* 22, the *True History* II. 17, and *Demonax* 6 Spence does use *irony* where Lucian had.[32] Dryden's Lucian also uses *irony* in *Fisher* 22 and *Demonax* 6,[33] and Dryden's Plutarch uses "Ironical" in *Pompey* 30[34] as the English equivalent for the Greek word. A convincing indication of how limited was the use of our word in this period is that in all his critical efforts of various kinds—essays, discourses, lives, prologues

---

Cawdry's *A Table Alphabeticall, conteyning and teaching the true writing, and understanding of hard usuall English wordes, borrowed from the Hebrew, Greeke, Latine, or French. etc. With the interpretation thereof by plaine English words....* 1604, had included "*ironie*, (g) a mocking speech."

[24] *Ibid.* (1639).

[25] Francis Hickes, *Lucian* (1634), p. 135.

[26] Thomas Heywood, *Lucian* (1637), p. 137.

[27] Jasper Mayne, *Lucian* (1663), p. 1.

[28] John Bulwer, *Chirologia and Chironomia* (1644), frontispiece, pp. 79-80, 95, 170, 177-78, 181-83, 183, 189. *Pathomyotomia* (1649), pp. 64-65.

[29] John Smith, *Rhetorique* (1657), pp. 45-48, 74-76, 77, 77-79, 79-80, 165, 203-4.

[30] Roger L'Estrange, *Tully's Offices* (1681), p. 53.

[31] Ferrand Spence, *Lucian* (1684-85), I, sig. A7ᵛ, C3ᵛ, D8ʳ, p. 7; III, 44.

[32] *Ibid.*, II, 31-32, 208; III, 44.

[33] Dryden, *Lucian* (1710-11), III, 358; IV, 130.

[34] Dryden, *Plutarch* (1683-86), IV, 140.

and epilogues—Dryden uses it only once, in his Life of Lucian; and in the collection of John Dennis' critical essays made by E. N. Hooker, it appears in a likely context only once.

The route by which *irony* entered general use is evident in *The Fox with his Fire-brand Unkennell'd and Insnared: Or, a Short Answer to Mr. Daniel Foe's Shortest Way with the Dissenters. As also to his Brief Explanation of the same* (London: 1703). Defoe had explained that the *Shortest Way* was an irony, and the author of this pamphlet replies:

> To be short and brief with him: It is granted him that he is a very *Ironical* Gentleman all over: That he has a very *Ironical* Name, but is still more Knave than Fool: That he has a very *Ironical* Style, but what abounds with more Malice than Wit: But that he is free from any *seditious Design*, is such an *Irony*, that it must move Laughter more than Attention or Belief, and make a Jest of himself and the Government together; at this rate of *Explanation*, Mrs. *Cellier's Meal-Tub*, *Fitz Harris's Libel, Robert Young's Flower-Pot-Association*, and *Fuller's Shams* upon the Parliament, and some of our best Ministers of State, were all *Ironies* too....[35]

The pamphlet continues in this vein, belaboring Defoe's defense of irony from all sides at once. It is probably accurate to say, however, that not until the decade 1720-30 did *irony* finally become a word one was likely to meet periodically, if not frequently, in the polite—and impolite—conversation and general literature of the day. Early in the decade Thomas Gordon wrote his essay "Of Libels," in which he specifies at length the rules to be followed by "all *Ironical Defamers*."[36] *The Art of Railing*, 1723, offers a nearly verbatim reprint of Gordon's essay,[37] and the hostile "Essay on Gibing" refers knowingly to the *irony* of Socrates and of the Bible.[38] During the years 1727-30 the *Craftsman*[39] carried on a

---

[35] *The Fox with his Fire-brand Unkennell'd* (1703), pp. 3-4.

[36] *Humourist* II (1725), pp. 96-105.

[37] This pamphlet of 27 pages consists of a history of railing (pp. 1-11), Gordon's essay presented without acknowledgment and with the change of only a few words (pp. 11-18), and a sample of political railing (pp. 19-27). It is possible that Gordon wrote the whole pamphlet, lifting material from himself. It was summarized in the *Free Briton* for July 22, 1731, and excerpts from this summary appeared in the *Gentleman's Magazine*, I (1731), 296-97.

[38] "An Essay on Gibing" (1727), pp. 5-10.

[39] *Craftsman* (1731), I, 102-4, 106 (No. 18, Feb. 7, 1727); II, 172-74 (No.

running attack against the injustice of the government's "interpreting" perfectly innocent statements as libelous ironies and in-
nuendoes. The *Craftsman*'s attack is sometimes straightforward but
more often tongue-in-cheek, and the word *irony* appears regularly.
The essay for February 7, 1727, explains just what irony is and how
it operates. In 1729 Orator Henley defended irony by name, along
with other ways of jesting, in *An Oration on Grave Conundrums,
and Serious Buffoons. . . ,*[40] and half a dozen of the notes added to
the 1729 edition of the *Dunciad* comment on the author's *irony.*[41]
In the same year appeared the longest and most elaborate defense
of irony made during this period, Anthony Collins' *A Discourse
concerning Ridicule and Irony in Writing.*[42] This 77-page controversial pamphlet is entirely derivative in thought, consisting largely
of multitudinous displays of irony and ridicule used by people of
reputation from Socrates and Christ to Shaftesbury and Swift, but
its wide-ranging and exhaustive use of examples, the representative
nature of its arguments, and the emphasis of its orientation make
it a milestone in the history of general concern over irony. The
word itself appears on nearly every page. The year 1729, then,
looks like a turning point. From the beginning of the *Gentleman's
Magazine* the word appears in its pages.[43] The Preface to *Select
Letters taken from Fog's Weekly Journal*, 1732, remarks: "It
will be observ'd that many of them are written in an ironical and
ludicrous Style. . . ." The *Prompter* for March 23, 1736 (No. 144)
complains that the *Grub-street Journal* had not maintained throughout its career the "ironical Transversion of Censure" with which
it had started, and the *Grub-street* for April 14, 1737, answered
this criticism with a short dissertation on the merits and short-
comings of irony. In the March 26, 1748 (No. 17) issue of the
Jacobite's Journal Fielding makes a similar explanation of why he
has stopped using a strictly ironic method of writing the paper.

68, Oct. 21, 1727); V, 210 ff. (No. 179, Dec. 6, 1729), 232-34 (No. 182, Dec. 27,
1729); VII, 94-95 (No. 226, Oct. 31, 1730).

[40] John Henley, *Oration on Grave Conundrums* (1729), pp. 1-4.

[41] Pope, *Dunciad* (Sutherland), pp. 62-63, 119, 186-91, 201-6.

[42] Anthony Collins, *Discourse concerning Ridicule and Irony* (1729).

[43] *Gentleman's Magazine*, I (March, 1731), 107; III (June, 1733), 282-83; X
(Nov., 1740), 547-48; XV (April, 1745), 207-8.

Smollett uses some form of the word *irony* eight times in *Peregrine Pickle*, not a particularly esoteric work.[44]   Such appearances of the word in the popular literature of the time indicate that it had finally achieved general currency.[45]

ii. *Stock definitions of* irony *and related terms*

Before the late eighteenth century little attempt was made to carry the explicit definition of *irony* beyond the type of the dictionary entry and the traditional rhetorical classifications; within this scope certain stock definitions, used by Quintilian and Cicero in their discussions of verbal irony, were passed down from dictionary to dictionary and from rhetoric to rhetoric and turned up in the unsystematic explanations of more casual writers.   By far the most popular of these stock formulations was that *irony* means *saying the contrary, or opposite, of what one means.*   This had first appeared in the *Rhetoric to Alexander,* moved on through Cicero, Quintilian, and the medieval rhetoricians,[1] and then settled down in English.[2]

[44] Smollett, *Peregrine Pickle*, I, 43-44, 204; II, 38, 68, 253; III, 31; IV, 101, 109-10.

[45] Nevertheless Ephraim Chambers, *Cyclopaedia* (1741, 1743), lists the four principal tropes as "the metaphora, metonymia, synecdoche and ironia;" not until the 1778-88 edition were the names of these tropes Anglicized.   But John Oldmixon, *Logick and Rhetorick* (1728) had discussed irony without once using the Latin form of the word, and Leonard Welsted, *Longinus* (1727), pp. 77-78, had used *irony* quite naturally as the English equivalent of the Greek word.   In his translations of Quintilian and of Cicero's *De Oratore* and *Academica,* all published at mid-century, William Guthrie uses *irony* as the equivalent of the Latin term wherever it seems appropriate.   William Guthrie, *Cicero De Oratore* (1822), pp. 197-200, 287; *Quinctilianus His Institutes* (1756), I, 229; II, 29-30, 56, 62, 235ff., 249, 279-80, 286; *Morals of Cicero* (1744), p. 377.

[1]Sedgewick, "Dramatic Irony" (1913), pp. 192-94.   Cicero *On Oratory* II. 67 ff.   Quintilian *Institutio* VIII. vi. 54-58; IX. ii. 44-53.

[2] *Thordynary of Crysten men* (1506), Part IV, sec. xxii.   Thomas More, *Works* (1557), chap. v, p. 939.   Hoby, *Courtier* (Everyman), pp. 159-61.   Abraham Fraunce, *Arcadian Rhetorike* (1588), Book I, chap. vi.   Puttenham, *Arte of English Poesie* (Willcock-Walker), pp. 186-91.   Peacham, *Garden of Eloquence* (1593), pp. 35-36.   Florio, *Worlde of Wordes* (1598) and (1611).   Richard Perceval, *Dictionarie* (1599).   John Hoskins, *Directions for Speech and Style* (Hudson), pp. 29-30.   John Bullokar, *English Expositor* (1621).   Henry Cockeram, *English Dictionarie* (Tinker).   William Whately, *Prototypes* (1640), Book III, chap xxxix, p. 21.   Thomas Fuller, *The Holy State* (1642), pp. 73-74.   John Bulwer, *Chirologia and Chironomia* (1644), pp. 181-83.   Thomas Blount, *Aca-*

It was usually stated baldly and without qualification. Dr. Johnson gives: "A mode of speech in which the meaning is contrary to the words."[3] The Earl of Chesterfield tells his son: "This is a figure of speech called Irony; which is saying directly the contrary of what you mean...."[4] Several of the early dictionaries and rhetorics offer "saying black is white" as an illustration, which cannot have been very illuminating to the uninstructed.[5] Their situation is made fun of by Middleton and Rowley, who use a tailor's rhetoric as representative of the learning of "Mechanick *Rabbies*" of the age:

> By his Needle he understands *Ironia*,
> That with one eye lookes two wayes at once:[6]

and Sir Thomas Browne points out a fallacy which arises from over-awareness of this device: "The circle of this fallacy is very large; and herein may be comprised all Ironical mistakes, for intended expressions receiving inverted significations...."[7] One distinction is recorded, however, in a few dictionaries: "a figure in speaking, when one means contrary to the signification of the word, or when a man reasoneth contrary to what he thinks, to mock him, whom he argues with...."[8]

A second, considerably less popular, formula was that *irony*

demie of Eloquence (1654), pp. 25-26. John Smith, *Rhetorique* (1657), pp. 45-48, 74-76. Hobbes, *The Art of Rhetoric* (Molesworth), p. 517. John Prideaux, *Sacred Eloquence* (1659), pp. 12-14. Edward Phillips, *New World of Words* (1662) and (1706). Robert Ferguson, *The Interest of Reason in Religion* (1675), pp. 299-300. *Art of Speaking* (1708), pp. 63, 305-11. George Granville, *Unnatural Flights in Poetry* (Spingarn), p. 296. Edward Cocker, *English Dictionary* (1704). John Harris, *Lexicon Technicum* (1704). Bailey, *Universal Etymological English Dictionary* (1724), (1733), (1745), (1757), (1766), (1790). Bailey, *Universal Etymological English Dictionary* II (1727). Bailey, *Dictionarium Britannicum* (1730). Anthony Blackwall, *Introduction to the Classics* (1728), pp. 176-79. John Oldmixon, *Logick and Rhetorick* (1728), pp. 21-28. J. K., *New English Dictionary* (1731). Thomas Dyche, *New English Dictionary* (1765). *Pocket Dictionary* (1753). *World* (Chalmers), XXVII, 277-79 (No. 104, Dec. 26, 1754). Warren Taylor, *Tudor Rhetoric* (1937), pp. 35-36.

[3] Johnson, *Dictionary* (1755-56).

[4] Chesterfield, *Letters to His Son* (Strachey-Calthrop), I, 36.

[5] John Bullokar, *English Expositor* (1621) and (1719). Henry Cockeram, *English Dictionarie* (Tinker), (1626) and (1639). John Smith, *Rhetorique* (1657), p. 45.

[6] Middleton and Rowley, *World tost at Tennis* (1620), sig. C^v-C2^r.

[7] Thomas Browne, *Works* (Sayle), *Pseudodoxia Epidemica*, Book I, chap. iv.

[8] Thomas Blount, *Glossographia* (1656). See also: Thomas Elyot, *Bibliotheca* (1552). Thomas Cooper, *Thesaurus* (1578). Benjamin Martin, *Lingua Britannica Reformata* (1749). Robert Ainsworth, *Thesaurus* (1751).

means *saying something other than one means*.[9] People were not always sure whether this was only a more general way of saying the same thing or the definition of another kind of irony. Cicero had said:

Ironical dissimulation has also an agreeable effect, when you say something different from what you think; not after the manner to which I alluded before, when you say the exact reverse of what you mean, as Crassus said to Lamia, but when through the whole course of a speech you are seriously jocose, your thoughts being different from your words. . . .[10]

Hoby's *Courtier* offers a modern version of this passage[11] and Prideaux seems to recognize the difference in a footnote to *"Ironia"*:

Simulatio, Because we speak one thing, and mean another. . . . It is likewise called by *Tully*, *Inversio*, a turning upside down of a thing, or contrary to the right form. A proper tearm to expresse this Trope where the contrary is meant to what is said. . . .[12]

Quintilian, however, had used this formula as another way of stating the first one,[13] and some of the dictionaries and rhetorics give it as their only definition of *irony*, apparently assuming that no difference is involved. It is this abstract formula which George Daniel has in mind as he describes the cloud of arrows that descended upon the French cavalry at Agincourt, and how the English archer aimed:

> Yet here: (and 'tis the Ironie of warre
> Where Arrowes forme the Argument;) he best
> Acquitts himselfe, who doth a Horse praefer
> To his proud Rider; and the object, Beast
>   Transfformes Philosophy but yet the Rule
>   Makes out, to Act, on the more Passive Soule.[14]

[9] The formula is stated in: Cicero *Academica* II. 15 and *On Oratory* III. 53. Quintilian *Institutio* VI. ii. 15-16. Miles Coverdale, *Remains* (Parker Soc.), II, 333. Thomas Wilson, *Rhetorique* (G. H. Mair), pp. 134-56. Richard Sherry, *Rhetorike* (1555), fol. xxiii, xxvi. John Marbeck, *Notes and Commonplaces* (1581), p. 560. Puttenham, *Arte of English Poesie* (Willcock-Walker), pp. 186-91. Edward Cocker, *English Dictionary* (1724). Ephraim Chambers, *Cyclopaedia* (1741, 1743) and (1778-88). Benjamin Martin, *Bibliotheca Technologica* (1737), pp. 178-80. John Lawson, *Lectures Concerning Oratory* (1760), pp. 257-68.
[10] Cicero *On Oratory* II. 67.
[11] Hoby, *Courtier* (Everyman), pp. 159-61.
[12] John Prideaux, *Sacred Eloquence* (1659), pp. 12-14. See also John Smith, *Rhetorique* (1657), pp. 45-48.
[13] Quintilian *Institutio* VIII. vi. 54-58.
[14] George Daniel, *Poems* (Grosart), IV, 149-50 ("Trinarchodia," stanza 198).

The clever archer aims at something other than he means to hit.

The third stock formula, used ordinarily to clear up the vagueness of the other two, was not only the most instructive but also the most variable in phrase. Quintilian had stated it in its persistent form: "It is permissible to censure with counterfeited praise and praise under a pretence of blame."[15] The seventeenth century enlivened it. *Irony* is "calling that foule which is faire, or that sweete which is sowre,"[16] *irony* "expresseth a thing by contrary, by show of exhortation when indeed it dehorteth,"[17] "An Irony is a nipping jeast, or a speech that hath the honey of pleasantness in its mouth, and a sting of rebuke in its taile."[18] Other more subdued versions appear occasionally throughout our period.[19] Giving the name of a virtue to a vice or of a vice to a virtue was a frequently offered subformula which seems to account for Fielding's peculiarly mechanical use of *irony* in the following passage:

By Wisdom here, I mean that Wisdom of this World, which St. Paul expressly tells us *is Folly;* that Wisdom *of the Wise,* which, as we read both in Isaiah and in the Corinthians, is threatned with Destruction: Lastly, I here intend that Wisdom in the Abundance of which, as the Preacher tells us, there is *much of Grief;* which, if true, would be alone sufficient to evince the extreme Folly of those who covet and pursue such Wisdom.

But tho' the Scriptures in the Places above cited, and in many others do very severely treat this Character of worldly or mock Wisdom, they have not, I think, very fully described it, unless perhaps Solomon hath done this ironically under the Name of Folly. An Opinion to which I am much inclined; and indeed what is said in the 10th Chapter of Ecclesiastes of the great Exaltation of a Fool, must be understood of a Fool in Repute, and such is the Wise Man here pointed at.

In the same Manner, the best Writers among the Heathens have obscurely and ironically characterised this Wisdom. *What is a covetous*

---

[15] Quintilian *Institutio* VIII. vi. 54-58.

[16] John Marbeck, *Notes and Commonplaces* (1581), p. 560.

[17] John Hoskins, *Directions for Speech and Style* (Hudson), pp. 29-30. Thomas Blount, *Academie of Eloquence* (1654), pp. 25-26, repeats this phrase.

[18] Edward Reyner, *Government of the Tongue* (1658), pp. 223-27.

[19] Cicero *On Oratory* II. 67. Thomas Wilson, *Rhetorique* (G. H. Mair), pp. 134-56. Edward Phillips, *New World of Words* (1706). Bailey, *Dictionarium Britannicum* (1730). Ephraim Chambers, *Cyclopaedia* (1741, 1743) and (1778-88). *Memoirs of Grub-street* (1737), I, viii-x. Chesterfield, *Letters to His Son* (Strachey-Calthrop), I, 36.

Man? says Horace, *he is both a Fool and a Madman.* Now Avarice is the very highest Perfection and as it were Quintessence of this Kind of Wisdom.[20]

At times, in the process of assimilating *ironia,* the English seem to have slipped into giving the word a more general definition than it had traditionally had. Both Cicero and Quintilian had discussed irony as a particular type of jest, and the function of the device was given as derision; it is not surprising then that some of the rhetorics and dictionaries extended the word's reference to any mock or scoff, regardless of rhetorical structure:

Now is *ironia* as much to say as a mockage, derision, or meaning of another thing, than is expressed in the words.[21]

ironie, (g) a mocking spaech.[22]

Ironically. Spoken scoffingly.
Ironie. Speaking by contraries, saying black is white.[23]

Ironia is taken for dissimulation, whereby one thing is thought and another spoken; it signifies also taunting speeches, or a speaking by contraries. . . .[24]

Ironical, (Greek) spoken in mockery, or by that figure called *Irony,* which is a speaking contrary to what a man means by way of bitter gibing or scoffing.[25]

Ironie . . . a speaking by contraries or mockingly.[26]

Ironia, a scoffe or flout. . . .[27]

Ironia . . . a mock or scoffe, also a trope.[28]

IRONICAL, spoken by way of Railery.
RALLERY, a close or secret Jibe, pleasant drolling, or playing upon another in discourse.[29]

---

[20] Fielding, *Covent-Garden Journal* (Jensen, 1915), II, 126.
[21] Miles Coverdale, *Remains* (Parker Soc.), II, 333.
[22] Robert Cawdry, *A Table Alphabeticall* (MLA facs.).
[23] Henry Cockeram, *English Dictionarie* (Tinker). Edward Cocker, *English Dictionary* (1704) gives the same kind of entries.
[24] John Smith, *Rhetorique* (1657), pp. 45-48. See also Puttenham, *Arte of English Poesie* (Willcock-Walker), pp. 154-55, 186-91; and Warren Taylor, *Tudor Rhetoric* (1937), pp. 35-36.
[25] Edward Phillips, *New World of Words* (1662).
[26] Elisha Coles, *English Dictionary* (1676).
[27] Angel Day, *English Secretorie* (1595), Part II, pp. 79-80.
[28] Francis Holyoke, *Dictionarium* (1627).
[29] B. N. Defoe, *Compleat English Dictionary* (1735).

Although after the Restoration such distinctions were pretty much ignored as being pedantry, Renaissance rhetoric involved *irony* in its complex classifications of rhetorical terms. In these irony was ordinarily classed as a trope, along with metonymy, metaphor, and synecdoche, and tropes were also divided into those consisting of a single word and those consisting of a sequence of words.

A Trope or turning is when a word is turned from his naturall signification, to some other.... The excellencie of tropes is then most apparant,
when either manie be fitlie included in one word, or one so continued
in manie, as that with what thing it begin, with the same it also end....[30]

There be two kindes of tropes. The first côteineth *Metonymia*, the
châge of name: and *Ironia*, a scoffing or jesting speach. The second
comprehendeth a *Metaphore* and *Synecdoche*.[31]

Irony was also occasionally classed as a figure—a term the meaning of which varied with the rhetorician using it[32]—but without any change in the status of irony. Within this framework a number of connections were made between irony and other rhetorical devices. The "ancient flirtation between rhetorical irony and allegory"[33] continued through Sherry,[34] Fraunce,[35] and Puttenham, but the pair went pretty much their own ways thereafter. Puttenham explains the relationship:

...*Allegoria*, which is when we speake one thing and thinke another,
and that our wordes and our meanings meete not.... Of this figure...
we will speake first as of the chief ringleader and captaine of all other
figures....[36]

[30] Abraham Fraunce, *Arcadian Rhetorike* (1588), Book I, chap. i.
[31] *Ibid.*, Book I, chap. ii. See also: Richard Sherry, *Rhetorike* (1555), fol.
xxiii. Peacham, *Garden of Eloquence* (1593), p. 1. Thomas Granger, *Divine
Logike* (1620), p. 175. John Smith, *Rhetorique* (1657), pp. 45-48. Hobbes, *The
Art of Rhetoric* (Molesworth), p. 515. John Prideaux, *Sacred Eloquence* (1659),
pp. 12-14. *Art of Speaking* (1708), p. 62. Anthony Blackwall, *Introduction to
the Classics* (1728), pp. 148 ff., 176-79.
[32] See: Puttenham, *Arte of English Poesie* (Willcock-Walker), pp. 137-38, 142-
43, 154-55, 158-60. Abraham Fraunce, *Arcadian Rhetorike* (1588), Book I,
chaps. i and xxvii. Peacham, *Garden of Eloquence* (1593), p. 1. Anthony Blackwall, *Introduction to the Classics* (1728), p. 148. The convolutions of rhetoric
during this period may be explored in W. P. Sandford, *English Theories of Public
Address* (1931).
[33] G. G. Sedgewick, *Of Irony* (1948), p. 6.
[34] Richard Sherry, *Rhetorike* (1555), fol. xxvi.
[35] Abraham Fraunce, *Arcadian Rhetorike* (1588), Book I, chaps. i and vi.
[36] Puttenham, *Arte of English Poesie* (Willcock-Walker), pp. 186-91. See also
pp. 154-55.

Puttenham lists enigma, proverb, irony, sarcasm, asteismus, micterismus, antiphrasis, and charientismus as "souldiers to the figure *allegoria*." In the rhetorics of the time *sarcasm*, "a nipping taunt," "a bitter kind of derision," was sometimes classified separately from irony,[37] sometimes said to be "neer to an Irony, but that it's somewhat more bitter,"[38] and sometimes listed as a subtype of irony.[39] Like *allegory*, *antiphrasis* was defined in the same words as *irony*: "a forme of speech which by a word exprest doth signifie the contrary,"[40] but unlike *allegory*, *antiphrasis* in actual use referred to the same strategy as *irony* did, although John Smith accepted this distinction: "*Antiphrasis* and this [*irony*] are of very nigh affinity, only differing in this, that Antiphrasis consists in the contrary sense of a word, and Ironia of a sentence."[41] *Asteismus*, "whan a thyng is polished with some mery conceit," *micterismus*, "a counterfayted laughter," and *charientismus*, "when thinges that be hardely spoken, be mollifyed with pleasaunte woordes"[42] were three other devices which frequently turned up in the company of *irony*, and Sherry, Smith, and Prideaux classify them as subtypes of irony.[43] *Preterition*, "when you say you let passe that which notwithstanding you touch at full,"[44] was also sometimes classed as a type of irony.[45] Indeed, the rhetoricians played something of a shell game with these terms—*irony, sarcasm, antiphrasis, asteismus, micterismus,* and *charientismus*—for an illustration used in one guidebook under *irony* was likely to turn up in another under *sarcasm* and in another under *antiphrasis*. The differences among these terms were not significant,

---

[37] *Ibid.* See also Peacham, *Garden of Eloquence* (1593), pp. 37-38.

[38] Thomas Hall, *The Schools Guarded* (1655), pp. 163-70. John Smith, *Rhetorique* (1657), pp. 79-80. Ephraim Chambers, *Cyclopaedia* (1728), (1741, 1743), under "Sarcasm."

[39] Richard Sherry, *Rhetorike* (1555), fol. xxvi. John Prideaux, *Sacred Eloquence* (1659), pp. 12-14.

[40] Peacham, *Garden of Eloquence* (1593), pp. 24-25.

[41] John Smith, *Rhetorique* (1657), pp. 45-48.

[42] Richard Sherry, *Rhetorike* (1555), fol. xxvi.

[43] *Ibid.* John Smith, *Rhetorique* (1657), pp. 77-79. John Prideaux, *Sacred Eloquence* (1659), pp. 12-14. Prideaux adds three other subtypes: chleuasmus, diasyrmus, and exutenismus.

[44] John Smith, *Rhetorique* (1657), p. 165.

[45] *Ibid.* Abraham Fraunce, *Arcadian Rhetorike* (1588), Book I, chap. vi. Anthony Blackwall, *Introduction to the Classics* (1728), pp. 195-98.

but the difference between *allegory* and *irony* was so considerable
that the association based on identity of abstract definition fell into
disuse.[46]

[46] In the 1778-88 edition of Ephraim Chambers' *Cyclopaedia* this distinction,
which had not appeared in earlier editions, was added to the article on "allegory":
"Scaliger considers *allegory* as one part, or side, of a comparison. It differs from
irony, in that *allegory* imports a similitude between the thing spoken and intended;
irony a contrariety between them."

THE DICTIONARY

1. *IRONY* AS PRETENSE AND DECEPTION

This earliest Greek sense of the word, which persisted in vary-ing forms and degrees in both Greek and Latin, was not carried over into common English usage. In translations *dissimulation*, or occasionally *hypocrisy*, was substituted for *irony*[1] in this sense (*dissimulation* could also be substituted for *irony* in the sense of blame by seeming praise,[2] as it had been in Latin). I have, how-

---

[1]"... very often the signification of a *Greek* Term translated word for word, is quite another thing in our Language; for example, Irony which with us is a raillery in conversation or Rhetorical Trope; with Theophrastus it signifies somewhat be-tween cheating and dissembling. ..."

— Bruyère, *Manners of the Age* (1699),
"Prefatory Discourse."

Dissimulation was substituted for the Greek *irony* in the following translations, except where otherwise noted:
Aristophanes *Clouds* 449: Thomas Stanley, *History of Philosophy* (1655-62), Part III, p. 76 (another substitute); Lewis Theobald, *Clouds* (1715), p. 25 (another substitute).
Aristotle *Rhetoric* II.v.11-12: Hobbes, *A Briefe of the Arte of Rhetoric* (1637?), pp. 82-83; Aristotle's *Rhetoric* (1686), p. 102.
Aristotle *Ethics* II.vii.12: John Wylkinson, *Ethiques of Aristotle* (1547), sig. C 2ʳ & ᵛ (another substitute).
Demosthenes *First Philippic* 7: Thomas Wilson, *Demosthenes* (1570), p. 35 (another substitute); *Demosthenes* (1702) (another substitute).
Theophrastus *Characters* (Loeb), pp. 41-43: Bruyère, *Manners of the Age* (1699), sig. Hh 7ʳ & ᵛ; Eustace Budgell, *Theophrastus* (1714), p. 5; Henry Gally, *Theophrastus* (1725), p. 120; John Healey, *Theophrastus* (1616), p. 4 ("Cavil-ling").
Plutarch *Lives*, "Demetrius" 18, "Agis" 19, "Pompey" 30: North, *Plutarch* (1595), pp. 948, 849 ("hypocrisy"), 688; Dryden, *Plutarch* (1683-86), IV, 264.
Lucian *True History* II.17: *True History from the Greek* (1744), p. 65 ("hypocrisy").
See also John Baret, *Alvearie* (1580), "dissimuling."
[2] Thomas Wilson, *Rhetorique* (G. H. Mair), pp. 184-85. Hoby, *Courtier* (Everyman), pp. 159-61. Edward Phillips, *New World of Words* (1706), under "Dissimulatio."

ever, encountered several English passages in which *irony* is used to mean genuine and thorough deception of some sort.

I.A. *Constant dissimulation*

This differs from most of the other ironies (Dict. III through x) in that actual deception, not indirect satire, is intended.

Gabriel Harvey, *Works* (Grosart), II, 294-318:

He would either wisely hold his peace: or smoothly flatter me to my face: or suerly pay-home with a witnesse: but commonly in a corner, or in a maze, where the Autour might be uncertaine, or his packing intricate, or his purpose some way excusable. No man could beare a heavy injury more lightly: or forbeare a learned adversary more cunningly: or bourde a wilfull frend more dryly: or circumvent a daungerous foe more covertly: or countermine the deepest underminer more suttelly: or lullaby the circumspectest Argus more sweetly: or transforme himselfe into all shapes more deftly: or play any part more kindly. He had . . . such an inextricable sophistry, as might teach an Agathocles to hypocrise profoundly, or a Hieron to tyrannise learnedly . . . . nothing but his fact discovered his drift; & not the Beginning, but the End was the interpreter of his meaning.

He could speake by contraries, as queintly as Socrates; and do by contraries, as shrewdly as Tiberius. . . .

Stephen Gardiners Fox, or Macchiavels Fox, are too-young Cubbes, to compare with him; that would seeme any thing, rather than a Fox, and be a Fox rather then any thing else.

. . . his curses, [were] like the blessinges of those witches in Aphrica, that forspoke, what they praysed, and destroyed, what they wished to be saved.

I have seene spannels, mungrels, libbards, antelops; scorpions, snakes, cockatrices, vipers, and many other Serpents in sugar-worke: but to this day never saw such a standing-dish of Sugar-worke, as that sweet-tongued Doctor; that spake pleasingly, whatsoever he thought; and was otherwhiles a fayre Prognostication of fowle weather. Such an autenticall Irony engrosed, as all Oratory cannot eftsoones counterpane. Smooth voyces do well in most societies; and go currently away in many recknings, when rowgh-hewne words do but lay blockes in their own way. He found it in a thousand experiences; and was the preciseststreet practitioner of that soft, and tame Rhetorique, that ever I knew in my dealings.

... if ever any were Hypocrisy incarnate, it was he. . . .

I twice, or thrise tryed him to his face, somewhat sawcily, and smartly: but the Picture of Socrates, or the Image of S. Andrew, not so un-mooveable. . . .

It is not the threatener, but the underminer, that worketh the mischief: not the open assault, but the privy surprize, that terrifieth the old souldiour. . . . [Cf. Aristotle *Rhetoric* II.v.11-12.]

Gabriel Harvey, *Marginalia* (Moore Smith), p. 138:

Pestilens Ironia. magae laudant arbores, animalia, pueros, puellas: eademque necant occultè.

ALSO: Gabriel Harvey, *Marginalia* (Moore Smith), pp. 139-40, 143. In his character of Dr. Perne quoted at some length here Harvey implies that the Doctor sometimes used verbal irony ("bourde a wilfull frend...dryly"), but Harvey's chief complaint is quite simply that Perne was a hypocrite and dissembler. The significant fact is that Harvey tends to define Perne's hypocrisy in terms of blame-by-praise. Perne spoke "by contraries"; his curses "forspoke, what they praised"; he was "a standing-dish of Sugar-worke." We know that Harvey claimed a wide Classical knowledge[3] and in the character quoted there are traces of Aristophanes' "foxy deceit" (*Clouds* 449) and of Aristotle's and Theophrastus' self-depreciator (Aristotle *Rhetoric* II.v.11-12; Theophrastus *Characters* [Loeb], pp. 41-43). What Harvey seems to have done, then, is to formulate the Classical sense of deception in terms of rhetorical blame-by-praise, so that Perne's "autenticall Irony" is insincere praise that is actually meant to deceive and thereby hide evil intentions. Several notes in the *Marginalia* use *irony* in the same way.

Thomas Browne, *Christian Morals* (1716), Part III, sec. 20, pp. 108-9:

Though the World be Histrionical, and most Men live Ironically, yet be thou what thou singly art, and personate only thy self. Swim smoothly in the stream of thy Nature, and live but one Man. To single Hearts doubling is discruciating: such tempers must sweat to dissemble, and prove but hypocritical Hypocrites. Simulation must be short: Men do not easily continue a counterfeiting Life, or dissemble unto Death. He

---

[3] See pp. 62-63 below.

who counterfeiteth, acts a part, and is as it were out of himself: which, if long, proves so ircksome, that Men are glad to pull of their Vizards, and resume themselves again; no practice being able to naturalize such unnaturals, or make a Man rest content not to be himself.

Browne uses *irony* here to mean simply lifelong deceit and hypocrisy. Since by his time *dissimulation* would have been a much more natural word to use, we may suppose that Browne chose "Ironically" for its esoteric connotation, the word probably suggesting itself to him by reason of its early Greek sense of foxy deceit and Theophrastus' use of it to name his character of the dissembler.

I.B. *Self-depreciation in order to achieve a practical end*

CLASSICAL PRECEDENTS: Aristotle *Ethics* IV.vii.1-17. Demosthenes *First Philippic* 7. Theophrastus *Characters* (Loeb), pp. 41-43. Plutarch *Lives*, "Pompey" 30.

Thordynary of Crysten men (1506), Part IV, sec. xxii:

Also a man fyndeth another maner of lyenge the whiche may be called jactaunce & is cõmytted in spekynge or ymagenynge of hymselfe more grete thynges than there is of godnes of nobles of prowesse or of vertues and after the grevousnes of the cyrcũstaunces it is oftentymes mortall synne. Also to saye of hym selfe ony thynge of his feblenesses & neces-sytes or of his synnes or to take bestymentes of abjeccyon to the ende that a man be renowmed & reputed humble abjecte & grete thynge in merytes & devocyons before god the which thynge is not suche as a man it sheweth that may be mortall synne and such synne is named yronye not that the whiche is of grammare by the whiche a man sayth one & gyveth to understande the contrarye....

ALSO: Dryden, *Plutarch* (1683-86), IV, 140.

I.C. *Falsely attributing some attitude or act to another*

The Fox with his Fire-brand Unkennell'd (1703), pp. 3-4:

Mr. *Foe*'s *Ironical* Vein has only this for Its Vindication, which must make it too the greater Jest, That those Knights of the Post only de-sign'd their Libels and Associations for the Pockets of particular Per-sons; but Mr. *Foe*, with a *Shorter Way* indeed, paums his upon the whole Government and Constitution at once; and very *Ironically* dresses up the Church and State in the Lions and Bears Skin, and such Ironical

Figures as are not to be found in the *Tropes* of our Modern Rhetorick, but a barbarous *Irony* that was much practised by the Old *Romans* on the Primitive Christians, the better to bring their Dogs to worry them.

ALSO: *Ibid.*, pp. 21, 23. The anonymous author here is saying that the ironical exaggerations of Defoe's *Shortest Way with the Dissenters* were not meant to act as the satiric vehicle of a "contrary" and supposedly genuine meaning; they were meant to be taken at face value and believed. Thus the *Shortest Way* was a pack of lies and libels knowingly foisted upon the public, and this was a kind of irony different from most rhetorical irony. (Cf. Dict. II.B, Shaftesbury.)

II. *IRONY* AS LIMITED DECEPTION

II.A. *A temporary deception which tricks one's interlocutor into revealing the truth*

This sense differs from Dict. I in that the deception lasts only long enough to produce the desired effect, but it differs from verbal irony (Dict. III.B, IV through VIII) in that the result is produced by the deception and not by seeing through an apparent deception.

William Whately, *Prototypes* (1640), Book III, chap. xxxix, p. 21:

[While Joseph rules in Egypt his brothers come to him for food; Joseph imprisons them, binds Reuben, hides his cup in Benjamin's sack and then accuses them of theft. Finally melted by Judah's oration, Joseph reveals himself. All this, says Whately, Joseph did "to bring them to thorough repentance for their sin."]

Againe, it may seeme to be lawfull by the example of *Joseph* in way of probation and tryall, to counterfeit discontent, and to lay grievous things to the charge of men, and presse them as if they were guilty, though one know the contrary: I still say, if it be done by way of tryall, so that at last it be made manifest, that it was meerely in tryall, and that which would seeme a lye, if it were affirmed expressely and not with reference to such an end, being said to such an end is not a lye, because it is indeed not an affirming, but a seeming to affirme for a time. So *Salomon* seemed angry, and commanded to divide the child betwixt the two wrangling harlots that came before him, our Saviour made as if he would have gone further, when the Disciples had him in with them at *Emmaus*. So if a Judge seeing great probability, and in a manner certainty of the guiltinesse of an offendour, shall affirme something to him, to draw a confession from him, as for example, that some companion of his hath confest it, and that it is in vaine for him any longer to deny, or that he was seene at such time in such a place, by such and such, when indeed these things were not so, but somewhat equivalent to them, was true, *viz.* Arguments convincing their guiltinesse, even as much as these things would, though not to make them confesse. I say such courses taken by way of probation and tryall, and finding out guiltiness, are not to be esteemed lyes, because here the meaning is to be taken according to the present show of words. These be but a kind of ironicall carryage, no more lies than an irony, that by affirming one thing in such and such a manner and gesture, doth affirme the quite contrary.

This unusual use of the word is obviously the product of overstrained rationalizing.

ii.b. *Ambiguous language intended to conceal part of its meaning from part of the audience*

This sense differs from Dict. i in that the underlying meaning is intended to be perceived by certain of the audience, even if only by the ironist as his own audience. It differs from the verbal ironies (Dict. iii.b, iv through viii) not only in the actual deception involved, but also in the motive, which is not so much rhetorical effectiveness attained through the use of certain verbal devices as it is the urge to self-expression through any kind of ambiguity which will pass the censor.

Christopher Ness, *History of the Old and New Testament* (1696), I, 234:

[Ness is discussing Jacob's answer to Isaac, "I am Esau."] Some say, that *Jacob* neither lyed, nor sinned in what he said. . . . They say that his Speech to *Isaac*, if expounded in the best sense, is no Lye, but an *Irony* . . . which is a witty way of speaking words, that in a strict acceptation sounds not true, yet importeth some great truth when taken by the right handle. . . . Thus *Jacob*'s Speech importeth, that he was the Person to whom the *Blessing* (which *Isaac* was to pronounce) belongeth, for Esau had resign'd it to him by the sale of his *Birthright;* which purchase gave *Jacob* a civil right to the *Blessing.*

Irony here is very close to allegory.

Craftsman (1731), VII, 94-95 (No. 226, Oct. 31, 1730):

[Caleb is giving examples of the way his historical essays are ridiculously forced into parallels of modern events.]

I often wonder that the *weekly Advocates for Power* have never insisted on two famous Instances of *Court Prosecutions* in the Reign of *Edward IV* to justify their *ironical Constructions.* One is that of a poor *Grocer,* who was hang'd in that Reign, for saying that He would make his Son *Heir of the Crown;* alluding, either innocently, or for the Sake only of a little Pun upon the Times, to his own House, which bore the sign of the *Crown.* The other Instance was of a *Gentleman,* who was condemn'd as a Traytor, upon the following Account. The *King* having kill'd a *favourite white Deer* in his Park, He was so much griev'd at his Loss, that he suffer'd himself to wish, in a Transport of Passion, *that the Horns of the Deer were in the Belly of Him, who advis'd the King to do it.* This was interpreted, by the *state Casuists* of those Times, into a Design of compassing the *Death of the King;* for, said They, the *King* kill'd the Deer without any Body's Advice; from whence it follow'd that the Gentleman *wish'd the Deer's Horns in the King's own Belly; innuendo,* He had an Intention of murthering the *King,* which is *high Treason;* and He was executed accordingly.

Shaftesbury, *Characteristics* (1714), I, 71-72:

If Men are forbid to speak their minds seriously on certain Subjects, they will do it ironically. If they are forbid to speak at all upon such Subjects, or if they find it really dangerous to do so; they will then redouble their Disguise, involve themselves in Mysteriousness, and talk so as hardly to be understood, or at least not plainly interpreted, by those who are dispos'd to do 'em a mischief. And thus *Raillery* is brought more in fashion, and runs into an Extreme.

Although the above passage is far from unequivocal, Shaftesbury seems to be following a tendency of his time to apply the word loosely to all kinds of derisive attack (Dict. ix) with the emphasis in this context on the deceptive function of some kinds. For a full discussion of Shaftesbury's use of *irony* see Dict. iii.A below.

ALSO: Anthony Collins, *Discourse concerning Ridicule and Irony* (1729), pp. 23-26.

iii. BLAME-BY-PRAISE AND PRAISE-BY-BLAME

iii.a. *Irony of manner*

The *irony of manner* may be the manner of an author in a work of art or the pervasive manner of a man in his relations with other men. In this sense *irony* refers to an expression of personality, a manner of speech and action which conveys to the observer a distinct image of character. That character is one of great modesty and self-effacement joined to sympathetic admiration of others, and as such represents the principles of praise-by-blame and blame-by-praise projected through the whole image of a personality. This sense differs from that irony of detachment which is one component of dramatic irony (Dict. x) in that it is an expression of an attitude rather than the attitude itself. It differs from the verbal ironies of blame-by-praise and praise-by-blame (Dict. iii.b) in that it is not a limited device. During the English classical period some references to Socrates' constant use of irony seem to imply an awareness of the irony of manner.

CLASSICAL PRECEDENTS: Plato *Symposium* 216 *de* [?], 218*d* [?]. Cicero *Brutus* 85-87. Cicero *Academica* II.15; II.74 [?]. Cicero *De officiis* I.30. Quintilian *Institutio* IX.ii. 44-53.

Roberte Whytinton, *Tullyes offyces* (1534), sig. Gi^r.
Gabriel Harvey, *Marginalia* (Moore Smith), p. 155:

A continual Ironist, like Socrates, Sanazarius, & owr Sir Thomas More: suer in the sweetist, & finist kinde.

Fulke Greville, *Sidney* (1652), pp. 174-77:

... to come particularly to that Treatise intitled: *The Declination of Monarchy.*. Let me beg leave of the favourable Reader, to bestow a few lines more in the story of this Changling, then I have done in the rest; and yet to use no more serious authority then the rule of *Diogenes,* which was, to hang the Posie where there is most need.

... when I had in mine own case well weigh'd the tendernesse of that great subject, and consequently, the nice path I was to walke in between two extremities; but especially the danger, by treading aside, to cast scandall upon the sacred foundations of Monarchy; together with the fate of many Metaphysicall *Phormio's* before me, who had lost themselves in teaching Kings, and Princes, how to governe their People: then did this new prospect dazzle mine eyes, and suspend my travell for a time.

But the familiar self-love, which is more or lesse born in every man, to live, and dye with him, presently moved me to take this Bear-whelp up againe and licke it. Wherein I, rowsing my selfe under the banner of this flattery, went about (as a fond mother) to put on richer garments, in hope to adorne them. But while these clothes were in making, I perceived that cost would but draw more curious eyes to observe deformities. So that from these checks a new counsell rose up in me, to take away all opinion of seriousnesse from these perplexed pedegrees; and to this end carelessly cast them into that hypocriticall figure *Ironia*, wherein men commonly (to keep above their workes) seeme to make toies of the utmost they can doe.

And yet againe, in that confusing mist, when I beheld this grave subject (which should draw reverence and attention) to bee overspangled with lightnesse, I forced in examples of the Roman gravity, and greatnesse, the harsh severity of the *Lacedemonian* Government; the riches of the *Athenian* learning, wit, and industry; and like a man that plaies divers parts upon severall hints, left all the indigested crudities, equally applied to Kings, or Tyrants: whereas in every cleere judgement, the right line had beene sufficient enough to discover the crooked; if the image of it could have proved credible to men.

Here, for the first time so far as I know, *irony* refers not to the habitual manner of a famous jester but to the image of his own personality which an author chooses to project throughout the whole of one of his works. The manner Greville seems to be thinking of is a sort of jesting self-depreciation not unlike Chaucer's or Socrates'. What can have inspired Greville to this use of *irony*? It may be that he had in mind that modesty which Aristotle had called understatement and grudgingly admitted to be more graceful than boasting, which Theophrastus and Demosthenes had described as a hypocritical method of evading responsibility, and which Cicero had liked because it marked a man as free from conceit. All these Classical notions about irony were available to Greville, his motives include modesty and the avoidance of responsibility, and his choice of "hypocriticall" to modify "*Ironia*" may have been suggested by Theophrastus' character of the Eiron, in the seventeenth century called a dissembler or hypocrite. If this was the course of

Greville's thinking, he did in fact, by applying a Classical sense of the word to the literary manner of an author, define one aspect of the irony of manner which has become prominent in twentieth-century criticism.

Thomas Stanley, *History of Philosophy* (1655-62), Part III, pp. 5-6:

... he [Socrates] taught onely by *Irony* and *Induction*: the first *Quintilian* defines *an absolute dissimulation of the will more apparent then confest, so as in that, the words are different from the words, in this, the sense from the speech, whilest the whole confirmation of the cause, even the whole life seems to carry an Irony, such was the life of* Socrates, *who was for that reason called* εἰρών; *that is, one that personates an unlearned man, and is an admirer of others as wise. In this Irony* (saith Cicero) *and dissimulation he far exceeded all men in pleasantnesse &. Urbanity* ... ; *He detracted from himself in dispute, and attributed more to those hee meant to confute, so that when he said, or thought another thing, he freely used that dissimulation which the Greeks call* Irony, *which* Annius *also saith, was in* Africanus.

Rapin, *Comparison of Plato and Aristotle* (1673), p. 17:

His [Socrates'] Conversation was always very pleasant; for he had a wonderful art of putting vizards upon things, and divertising people with their own reproof; in which the Irony which was so familiar and natural to him, stood him in excellent stead, especially against the Sophists, whom he loved to render ridiculous; for they were a sort of people, as himself used to say, of a depraved pallate in all things. The ignorance he affected with them, was a mark of the scorn he put upon them; for when he treated with reasonable men, he changed his manner of converse; he transformed himself as it were into their humour, to enter better into their conceptions.

Shaftesbury: The most illuminating context in which Shaftesbury uses the word *irony* is a part of his *Regimen*,[4] that very personal work in which he puts aside the affectations of his public mission and speaks with intense directness. We can enter that context through this admonition:

... go to those simple but Divine operations, those simplicities of nature which for want of simplicity are so little felt. .... Only a right disposition is wanting, and simplicity to judge of these simplicities, these only beauties, truths, excellences. What is the rest but grotesque? what is atheism but

[4] Shaftesbury, *Life, Letters, Regimen* (Rand).

nature-grotesque?   Nature seen thus in masquerade, disfigured, charged, as they say in painting, and after a kind of caricature?   And how this grotesque *without?*   How but from the grotesque-work *within?*   See the effect of those masks, the buffoonery, drollery, and burlesque.— Beware!—[5]

Here is the mathematically beautiful universe of Plato and the Enlightenment, a universe to be contemplated only by the steadfast and simple mind undisturbed by the world's mutability.   By contrast, the frenetic mind which plays upon every passing wave of appearances, of hopes and fears, exists not only in a world of grotesquerie but also in a storm of fiercely restless joys.   But there is "another sort of joy which is soft, still, peaceable, serene,"[6] and to achieve this joy the simple mind must avoid involvement— "the excrescences and funguses of the mind, endeavour to cut wholly off, much rather than the warts or corns from off thy body."[7]   And if the baser temper *will* involve itself in passing delights and hopes and fears?   "Beware, then, and for safety's sake apply contraries. . . . Turn the edge the other way, present the point, and keep temper aloof.   Thwart, cross, perplex, and break it. . . ."[8]

Thus at last hardly can any appearance arise, hardly can there be any object ever so remote or foreign, but what the mind will accommodate to itself and turn to its own use. . . .   This is just the reverse of what happens to those who are grown into the thorough buffooning habit.   Everything that they see, be it ever so grave or serious, has a ridiculous appearance, and whether they will or not becomes burlesque. . . . The difference here is that, as that other glass crooks and distorts the objects, so this continually straightens and redresses what is amiss, and sets everything in its due light, so as to hinder all confusion.[9]

Thus the steadfast, uninvolved mind sees all things from one clear point of view which is neither comic nor tragic, whereas the involved mind distorts the truth by seeing it from a too-serious or too-comic viewpoint which Shaftesbury habitually thinks of in terms of buffoonery and burlesque.

[5] *Ibid.,* p. 186.
[6] *Ibid.,* pp. 151-54.
[7] *Ibid.,* p. 164.
[8] *Ibid.,* pp. 196-97.
[9] *Ibid.,* pp. 171-72.

In social intercourse there is for the Stoic a difficult problem, especially for the eighteenth-century English gentleman Stoic. In addition to combating his internal joy or concern over external events, he must deny himself the revelation of this struggle to others. To reveal to the world his "disordered false self" is to disgrace the art which should make him happy and reveal his happiness to others.[10] If, on the other hand, he maintains his self-control he can achieve the ideal social carriage:

What can be an easier, happier part than to live disinterested and un-concerned, as being loose from all those ties and little mean regards which make us to depend so much on others? What can be more generous and of a better feeling than to go through companies, conversations, and affairs in the security and simplicity of mind? ... he who is secure as to the great events and is concerned but for one thing (which if he will himself, he need not miss), he, and he alone, is truly free; and with respect to things within, is becoming, beautiful. He alone has every-thing orderly, still, quiet; nothing boisterous, nothing disturbed; but every motion, action, and expression decent, and such as is becoming that more noble and far superior character of one who in another sense is called *well bred*, with respect to a different discipline and breeding.

Imitation, gesture, and action in discourse; different tones of voice, alterations of countenance, odd and humoursome turns of speech, phrase, expressions;—all this is agreeable in company, and may set off a story, help in an argument, or make anything to be felt which one would de-sire should be so. But all this is utterly wrong, harsh, dissonant; out of measure and tone. All that is vehement, impetuous, turbulent must needs be so: as well as all that which in any degree borders upon mimicry, buffoonery, drollery.[11]

But there is a social problem to be faced: How is one to maintain an inner gravity and equanimity, concealing the struggles that at-tend it, and yet live in a society of men who grasp at passing joys and delight in drollery and buffoonery?

Remember that sort of dissimulation which is consistent with true simplicity: and besides the innocent and excellent dissimulation of the kind which Socrates used, remember that other sort (not less his) which hides what passes within, and accommodates our manners to those of our friends and of people around us, as far as this with safety can be

[10] *Ibid., pp.* 198-200.
[11] *Ibid.,* pp. 180-81.

allowed. Remember, therefore, what countenance is to be shown even then when all is grave and solemn within.[12]

If the first [Socrates] of the three *great ones* ... involved himself as he did, and in those times, how much more thou? and in these? If the age then bore not a declaration, how much less now?—Then not ripe: now rotten.

Remember, therefore, in manner and degree, the same involution, shadow, curtain, the same soft irony; and strive to find a character in this kind according to proportion both in respect of self and times. Seek to find such a tenour as this, such a key, tone, voice, consistent with true gravity and simplicity, though accompanied with humour and a kind of raillery, agreeable with a divine pleasantry.—This is a harmony indeed! What can be sweeter, gentler, milder, more sociable, or more humane?[13]

No apologising; no show of inward work; no hint; no glance.—The purple only. No earnest, clearings, &c., cares, mystery.—The honest irony, jest.

Return, therefore, again, as above, and remember the involution, the shadow, the veil, the curtain.[14]

Is it possible to describe a circle around this manner of Shaftesbury's? It involves "gravity and a certain becoming reservedness,"[15] it may even appear by contrast to be "dulness and stupidity."[16] And yet the attitude behind the manner cannot be really grave, for the only really serious things, the internal things, are never revealed. What are talked of are the external things, and these, in Shaftesbury's philosophy, cannot be taken seriously. Though he may *appear* grave in discourse, he is not really so—at least within the context of that discourse.[17]

... this simple and (in appearance) humble, mean, insipid character; this middle genius, partaking neither of hearty mirth nor seriousness. ... This, as difficult as it may seem, yet by attention and hearty application may most easily be preserved, if on the one hand thou strenuously resist what offers from the vulgar side and that facetious comic kind, whatever it be of wit, jest, story, and the like; and if, on the other hand,

[12] *Ibid.*, p. 182.
[13] *Ibid.*, pp. 192-94.
[14] *Ibid.*, p. 205.
[15] *Ibid.*, p. 183.
[16] *Ibid.*, p. 153.
[17] *Ibid.*, p. 194.

thou as strenuously resist and abstain from that as ridiculous seriousness and solemnity in these affairs, eager contention and striving in the concerns of others, and for the reformation and conviction of others.[18]

If at times this middle character may extend itself to a soft raillery, it never indulges in buffoonery:

If there be, however, a facetiousness, a humour, a pleasantry of a right kind, proportionable and always in season, just, even, and spread alike through a whole character and life, sweet, gentle, mild, and withal constant, irrefragable, never inwardly disturbed whatever outward economy may require; if there be this thing, this true, innocent, excellent jest and pleasantry; let this be the care, how to preserve this jest and keep it the same; how never to be false to it; never to betray it, sacrifice it, prostitute it; never basely to yield it up to that other vile and scurrilous jest, most incompatible with it, its bane, destruction, and extinction. Let there be no raillery of that sort, no drollery, no buffoonery, nor anything that but borders upon it. . . .

Remember another character, another dignity, another humour, pleasantry. The Socratic genius, this mirth, these *jests,* these turns, and this simplicity. The chatter of the Roman comic poet and what he borrowed hence, and from his Socratic masters. But for Aristophanes, a Plautus, a modern play, modern wit, raillery, humour, away![19]

In the above quotation we have perhaps the soft pleasantry to which the middle character may extend itself, but in another place Shaftesbury gives us the core of it: ". . . therefore do thou *seem* in earnest."[20] And we have the description quoted above: ". . . this simple and (in appearance) humble, mean, insipid character." Thus when Shaftesbury invokes the Socratic manner, "besides the innocent and excellent dissimulation of the kind which Socrates used, remember that other sort (not less his) which hides what passes within, and accommodates our manners to those of our friends and people around us," we may with some assurance assume that the first dissimulation is Socrates' pose as a "humble, mean, insipid character," and the second his frequently but not always mocking accommodation of his mind to the minds of those he discoursed with.

[18] *Ibid.*
[19] *Ibid.,* pp. 196-97. Cf. *ibid.,* pp. 225-27.
[20] *Ibid.,* pp. 198-200.

There seem to be three distinct ironies waiting to be plucked out of the attitude and manner Shaftesbury describes. There is first of all the simple verbal irony of blame-by-praise and praise-by-blame (Dict. III.B), a device which Socrates often used. In its mildest form this verbal device is no doubt such a pleasantry and jest as Shaftesbury's manner may extend itself to, but in any virulent form it would partake of the buffoonery he abhors.

The second irony inherent in Shaftesbury's ideas would be that pervasive irony of manner which is a fusion of modest self-abnegation, a kind of gravity, and an apparent tolerance of all things behind which hide reservations about all things. As Shaftesbury theorizes about it, this manner becomes an elaborate flowering of the traditional concept of verbal blame-by-praise and praise-by-blame. The motive is to defend one's soul against prying by the world, to defend oneself from one's own temporal interests and passions, and yet to seem to live in accommodation with the society one belongs to. It is a constant way of life which is not intended to issue in verbal warfare; indeed the reservations beneath the tolerance are hidden to all except the acutest observer, the general effect being one of simple and true, though slightly peculiar, character. Nevertheless the simulations of modesty and tolerance are the subtlest of parallels to ironic self-depreciation and blame-by-praise, and in Shaftesbury's repeated admonition to himself to react to social stimuli in a *contrary* manner we find an echo of the traditional definition of blame-by-praise.

Shaftesbury uses the word *irony* only twice in the *Regimen*, in passages I have quoted above. His "honest irony" may refer only to that best verbal irony of praise and blame (Dict. III.B) which Socrates used and Shaftesbury could approve. But his "soft irony" brings the word very close indeed to the underlying manner he is describing and thereby to the irony of manner as it has been thought of in connection with Socrates.

The third irony inherent in Shaftesbury's philosophy is Sedgewick's irony of detachment or spiritual freedom. Although this irony inheres in a philosophical attitude not unlike Shaftesbury's detachment from the "immediate changes and incessant eternal conversions, revolutions of the world,"[21] Shaftesbury does not seem to connect the word to this attitude itself. He associates it only with the unique manner which this attitude may underlie.

It is easiest to understand the range of Shaftesbury's uses of *irony* in his other writings as well as in the *Regimen* when we see them in relation to a continuum which begins with the Socratic manner described above, modulates into mild raillery, thence into gross raillery, and ends in obscurity. Outside the *Regimen* Shaftesbury comes nearest to describing the Socratic manner in "Soliloquy," where he describes Socrates as

a perfect Character; yet, in some respects, so veil'd, and in a Cloud, that to the unattentive Surveyor he seemed often to be very different from what he really was: and this chiefly by reason of a certain exquisite and refin'd Raillery which belong'd to his Manner, and by virtue of which he cou'd treat the highest Subjects, and those of the commonest Capacity both together, and render 'em explanatory of each other. So that in this Genius of writing, there appear'd both *the heroick* and *the simple, the tragick* and *the comick Vein.*[22]

Presumably such "exquisite and refin'd Raillery" was the "pleasantry of a right kind, proportionable and always in season . . . sweet, gentle, mild" which in the *Regimen* he feels is appropriate to the middle character, the simple, steadfast mind. Unfortunately

To describe true *Raillery* wou'd be as hard a matter, and perhaps as little to the purpose, as to define *Good Breeding.* None can understand the Speculation, beside those who have the Practice.[23]

Nevertheless, Shaftesbury's notion of true raillery seems to involve "a free and familiar style,"[24] a "random *Miscellaneous* Air"[25] in contrast to the "dogmaticalness of the schools,"[26] the "looking freely into all subjects"[27] with sweet reasonableness and without passion, the use of "parables, tales, or fables,"[28] a preference for indirection

---

[21] *Ibid.,* pp. 192-94.

[22] Shaftesbury, *Characteristics* (1714), I, 194-95.

[23] *Ibid.,* I, 65. Shaftesbury realized that such raillery was to be found only in select company. See *ibid.,* I, 47-48, 52-54.

[24] Shaftesbury, *Characteristics* (Robertson), I, 51.

[25] *Ibid.,* II, 240.

[26] *Ibid.,* I, 52-54.

[27] *Ibid.*

[28] *Ibid.,* II, 283. Cf. *ibid.,* pp. 217-37.

rather than direct exposition, and finally, the softer forms of under-statement, blame-by-praise, and other methods of "milder censure and reproof."[29] We hear the voice of Socrates very plainly in such divine pleasantry.

Since not all men are either Socrates or even gentlemen, nor are they free to speak as they like, much pleasantry passes over into that buffoonery which distorts the truth and gives real pain to its object,[30] that frenetic involvement which in the *Regimen* Shaftesbury warns himself to avoid at all costs. He excludes most of the greatest satirists—Aristophanes, Lucian, Cervantes, Swift—when he is measuring by this ideal standard. But Shaftesbury's practical attitude toward the use of gross raillery is mixed: though he deplores its grossness, he feels that under many circumstances it is probably the most effective weapon available.[31] Even he is driven to use it occasionally.[32] Under the head of such gross rail-lery would come any except the gentlest and politest of gambits.

When raillery is carried to such an extreme of mystification that the real meaning is obscure to all or most of the audience, it is "a gross, immoral, and illiberal way of abuse."[33]

We saw above that in the *Regimen* the word *irony* occurs twice in the immediate neighborhood of Shaftesbury's true philosophic manner; in this association he modified it with "honest" and "soft." He uses the word twice elsewhere (Dict. III.B.ii) to mean only verbal blame-by-praise, both times distinguishing between good-humored irony and gross, buffooning irony. In two other places[34] he uses the word without modification or distinction in the vicinity of gross raillery, and once he uses it in relation to the obscurity of meaning which carries raillery beyond the bounds of wit into abuse (Dict. II.B). Thus *irony* for Shaftesbury is associated with a Socratic

---

[29] *Ibid.*, II, 217-37.

[30] *Ibid.*, I, 44-45, 47-48, 51.

[31] *Ibid.*, I, 21-22, 157-70.

[32] Shaftesbury, *Second Characters* (Rand), p. 140. Shaftesbury, *Life, Letters, Regimen* (Rand), pp. 504-5.

[33] Shaftesbury, *Characteristics* (Robertson), II, 295.

[34] *Ibid.*, I, 44-45. Shaftesbury, *Life, Letters, Regimen* (Rand), pp. 504-5. It also appears in the Index to *Characteristics* (1714) and on page 365 of Rand's *Life, Letters, Regimen*. In none of these places does the context supply any definite clue to the method of the irony, if any, Shaftesbury had in mind.

irony of manner, the verbal device of blame-by-praise which can produce either true or gross raillery, and certain kinds of verbal deception or mystification which are gross abuse. The dominant connotation of the word is for him pejorative, associating it as he does primarily with the caustic controversial irony he dislikes. A mitigating factor is the word's traditional association with Socrates, which leads him to extend it to Socrates' pervasive manner, prefacing it with favorable adjectives. It is possible that the disparaging connotation of the word prevents him from associating it more definitely with Socrates' manner.

ALSO: Anthony Collins, *Discourse concerning Ridicule and Irony* (1729), p. 46, quoted on p. 103 below. William Guthrie, *Cicero His Offices* (1755), p. 61. William Guthrie, *Quinctilianus His Institutes* (1756), II, 236ff.

III.B. *Limited discourse*

III.B.i. *Praise-by-blame.* First defined in the *Rhetoric to Alexander*, this sense of *irony*, as half the dichotomy praise-by-blame: blame-by-praise, stood from its early formulation through the mid-eighteenth century as the central meaning of the word.[35] *Irony* sometimes referred to a fusion of the two approaches, as in "the irony of Socrates." As a separate entity, however, praise-by-blame was a much less frequently invoked meaning than blame-by-praise.

The technique of praise under the pretense of blame was developed in obvious ways by the prose and verse satirists of late Elizabethan times as part of their satiric arsenal. Later, under the hands of the Scriblerus group and pre-eminently of Swift, taking their lead from French letter writers, this irony became a pervasive and delightful mode of letter writing, conversation, and *jeux d'ésprit*. The result was to give the word itself a wider area of reference in social intercourse and almost to give it a pleasant connotation. But *raillery* was the more popular term for such playful

[35] G. G. Sedgewick, "Dramatic Irony" (1913), pp. 127-29, 136-38, 143-44, 191-94.

compliment and *irony* never lost its overtones of contention and spite.

CLASSICAL PRECEDENTS: *Rhetoric to Alexander.* Quintilian *Institutio* VIII.vi.54-58.

Abraham Fraunce, *Arcadian Rhetorike* (1588), Book I, chap. vi. [Illustration under "Ironia"]:

> Of Mopsa.
> So that the pretie pig, laying her sweet burden about his necke; my *Dorus,* sayd she, tell me these wonders.

ALSO: John Marbeck, *Notes and Commonplaces* (1581), p. 560.

Gabriel Harvey, *Works* (Grosart), II, 243-45:

> ... the Ironyes of Erasmus in his prayse of Folly; of Agrippa in his disprayse of Sciences...

ALSO: Gabriel Harvey, *Marginalia* (Moore Smith), p. 143.

Bacon, Works (Spedding), III, 388:

> ... it was not without cause, that so many excellent philosophers became Sceptics and Academics, and denied any certainty of knowledge or comprehension, and held opinion that the knowledge of man extended only to appearances and probabilities.   It is true that in Socrates it was supposed to be but a form of irony, *Scientiam dissimulando simulavit,* [an affectation of knowledge under pretence of ignorance: —editor's trans.] for he used to disable his knowledge, to the end to enhance his knowledge.... [Cf. J. A. K. Thomson, "Erasmus in England" (1930-31), pp. 73-74 n., and Johnson, *Dictionary* (1755-56) under "Ironically."]

ALSO: Bacon, *Works* (Spedding), III, 293; IV, 68-69; VII, 158. John Stephens, *Satyrical Essayes* (1615), pp. 1-5, and *Essayes and Characters Ironicall* (1615), pp. 1-7, 29-30 (see discussion under Dict. III.B.ii).   C. H. Spurgeon, *Treasury of David* (1885), p. 420, quoting "William Gurnall's Funeral Sermon for Lady Mary Vere, 1671." *Aristotle's Rhetoric* (1686), p. 257 (the *Rhetoric to Alexander*).   Charles Leslie, *Best Answer Ever was Made* (1709), p. 24.   Bailey, *Universal Etymological English Dictionary* II (1727).   Bailey, *Dictionarium Britannicum* (1730).

Pope, *Works* (Elwin-Courthope), VII, 412:

> Dr. Swift much approves what I proposed, even to the very title, which I design shall be, The Works of the Unlearned, published monthly, in

which whatever book appears that deserves praise, shall be depreciated ironically, and in the same manner that modern critics take to under-value works of value, and to commend the high productions of Grub-street.

ALSO: *Ibid.*, VII, 306-7, Warburton's note.　Pope, *Works* (1751), VI, 192 ("Memoirs of ... Scriblerus").

Swift, *Poems* (Williams), I, 214-19:

> Our Conversation to refine
> True Humor must with Wit combine:
> From both, we learn to Railly well;
> Wherein French Writers most excell:
> Voiture in various Lights displays
> That Irony which turns to Praise,
> His Genius first found out the Rule
> For an obliging Ridicule:
> He flatters with peculiar Air
> The Brave, the Witty, and the Fair;
> And Fools would fancy he intends
> A Satyr where he most commends.

Swift, *Correspondence* (Ball), IV, 163-66:

[Lord Bathurst to Swift, Cirencester, Sept. 9, 1730:]

I receive so much pleasure in reading your letters, that, according to the usual good-nature and justice of mankind, I can dispense with the trouble I give you in reading mine. But if you grow obstinate, and will not answer me, I will plague and pester you, and do all I can to vex you. I will take your works to pieces, and show you that they are all borrowed or stolen. Have you not stolen the sweetness of your numbers from Dryden and Waller? Have not you borrowed thoughts from Virgil and Horace? At least, I am sure I have seen something like them in those books. And in your prose writings, which they make such a noise about, they are only some little improvements upon the hu-mour you have stolen from Miguel de Cervantes and Rabelais. Well, but the style—a great matter indeed, for an Englishman to value him-self upon, that he can write English; why, I write English too, but it is in another style.

But I will not forget your political tracts. You may say, that you have ventured your ears at one time, and your neck at another, for the good of your country. Why, that other people have done in another manner, upon less occasion, and are not at all proud of it. You have overturned and supported Ministers; you have set kingdoms in a flame by your pen. Pray, what is there in that, but having the knack of hitting the passions of mankind? With that alone, and a little knowledge of ancient and modern history, and seeing a little farther into the inside of things than the generality of men, you have made this bustle. There is no wit in any of them: I have read them all over, and do not remember any of those pretty flowers, those just antitheses, which one meets with so frequently in the French writers; none of those clever turns upon words, nor those apt quotations out of Latin authors, which the writers of the last age among us abounded in; none of those pretty similes, which some of our modern authors adorn their works with, that are not only a little like the thing they would illustrate, but are also like twenty other things. In short as often as I have read any of your tracts, I have been so tired with them, that I have never been easy till I got to the end of them. I have found my brain heated, my imagination fired, just as if I was drunk. A pretty thing, indeed, for one of your gown to value himself upon, that with sitting still an hour in his study, he has often made three kingdoms drunk at once.

[Swift to Lord Bathurst, October, 1730:]
... I would give the best thing I ever was supposed to publish, in exchange to be author of your letters. I pretend to have been an improver of irony on the subject of satire and praise, but I will surrender up my title to your Lordship.

ALSO: *Ibid.*, V, 269-71. *Prompter*, No. 144 (March 23, 1736). *Memoirs of Grub-street* (1737), I, viii-x. William Guthrie, *Quinctilianus His Institutes* (1756), II, 235-36. *Monthly Review*, IX (July, 1753), 67-68. Letitia Pilkington, *Memoirs* I and II (1749), I, 59. Patrick Delaney, *Observations upon Orrery's Remarks* (1754), pp. 16-17. Deane Swift, *Essay upon Swift* (1755), pp. 135-36.

Johnson, *Lives* (Birkbeck-Hill), III, 60:

On all common occasions he [Swift] habitually affects a style of arrogance, and dictates rather than persuades. This authoritative and magisterial language he expected to be received as his peculiar mode of jocularity; but he apparently flattered his own arrogance by an assumed imperiousness, in which he was ironical only to the resentful, and to the submissive sufficiently serious.

Johnson's "ironical" above might also be taken as Dict. VIII, "any discourse not meant to be taken seriously."

III.B.ii. *Blame-by-praise.* In nearly two-thirds of the passages which I have collected for the years 1500-1755, *irony* denotes some mode of blame-by-praise. The thing itself was also discussed in the sixteenth- and early seventeenth-century handbooks under various other names, particularly *dissembling* and *antiphrasis*.[36] The illustrative examples given by Cicero and Quintilian passed from one sixteenth-century handbook to another, and a small group of scriptural examples descended through seventeenth-century handbooks.[37] So familiar were these stock illustrations to his readers that Hobbes could call the roll with confident brevity:

The mocking trope is, when one contrary is signified by another; as God said, *Man is like to one of us.* So Christ saith, *Sleep on*; and yet by-and-by, *Arise, let us go.* So Paul saith, *You are wise, and I am a fool.*

This trope is conceived either by the contrariety of the matter, or the manner of utterance, or both. So Elijah said to the prophets of Baal, *Cry aloud,* &c. So the Jews said unto Christ, *Hail, King of the Jews.*[38]

As the most frequently used sense of *irony*, blame-by-praise tended to dominate thought about the word's meaning; consequently it was sometimes assumed automatically that the word referred to blame-by-praise in instances in which the actual reference, if carefully distinguished, utilized another sense of the word. For instance, John Hoskins and his followers classed examples of understatement under the irony of blame-by-praise (see Dict. v.b). Ordinarily, however, *irony* as blame-by-praise referred to a limited piece of discourse or action which conveys a critical attack under the guise of

[36] Thomas Wilson, *Rhetorique* (G. H. Mair), pp. 121 ("diminishing"), 134-56 ("dissembling"), 184-85 ("Dissembling or close jesting"). Hoby, *Courtier* (Everyman), pp. 159-62 ("dissimulation"). Guazzo, *Civile Conversation* (Tudor Trans.), I, 68 ("Antiphrasis"), 82 ("mockerie"). Puttenham, *Arte of English Poesie* (Willcock-Walker), pp. 186-91 ("drye mock," "fleering frumpe" or "Micterismus," "broad floute" or "Antiphrasis"). Peacham, *Garden of Eloquence* (1593), pp. 24-25 ("Antiphrasis"), 35-36 (he gives the Latin names "Dissimulatio," "Irrisio," "Illusio"). Angel Day, *English Secretorie* (1595), Part II, pp. 79-80 ("Antiphrasis"). Philemon Holland, *Plutarch's Morals* (1603), p. 59 ("Mocker"), 433 ("mocke"), 474 ("mockerie"). Burton, *Anatomy of Melancholy* (1621), pp. 196-99 ("scoffing"). John Smith, *Rhetorique* (1657), pp. 79-80 ("Sarcasme"). *Art of Complaisance* (1673), pp. 81-82 ("poisonous praises").

[37] John Hoskins, *Directions for Speech and Style* (Hudson), pp. 11-12, 29-30. Thomas Blount, *Academie of Eloquence* (1654), pp. 5-6, 25-26. Thomas Hall, *The Schools Guarded* (1655), pp. 163-70. John Smith, *Rhetorique* (1657), pp. 45-48. Edward Reyner, *Government of the Tongue* (1658), pp. 223-27.

[38] Hobbes, *The Art of Rhetoric* (Molesworth), p. 517.

ostensible praise. The ironist intends his audience to understand his real intention—to be deceived only fleetingly—and the relationship is of rebuker and rebuked, perhaps surrounded by amused onlookers. If the rebuked does not realize his predicament the reason is not that he has not been offered the handle to it by the ironist, but that he is ridiculously obtuse. Of course the ironist may count on this density to make game for himself and the onlookers, but deception for a practical purpose (Dict. I, II) is not his intent. This irony differs from that of understatement in that its method is to say something contradictory of its real meaning, rather than somewhat less than its real meaning (Dict. v), yet it cannot be defined simply as stating an opposite, as was frequently done during our period, because the elements involved are not *any* logical opposites but can be only the opposites of praise and blame. However, irony did sometimes refer to a statement of any logical opposite, thus producing a distinct meaning (Dict. IV). But of course a complex ironic structure often involved both understatement (Dict. v) and the opposing of contrary terms (Dict. IV) within a dominant pattern of blame-by-praise and thus encouraged casual reference to the whole complex as blame-by-praise.

The irony of Socrates, which as we have seen has meant many things to many people, was usually referred to during the English classical period as simply the rhetorical device of blame-by-praise. Although people were of course aware that Socrates used this device repeatedly, there was no strong awareness of a pervasive ironic manner (Dict. III.A); Socrates' irony like most irony was simply a verbal device of blame-by-praise used either frequently or infrequently.[39]

[39] The extent to which the English classical period could resist thinking of Socrates' dialectical method, which is what Sedgewick offers as the meaning of *Socratic irony*, as irony is well illustrated by James Geddes, who discusses Plato for over 200 pages and perfectly describes his ironic handling of an opponent, yet does not call this method ironic.

"Socrates, the better to oppose those Dogmatists, and beat down their presumptuous vanity, disputed with them often. He affirm'd nothing himself, but thoroughly confuted their arguments. They pretended, they knew every thing, he on the other hand, said, he only knew that he was ignorant of every thing, and for this was declared by the oracle, to be the wisest of men: not that he intended to confound, and destroy all truths human and divine."

"It is pleasant to observe how Plato (or Socrates) defeats the Sophists by their own weapons. Those mighty champions, who valued themselves on puzzling

The methods of blame-by-praise familiar to the English classical age are discussed in Chapter III below.

CLASSICAL PRECEDENTS: Plato *Republic* 337a. Plato *Gorgias* 489*de*. Aristotle *Rhetoric* III.xix.5. Cicero *On Oratory* II. 65, 67 ff. Cicero *Letters to Quintus* III.iv.4. Cicero *Brutus* 85-87. Cicero *Academica* II.15. Quintilian *Institutio* VI.ii.9-16; VIII.vi.54-58; IX.ii.44-53; IX.iii.29. Plutarch *Lives*, "Timoleon" 15. Plutarch *Moralia* 44*d*, 236*c*. Lucian *A Literary Prometheus* 1; *Lexiphanes* 1; *Zeus Tragœdus* 52; *Anacharsus* 17-18.

Thordynary of Crysten men (1506), Part IV, sec. xxii:

. . . suche synne is named yronye not that the whiche is of grammare by the whiche a man sayth one & gyveth to understande the contrarye for the maner & the purpose in the whiche a man speketh the wordes as to saye alas that thou arte a good man or thynge semblable the whiche is as moche to saye that he is nothynge worthe. . . .

ALSO: Thomas More, *Works* (1557), chap. v, p. 939. Thomas More, *Lucian* (C. R. Thompson), pp. 24-27. Miles Coverdale, *Remains* (Parker Soc.), II, 331, 333. John Hooper, *Early Writings* (Parker Soc.), p. 420. Thomas Cranmer, *Answer unto . . . Gardiner* (1551), p. 69. John Philpott, *Writings* (Parker Soc.), pp. 418-19.

---

every one else, and perplexing the clearest question, when engaged with him, are soon sensible how unequal the match: at first, he deals with them gently, extols them for their knowledge, and leads them on step by step: they seem mighty fond of one who makes them such high compliments, and deign to inform him of every thing they know. In the midst of their triumph, Socrates begs leave to ask a question or two; desires them, in a few words to explain their meaning, and define some expression, or term of art: this perhaps they chearfully do for once: the absurdity of the definition is exposed; a second attempted; and found equally ridiculous; then a third, just as bad as the former. By this time, the antagonist, if modest, withdraws as softly as he can: but, if insolent and proud of his fame for eloquence, he turns in a fury, accuses Socrates of sophistry, pedantry, dullness, and pours forth all the ill-natured language he is master of. . . . A dialogue thus carried on, and the justness of character all along preserved, becomes equally entertaining to a man of taste, with the most facetious comedy. In such discourses Plato's style is natural, easy, often witty, and full of humour; his raillery exquisite, and such as becomes a gentleman; his reasoning refin'd, and metaphysical: the ingenuity and good humour of Socrates, his lively descriptions, frequent ironys, and just strokes of satyr, when set in opposition to the intemperance of language, the passionate surly behaviour, clumsy wit, sour repartees, and personal invectives of his adversaries, form an agreeable contrast, and wonderfully enliven the whole discourse." —James Geddes, *Composition and Manner of Writing of the Antients* (1748), pp. 98-101.

Richard Sherry, *Rhetorike* (1555), fol. xxvi:

Ironia, dissimulacion.... His kinds be these.

Sarcasmus, a scorne of our enemye, and a nipping taunt. As the Jewes said to Christ: now let him come down from the crosse, and save hymselfe, that saved other.

ALSO: Thomas Cooper, *Thesaurus* (1578), under "Ironia." Spenser, *Minor Poems* (Sélincourt), pp. 99 and 103: E. K.'s note on "October." John Marbeck, *Notes and Commonplaces* (1581), p. 560. Abraham Fraunce, *Arcadian Rhetorike* (1588), Book I, chap. vi. Puttenham, *Arte of English Poesie* (Willcock-Walker), pp. 186-91.

Thomas Nashe, *Works* (McKerrow), I, 306-7:

With the first and second leafe hee [Gabriel Harvey] plaies verie pretilie, and in ordinarie termes of extenuating verdits *Pierce Pennilesse for a Grammer Schoole wit*; saies *his Margine is as deepelie learnd as* Fauste praecor gelida, that *his Muse sobbeth and groneth verie piteouslie, bids him not cast himself headlong into the horrible gulph of desperation,* comes over him *that hee is a creature of wonderfull hope, as his own inspired courage divinely suggesteth, wils him to inchaunt some magnificent* Mecenas, *to honour* himselfe in honouring him, with a hundred such *gracewanting* Ironies cutte out against the woll, that woulde jeopard the best joint of *Poetica licentia* to procure laughter, when there crinckled crabbed countenance (the verie resemblance of a sodden dogges face) hath sworne it woulde never consent thereunto.

Not the most exquisite thing that is, but the Coūsel Table Asse, Richard Clarke, may so Carterly deride.

Everie Milke-maide can gird with, Ist true? How saie you, lo? who would have thought it? Good Beare, bite not. A man is a man though hee hath but a hose on his head.

Gabriel Harvey, *Works* (Grosart), II, 243-45:

The Ironyes of Socrates, Aristophanes, Epicharmus, Lucian, are *but Carterly derisions*: the Ironyes of Tully, Quintilian, Petrarch, Pontane, Sanazarius, King Alphonsus, but the sory *Jestes of the Counsell-table Asse, Richard Clarke*: the Ironyes of Erasmus in his prayse of Folly; of Agrippa in his disprayse of Sciences: of Cardan in his Apology of Nero, like Isocrates commendation of Busiris, or Lucians defence of Phalaris the Tyrant, but *Good Beare bite not*: the Ironyes of Sir Thomas More in his Utopia, Poemes, Letters, and other writings; or of any their Imitatours at occasion, but the *girdes of every milke-maide*. They were silly country fellowes that commended the Bald pate, the Feaver quartane; the fly, the flea, the gnat, the sparrow, the wren, the goose, the asse;

flattery, hypocrisie, coosinage, bawdery, leachery, buggery, madnesse it-
selfe. What Dunse or Sorbonist cannot maintaine a Paradoxe? What
Pesant cannot say to a glorious Soldiour? *Pulchrè me herculè dictum, &*
sapienter: or, *Lautè, lepidè, nihil supra*: or, *Regem elegantem narras*:
or, a man is a man, though he have but a hose upon his head: or so forth.
No such light payment Gabriell, at Pierce Penniles, or Thomas Nashes
hand. They are rare, and dainty wittes, that can roundly call a man
Asse at every third word; and make not nice, to befoole him in good
sullen earnest, that can strangle the prowdest breath of their pennes, and
meaneth to borrow a sight of their giddiest braines, for a perfect Anatome
of Vanitie, and Folly. Though strõg drinke fumẽth, & Aqua fortis fret-
teth; yet I will not exchaunge my Milke-maides Irony, for his Draff-
maides assery.

ALSO: Thomas Nashe, *Works* (McKerrow), III, 125-26. Gabriel
Harvey, *Works* (Grosart), II, 294-318. Gabriel Harvey, *Marginalia* (Moore Smith), pp. 143 (description of Sanazarius), 153, 155.
Peacham, *Garden of Eloquence* (1593), pp. 35-36. Angel Day, *English Secretorie* (1595), I, 44-45, 110-11, 138; II, 45-47, 79. Thomas
Danett, *Comines* (Whibley), II, 200. Joseph Hall, *Works* (Talboys), II, 71. Florio, *World of Words* (1611), under "Catálogo
d'ella glória d'el móndo." John Hoskins, *Directions for Speech
and Style* (Hudson), pp. 11-12, 29-30 (see below under Dict. v.B).

Bacon, *Works* (Spedding), IV, 68-69:

The school of Plato, on the other hand, introduced *Acatalepsia*, at
first in jest and irony, and in disdain of the older sophists, Protagoras,
Hippias, and the rest, who were of nothing else so much ashamed as of
seeming to doubt about anything.

Ibid., VI, 296-97:

... vain and supercilious arrogancy is justly derided in Plato, where he
brings in Hippias, a vaunting Sophist, disputing with Socrates, a true and
unfeigned inquisitor of truth; where, the discourse being touching beauty,
Socrates, after his loose and wandering manner of inductions, put first
an example of a fair virgin, then of a fair horse, then of a fair pot well
glazed. Whereat Hippias was offended, and said, "Were it not for
courtesy's sake, I should be loth to dispute with one that did allege
such base and sordid instances." Whereunto Socrates answered, "You
have reason, and it becomes you well, being a man so trim in your vest-
ments, and so fairly shod;" and so goes on in irony. [Cf. III, 332]

ALSO: *Ibid.,* V, 72, and above under Dict. III.B.i. Bacon usually thought of the term *irony* in connection with Socrates. He viewed Socrates' self-depreciation and his deferential manner as a reaction against the arrogant self-confidence of the Sophists. By depreciating his own knowledge, Socrates enhanced it in the minds of others; he also forced comparison with the confident manner of his antagonist, and with the addition of a little judicious but obviously misplaced compliment, he could bring that antagonist tumbling down.

Thus Bacon's central conception of the *irony* of Socrates was of a verbal weapon mixing blame-by-praise (of the antagonist) with praise-by-blame (of himself). Insofar as Bacon was thinking of Socrates' repeated use of this verbal device, he was using *irony* in a sense related to the *irony of manner* (see Dict. III.A), but his conception of an ironic "manner" went no deeper than the repeated use of the verbal device. Bacon was aware of Socrates' dialectical method, as the above quotations indicate, but he does not call it *irony;* he spoke of Plato as "a man of sublime wit (and one that surveyed all things as from a lofty cliff) . . . ,"[40] but he does not call this spiritual freedom *irony.*

ALSO: Jonson, *Works* (Herford-Simpson), III, 546; IV, 130-32. John Manningham, *Diary* (Camden Soc.), p. 74. Philemon Holland, *Plutarch's Morals* (1657), p. 526. Andrew Willet, *Hexapla in Genesin* (1608), p. 377.

Edward Topsell, *Four-Footed Beastes* (1607), pp. 2-5:

. . . generally they [apes] are held for a subtill, ironicall, ridiculous and unprofitable Beast. . . .

Moreover Apes are much given to imitation and derision, and they are called *Cercopes,* because of their wicked crafts, deceipts, impostures and flatteries. . . . Apes have beene taught to leape, singe, drive Wagons, raigning and whipping the Horses very artificially, and are very capable of all humaine actions. . . .

And as the body of an Ape is ridiculous by reason of an indecent likenesse and imitation of man, so is his soule or spirit . . . following every action he seeth done, even to his owne harme without discretion.

They are full of dissimulation, and imitation of man, they readiler folow the evill then the good they see.

[40] Bacon, *Works* (Spedding), IV, 360.

The word "ironicall" here may mean any kind of derision an ape might think of (Dict. ix), or more specifically the burlesque methods of mock praise. What is especially interesting about Topsell's use is that he applies the word to exclusively nonverbal actions. A few years later John Bulwer's treatises on gestures apply *irony* to certain motions which are meaningful without the accompaniment of words.

ALSO: Sandys, *Relation of a Journey* (1615), p. 83. William Warner, *Albions England* (1612), Book IX, chap. xxxv, pp. 238-39. Samuel Purchas, *Pilgrimage* (1614), pp. 877-78.

John Stephens, *Essayes and Characters Ironicall* (1615), p. 29:

> My labour I renew: but having seene
> How ill dispos'd my former truth hath been
> I grow a little wiser; and agree
> To make an Essay prove an Ironie.

So far as I know this was the first time *irony* was used in the title of an English book. Since Stephens presumably felt the word fitted his book in some way it is important that we know how. What is there in the book itself that would justify being called "Ironicall"? Or was the crucial factor in his choice of words an external one?

Essayes and Characters Ironicall, and Instructive. The second impression... 1615 was a revised edition of *Satyrical Essayes Characters and Others. Or Accurate and quick Descriptions, fitted to the life of their Subjects... 1615.* In both editions there is a tantalizing connection with the early meaning of *irony* as hypocrisy and deception (Dict. i). Thus on the title page of *Satyrical Essayes* appears a sentence from Theophrastus' character of the ironist: "It is more necessary to guard against those of this disposition than against serpents,"[41] two other mottoes emphasize the theme of dissimulation and hypocrisy, and the book opens with "Three Satyricall Essayes of Cowardlinesse":

> For who in Vertues troope was ever seene,
> That did couragiously with mischiefes fight
> Without the publicke name of hipocrite?

[41] Translated by Benjamin Boyce, *The Theophrastan Character in England to 1642*, p. 227 n.

Vaine-glorious, Malapert, Precise, Devout,
Be tearmes which threaten those that go about
To stand in opposition of our times
With true defiance, or Satyricke rimes.
Cowards they be, branded among the worst,
Who (through contempt of Atheisme) never durst
Crowd neere a great-Mans elbow, to suggest
Smooth tales with glosse, or Envy well addrest.
These be the noted cowards of our age;
Who be not able to instruct the Stage
With matter of new shamelesse impudence:
Who cannot almost laugh at innocence;
And purchase high preferment by the waies,
Which had bene horrible in Nero's dayes.
They are the shamefull cowards, who contemne
Vices of State, or cannot flatter them;
Who can refuse advantage; or deny
Villanous courses, if they can espye
Some little purchase to inrich their chest,
Though they become uncomfortably blest.[42]

In this first essay we see that Stephens is mimicking contemporary corruption in its appropriation of moral sanction to itself while applying unfavorable epithets to good men; in the second essay he makes a more direct attack on the "front" put up by these hypocrites, which is false, for behind it lurk evil, deceit, corruption. Those whom the popular voice calls cowards are really courageous men; the fine-appearing dissemblers are the real cowards, for they are afraid to reveal their own natures.[43] What Stephens is attacking, then, is that particular reversal of terms which is giving to a virtue the name of a vice and the giving to a vice the name of a virtue. This abstracted characteristic was one of the stock definitions of blame-by-praise *irony*;[44] moreover, such hypocrisy might have seemed to be the kind of irony described by Theophrastus. But the allusion to Theophrastus actually leads to nothing; nowhere in his book does Stephens apply the word *irony* to such hypocrisy.

On the other hand, passages like that quoted above do demonstrate Stephens' *use* of the irony of blame-by-praise. In mimicking

---

[42] John Stephens, *Satyrical Essayes* (1615), pp. 1-5.
[43] *Ibid.*, p. 15.
[44] See p. 33 above.

the attitude he attacks, Stephens works through simulated approbation of it; in applying the hypocrites' word "coward" to good men,
Stephens praises them under the guise of blaming them. His irony
is illustrated again in the passage below ("My labour I renew...")
when he mimics his critics ("Then what Profession shall I now
disgrace?") and depreciates himself ("Alas I am too modest...").
Stephens did in fact feel that "darke reproofe," a conventional description of irony at this time, was the proper method of satire.
This is evident in his rejections of "extreame reproofe," "Libell-
lashing measures," "triviall spleane," "cursing," "long invectives,"
"bitter malice," and "reviling phrase,"[45] and if Stephens' irony does
not strike us as "milde reproofe" or even very "darke reproofe,"
we must remember that his own age would have compared it with
the "clamorous rayling" of which the invectives of Nashe and
Harvey were educated examples.

As one object of his satire in the first edition Stephens included
the character of "A common Player,"[46] an attack on actors com-
pounded of insulting description, libelous insinuation, and ironic
praise of, for instance, the Player's "delicate quirkes against the
rich Cuckold." A second object of Stephens' attention was the lawyers, attorneys, and clerks who crop up regularly throughout the
Satyrical Essayes for the good reason that Stephens himself was a
member of Lincoln's Inn from Gloucestershire and associated with
inns-of-court men.[47] He attacks abuses of the law and of the profession with full satiric force, albeit with an occasional apology to
honest lawyers.[48] As a result of these attacks Stephens apparently
got into hot water with the actors and more importantly with his
friends the lawyers. There are a number of oblique references to
these difficulties, and one or two open ones.[49] Whatever forms the
trouble took, it produced a number of additions, deletions, and revisions in Stephens' second edition. In the character "A common

---

[45] John Stephens, *Essayes and Characters Ironicall* (1615), title page, pp. 18, 46, 71-72.
[46] John Stephens, *Satyrical Essayes* (1615), pp. 244-49.
[47] Benjamin Boyce, *op. cit.*, pp. 220-28.
[48] John Stephens, *Satyrical Essayes* (1615), pp. 1-5, 11-14, 29, 244-49, 280-83. John Stephens, *Essayes and Characters Ironicall* (1615), pp. 197, 333.
[49] Benjamin Boyce, *op. cit.*, p. 226. John Stephens, *Essayes and Characters Ironicall* (1615), sig. A3^r-A8^v, pp. 6-7, 18, 20-22, 29-30, 295-301, 335-41, 352.

Player" he made eleven changes, all but one aimed at exacerbating rather than diminishing the offense. But his changes in the legal satire followed a different line. In Essay I he added a long attack on merchants, embedded in which is a reference to "true Divines and honest Lawyers."[50] Out of Essay II Stephens cut the whole of the long attack on lawyers, substituting for it a brief attack on "the brag Civilian" who thinks himself better than "any common Lawyer."[51] In Essay III the lawyer of an uncomplimentary passage is replaced by a scholar.[52] Essay IV is entirely new and its title accurately represents its quite unironic message: "Essay the fourth entituled Reproofe. Or a defence for common Law & Lawyers mixt with reproofe against the Lawyers common Enemy." One can only conclude that a main purpose of these revisions was mollification of Stephens' friends in the legal profession.

Now let us turn again to the one passage other than the title in which the word *irony* appears:

> My labour I renew: but having seene,
> How ill dispos'd my former truth hath been
> I grow a little wiser; and agree
> To make an Essay prove an Ironie.
> Then what Profession shall I now disgrace?
> Reproofe is thought to have no better face
> Then *Impudence* or *Malice*; and is thought
> To be a scandall by corruption wrought.
> Tis true: a thriving knowledge hath by some
> Who lack'd such happy wit, been thought a scum;
> And, under shadow of reproofe, hath beene
> Made an extreame derision to be seene:
> Nay made a publike injury, to please
> Them, who should punish the contempt; & squese
> That shamefull envy, till it doth remaine,
> As empty as the rugged Authors braine,
> Alas I am too modest and obscure:
> I shew in darke reproofe what is impure;
> And therefore have beene blamed: but I will now
> Speake with an open zeale; and disavow
> The mincing tearmes of caution: if I faile

[50] *Ibid.*, pp. 1-7.
[51] *Ibid.*, pp. 7-19.
[52] *Ibid.*, p. 25.

To speake my meaning, let me nere prevaile
To speake a righteous thought: And if I misse
Opinion of a tempered zeale in this,
I shall account it glory; for the thing,
Needs such a Poets vehemence to sing
Her hated tropheies, that will neither care
To purchase hate; nor will his knowledge spare:
Nay such a Poet that will be most glad,
In her defence to be accounted mad.
In her? in whose defence? thine (sacred Law)
Thine, whose provoking rarity doth draw
My soule unto thy rescue.[53]

At first glance the opening four lines seem to say: since my first edition went about things in the wrong way I am going to write this new essay in a different style, the ironic style. The larger context offers two contradictions to this reading. He has renamed the whole book "Ironicall," but if the first edition was not ironical he has not made enough revisions to change its basic character. And in this passage he asserts bitterly that since he has been blamed for obscurity and dark reproof, he will now speak with open zeal. Considering all the traditional meanings of *irony*, one finds it impossible to believe that the word could at this time mean "openness." We begin again. If Stephens meant "prove" in the sense of "proving a will" or "proving a case," as he very well might, he was saying: since people misunderstood my first edition I will now speak plainly in order to prove that what I said was ironic.

Perhaps we can recapitulate Stephens' intentions in the following way. A primary object of his satire—the hypocritical reversal of moral terms—and his own tastes as a satirist led him, in his first edition, to use a certain amount of rather elementary blame-by-praise and praise-by-blame irony. Since this was not well received in all quarters he set out to repair the damage in his second edition. What better defense than to argue he had been misunderstood? He could add and delete material to make his meaning clearer (and show the essential goodness of his heart) and he could emphasize the fact that the body of his satire was not to be taken literally, at face value. It reproved indirectly and more gently than harsh

[53] *Ibid.,* pp. 29-30.

invective would, but it had to be interpreted correctly—it some-times said something different from what it really meant. And we arrive at the word *irony*, perhaps brought especially to Stephens' attention by Theophrastus' use of it in an older sense. This line of reasoning seems all the more convincing when we compare the new title with the title of the first edition: *"Accurate and quick Descriptions, fitted to the life of their Subjects." Irony* as Stephens used it, then, seems to have meant "saying something different from what one means," especially blame-by-praise and praise-by-blame (Dict. III.B).

ALSO: John Brinsley, *Tullies Offices* (1631), p. 221 [?]. Fynes Moryson, *Itinerary* (1617), p. 160. Thomas Granger, *Divine Log-ike* (1620), pp. 381-82. *Douay Bible* (1635), Jeremiah 46:3-16. Jasper Mayne, *Lucian* (1663), p. 1. John Dove, *Atheism Defined* (1656), chap. vi, p. 88. William Whately, *Prototypes* (1640), Book I, chap. xi, p. 147. Thomas Fuller, *Two Sermons* (1654), pp. 2-4.

John Bulwer, *Pathomyotomia* (1649), pp. 64-65:

> When we would *mock, deride, contemne, disdaine, threaten* or *rebuke,* we use an ironicall motitation or wagging Nod by the flexion and reflection of our Head in turnes in a quick succession, both which motions, peculiar to the Head, are done in sequence by the *Muscles* of *Assent* and *Deniall* making as 'twere a mixt motion, and that emphatical and proper enough, for an ironie, where the first action imports approbation, and the second coming in the interim and immediately upon the nick of it before it is fully done, by a contradictory motion compounds it into an ironie.

ALSO: John Bulwer, *Chirologia and Chironomia* (1644), pp. 181-83 (see also Dict. IX). Stephen Marshall, *Emanuel* (1648), pp. 1, 7-8. Milton, *Works* (Columbia), XVII, 299-303; XVIII, 331. Thomas Blount, *Academie of Eloquence* (1654), pp. 5-6, 25-26. Thomas Hall, *The Schools Guarded* (1655), pp. 163-70. Cowley, *Poems* (Waller), pp. 202-3, 204. John Smith, *Rhetorique* (1657), pp. 45-48, 74-76, 203-4. Hobbes, *The Art of Rhetoric* (Moles-worth), pp. 515, 517. Edward Reyner, *Government of the Tongue* (1658), pp. 223-27. Obadiah Walker, *Art of Oratory* (1659), p. 93. Daniel Pell, *Nec inter Vivos* (1659), pp. 407-8. Owen Fell-tham, *Resolves* (1661), pp. 284-85. Edward Phillips, *New World of Words* (1706), under "Irony." Rapin, *Comparison of Plato and Aristotle* (1673), p. 17.

Marvell, *Rehearsal Transpros'd* (1672), p. 129:

But that which I confess would vex me most, were I either an ill or a well-meaning Zealot, would be, after all to hear him [Parker] (as he frequently does) sneering at me in an ironical harangue, to perswade me, forsooth, to take all patiently for Conscience-sake, and the good example of Mankind: Nay, to wheedle one almost to make himself away to save the Hangman a labour. It was indeed near that pass in the Primitive times, and the tyred Magistrates ask'd them, whether they had not Halters and Rivers and Precipices, if they were so greedy of Suffering? But, by the good leave of your Insolence, we are not come to that yet.

ALSO: *Ibid.,* pp. 123-24. *Raillerie a la Mode* (1673), pp. 36-40. Richard Baxter, *A Paraphrase on the New Testament* (1701), Acts 23:5. *Somers Tracts* (1748), pp. 153-58. *Art of Speaking* (1708), pp. 63, 305-11. Otway, *Works* (Summers), "Don Carlos," Act II, scene i. Guilletiere, *Voyage to Athens* (1676), p. 348. Thomas Herbert, *Travels* (1677), pp. 198, 364, 392. Allen Apsley, *Order and Disorder* (1679), pp. 65-66. John Sergeant, *Reason against Raillery* (1682), Preface C4^v-D1^v. *Aristotle's Rhetoric* (1686), pp. 212, 257. Hugh Macdonald, *John Dryden: A Bibliography* (1939), p. 215 n. *Plutarch's Morals* (1691), I, 520. Christopher Ness, *History of the Old and New Testament* (1696), I, 234. Bruyère, *Manners of the Age* (1699), p. 413. Tom Brown, *Amusements and Letters* (Hayward), p. 75. Dennis, *Critical Works* (Hooker), II, 33-34. George Granville, *Unnatural Flights in Poetry* (Spingarn), p. 296. Defoe, *True-Born Englishman* (Morley), p. 195. Defoe, *Explanation of the Shortest Way* (Trevelyan), p. 56. *The Fox with his Fire-brand Unkennell'd* (1703), pp. 3-4, 5 [?], 6, 7, 16, 20 [?]. *The Shortest-Way with the Dissenters . . . Consider'd* (1703), pp. 3, 16. John Harris, *Lexicon Technicum* (1704), under "Irony." Bellegarde, *Reflexions upon Ridicule* (1717), I, 170, 179, 217, 221, 222; II, 47, 62, 149-50. Bayle, *Dictionary* (1710), I, 324C. Bayle, *Dictionary* (1734-41), I, 648a; IV, 408-9. Charles Leslie, *Best Answer Ever was Made* (1709),

p. 24.   White Kennett, *A Panegyrick upon Folly* (1709), pp. xiv-xvi.

Shaftesbury, *Life, Letters, Regimen* (Rand), pp. 356-66:

It is very unnatural to Mons. Dacier to assign to Horace any religion at all, after he has represented him as regardless of all religion or religious rites of his country, as to make an open jest of it, and of all things sacred in that pretended mock recantation of Epicureanism, Ode 34, Bk. I, which, in Mons. Dacier's sense, would be the poorest triumph and most affected piece of profaneness in the world, considering the gravity of the ode, and of all those its fellow odes in honour of the gods, and of the religion then established. . . .   There is a due proportion in irony well known to all polite writers, especially Horace, who so well copied that noted Socratic kind.   Go but a little further with it, and strain it beyond a certain just measure, and there is nothing so offensive, injurious, hypocritical, bitter, and contrary to all true simplicity, honesty, or good manners.   And such would be Horace's 34th Ode if Mons. Dacier's admired discovery were any discovery at all.

. . . it was actually a truth, and a sincere one in his mouth, that he had, to his sorrow, "Parcus deorum cultor et infrequens," by having fallen from his first principles, with which he began the world; but that in process of time, after having experienced all that pleasures and a Court with looser morals and a more flattering philosophy could afford him, he did at last "Retrorsum vela dare atque iterare cursus relictos." Nor was it necessary that Horace in such a recantation as this should treat religion any otherwise than according to the vulgar notions.   It had been ridiculous to philosophize profoundly in the ecstasy and rapture of an ode. Enthusiasm could never be more becoming than here; and it is in this spirit that this ode is written.

Shaftesbury, *Second Characters* (Rand), p. 170:

Inveigh here (but with modesty and socratic irony) against High Church and Popish toleration and inquisition of that horrid representation (viz. crucifixion) and other saints adored in those agonies and made altar-pieces, church-ornament and for rock closets.

What *irony* means for Shaftesbury here is simply the restricted verbal device of blame-by-praise often used by Socrates.   Shaftesbury's taste required that he distinguish between the graceful irony of Socrates and Horace, and such heavy-handed irony as Ode 34 would be if Dacier's interpretation were correct.   For a full discussion of Shaftesbury's use of *irony*, see Dict. III.A.

ALSO: *Spectator* (G. G. Smith), No. 266 (Jan. 4, 1712); No. 438 (July 23, 1712). Myles Davies, *Athenae Britannicae* (1716), II, 388-90. Blackmore, *Essays* I (1716), p. 149. Blackmore, *Essays* II (1717), pp. 252-53. *Humourist* II (1725), pp. 99-102, 103-4. *Art of Railing* (1723), pp. 11-18. Bailey, *Universal Etymological English Dictionary* II (1727), (1760), under "Irony." Bailey, *Dictionarium Britannicum* (1730), under "Irony."

"Memoirs of ... Scriblerus" in Pope, *Works* (1751), VI, 192:

> In *Politicks*, his Writings are of a peculiar Cast, for the most part Ironical, and the Drift of them often so delicate and refin'd as to be mistaken by the vulgar. He once went so far as to write a Persuasive to people to eat their own Children, which was so little understood as to be taken in ill part. He has often written against *Liberty* in the name of *Freeman* and *Algernoon Sydney*, in vindication of the Measures of *Spain* under that of *Raleigh*, and in praise of *Corruption* under those of *Cato* and *Publicola*.

> > ["Ralph Freeman" and "Algernon Sidney" were pen names signed to articles appearing at intervals in the *Daily Gazetteer* between . . . 1734 and 1738. . . . The reference is ironic, both writers strongly advocating liberty. "Algernon Sidney," of course, took his name from the famous advocate of republican doctrines who . . . was beheaded for treason on December 7, 1683.
> > The name "Walter Raleigh" was signed to a series of letters appearing in the *Craftsman* . . . during . . . 1728-29 in which Walpole's pusillanimous policy toward the aggressions of Spain was severely attacked.
> > "Cato" was the name used by John Trenchard and Thomas Gordon in a famous series of letters in defense of Whig policies and the Walpole regime, which appeared in the *London Journal* in 1721 and 1722. "Publicola" was the name signed to another series appearing in the same journal during . . . 1728 and 1729 in which Walpole was supported and the attacks of the *Craftsman*, especially those signed by "Walter Raleigh," were answered.
> > —Charles Kerby-Miller, ed., *Memoirs of Scriblerus* (New Haven, 1950), p. 348]

ALSO: Pope, *Works* (Elwin-Courthope), VII, 41-42, 235 and 236 and 249, 358-59. Pope, *Prose Works* (Ault), p. 307. Pope, *Dunciad* (Sutherland), pp. 119, 186-91 (n. to l. 328). Pope, *Iliad* (1756), IV, 36-38 (n. to l. 471); VI, Index of "Speeches or Orations" under "In the irony, or sarcasm": see especially II, 56-58; IV, 119-22, 137, 232, 239-40. Swift, *Letters to Ford* (Nichol Smith), p. 29 and Swift, *Correspondence* (Ball), II, 172-73. Swift, *Prose Works* (Temple Scott), X, 371-72; XI, 360. Irony as blame-by-praise and vice versa seems to have been the central meaning of the word for Pope and Swift although their use of it does extend to several other senses, for which see Dict. iv.b, v.b, and vii.

ALSO: *Gulliver Decypher'd* (1726?), pp. 33-34. Anthony Blackwall, *Introduction to the Classics* (1728), pp. 176-79, 195-98 (see Dict. iv), 212. Anthony Blackwall, *Sacred Classics Defended* (1727), pp. 254 and 256. Anthony Blackwall, *Sacred Classics Defended* II (1731), p. 81. "An Essay on Gibing" (1727), pp. 5-10. *Craftsman* (1731), I, 102-6 (No. 18, Feb. 7, 1727); II, 172-74 (No. 68, Oct. 21, 1727); V, 230-34 (No. 182, Dec. 27, 1729). *Gulliveriana* (1728), pp. 285-86. Ephraim Chambers, *Cyclopaedia* (1728), (1741, 1743), (1778-88), under "Irony." John Oldmixon, *Logick and Rhetorick* (1728), pp. 21-28 (see Dict. viii). John Henley, *Oration on Grave Conundrums* (1729), p. 7.

A Discourse concerning Ridicule and Irony in Writing, in a Letter to the Reverend Dr. Nathanael Marshall. London: 1729.

Although this pamphlet by Anthony Collins is significant because of the unusual prominence it gives *irony*, the word is used throughout in a loose and casual way. Collins seems to think of it as interchangeable with *banter, raillery, ridicule, drollery, satire,* and so on, so that frequently it has to be taken as meaning no more than a derisive attack of some kind (Dict. ix). On occasion, however, Collins uses *irony* alone and with emphasis to refer to a specific piece of writing (he never formally defines the word). Usually the referents turn out to be blame-by-praise of some sort, but see also Dict. v and vii. See pp. 6 and Edward Stillingfleet, *Works* (1709), II, 458-59; 10-13; 16-17; 22-23; 30 and 10 (see also under Dict. v.b); 45-46 and Francis Hare, *Difficulties and Discouragements* (1716) and Francis Hare, *New Defence of Bangor* (1720); 47 and *D—n of W—r still the same* (1720), pp. 5-6 (see also under Dict. vii), 6-7, 8, 10, 14-15, 21-22, 100-101; 58-59 and Charles Leslie, *Salisbury's Proper Defence* (1704); 61.

ALSO: *Memoirs of Grub-street* (1737), I, viii-x. *Grub-street Journal*, Nov. 26, 1730; April 8, 1731; June 28, 1733. *Gentleman's Magazine*, I (March, 1731), 107; III (June, 1733), 282-83; X (Nov., 1740), 547-48; XIV (Jan., 1744), 6-15; XV (April, 1745),

207-8; XXI (Oct., 1751), 456. *Fog's Weekly Journal*, No. 239
(June 2, 1733). *Prompter*, No. 144 (March 23, 1736). Benjamin
Martin, *Bibliotheca Technologica* (1737), pp. 178-80. *London
Journal*, No. 938 (July 9, 1737). Friedrich Dedekind, *Grobianus*
(1739), Dedication. Chesterfield, *Letters to His Son* (Strachey-
Calthrop), I, 36, 61. Fielding, *Joseph Andrews* (Mod. Lib.), pp.
21-22. Fielding, *Works* (Stephen), VII, 274-75. Fielding, *Amelia*
(Navarre Soc.), I, 183. Fielding, *Jacobite's Journal*, No. 17
(March 26, 1748). Fielding, *Plutus* (1742), pp. 33, 55-57. Charles
Jarvis, *Don Quixote* (1742), I, vi-vii, 105; II, 27 n. William
Guthrie, *Cicero De Oratore* (1822), pp. 197-200. William Guthrie,
Quinctilianus His Institutes (1756), II, 29-30, 235-36, 236 ff., 286.
Female Spectator (1755), IV, 122-23.

John G. Cooper, *Socrates* (1750), pp. 87-88:

... above all things, *Socrates* was most averse to assuming the Air or
Name of a Preceptor. Thus when *Demonicus* an *Athenian* brought his
Son *Theages* to be instructed in Wisdom, after having rallied him by
that beautiful Irony, which he used so often, upon the absurd Custom
of the *Grecians* of running after the Sophists, who profess'd to teach Wisdom, and having in the same Strain recommended Gorgias, Polus, and
others, "From among these, says he, you should chuse a Preceptor for
your Son; but to call me to that Office is by no means proper."

ALSO: *Ibid.*, p. 168 n. *Monthly Review*, I (July, 1749), 172; IV
(Feb., 1751), 302; V (July, 1751), 117-19; VII (Nov., 1752),
355, 357; IX (July, 1753), 67-68. John Ozell, *Don Quixote*
(Mod. Lib.), p. 478 n. Letitia Pilkington, *Memoirs* III (1754), p.
73. John Brown, *Essay on Satire* (1770), p. 329 (Part II, ll. 255-
68). Smollett, *Peregrine Pickle* (Shakespeare Head), I, 43-44,
204; II, 38, 68, 253; III, 31; IV, 101, 109-10. Christopher Smart,
Hilliad (Chambers), p. 45. Cambridge, *Scribleriad* (1752), pp.
iii-iv[?]; pp. xiii-xv and notes to Book II, l. 123 (p. 29), Book III,
l. 11 (p. 45), Book III, l. 25 (p. 46), Book III, l. 37 (p. 46),
Book III, l. 103. Orrery, *Remarks on Swift* (1752), pp. 262, 282-
85. John Lawson, *Lectures Concerning Oratory* (1760), pp. 257-68.
World (Chalmers), Table of Contents and No. 49 (Dec. 6, 1753),
XXVI, 262-68; Table of Contents and No. 89 (Sept. 12, 1754),
XXVII, 193-98. Allan Ramsay, *Essay on Ridicule* (1762), pp.

34-37. Deane Swift, *Essay upon Swift* (1755), pp. 135-36. Smollett, *Don Quixote* (1755), II, 270, 376. Johnson, *Dictionary* (1755-56), under "Irony," "Ironical," "Ironically," "Sarcasm." Johnson, *Lives* (Birkbeck-Hill), III, 12. Joseph Warton, *Essay on Pope* (1806), I, 163-64, 178-79; II, 111-12, 154, 234 n., 242, 341-42.

IV. *IRONY* AS SAYING THE CONTRARY OF WHAT ONE MEANS
FOR EMPHASIS, THE CONTRARY BEING NEITHER
FALSE PRAISE NOR FALSE BLAME

Irony as "saying the opposite of what one means" nearly always reduced itself to blame-through-praise or vice versa. Occasionally, however, the opposing element was not transparently false praise or blame, but an assertion of some other kind that would serve as effective contrast to the real meaning. But it is seldom easy to eliminate the mock value judgment from statements called ironic.

The difficulty can be illustrated through analysis of an example of irony used by Anthony Blackwall, *Introduction to the Classics* (1728), pp. 195-98:

Omission *is when an Author pretends, that he conceals and omits what he declares.*

This *Figure* is related to the *Irony*. *Tully* in his first *Oration* against *Cataline* points it at that *Monster* with a just Severity and Satire.

What? When upon the Death of your former Wife you had made room in your House for a new Marriage, did not you enhance and consummate that *Deed* of *Horror* with another piece of *Wickedness* monstrous and incredible? Which I pass by, and am willing it should be suppress'd in Silence. . .

Thus far Cicero is satisfied with the conventional denial of his real intention, a denial likely to pique more interest than an impassioned attack would. But nearly always in such willingness to pass over a thing there is implied a deference which is in some sort praise. In this passage Cicero goes on to make his mock praise explicit:

. . . lest it should be thought either that such an outragious Impiety cou'd be committed in this *City;* or if committed, cou'd be carry'd off with Impunity.

Thus this irony has become predominantly blame-through-praise (Dict. III.B) rather than conventional negation (Dict. IV.A), and in most uses of *irony* in this way there is some sense of the opposition between good and bad.

IV.A. *Pretending to omit what one is all the while asserting*

This was a conventional rhetorical device sometimes classified as irony.

CLASSICAL PRECEDENTS: Quintilian *Institutio* IX.ii.44-53.

Abraham Fraunce, *Arcadian Rhetorike* (1588), Book I, chap. vi:

There is also a kinde of *Ironia* called ... *Praeteritio* in Latin, a kind of pretĕded omitting or letting slip of that which indeed wee elegãtly note out in the verie shewe of praetermission, as when we say; I let this passe; I passe it over with silence. Like unto this is that which is called ... of the Latinists *Negatio,* a denial or refusall to speake, as, I will not say that which I might, I will not call you, &c. when neverthelesse we speake and tell al.

[Fraunce illustrates this device from, among others, Philip Sidney:]
     Sir P. Syd. 2. of Musidorus.
To tell you what pitifull mishaps fell to the yong Prince of *Macedon* his cosyn, I shoulde too much fill your eares with strange horrors: neither will I stay upon those laboursom adventures, nor lothsom misadventures, to which and through which his fortune and courage conducted him: my speach hasteth it selfe to come to the point of all *Musidorus* misfortunes.

ALSO: John Smith, *Rhetorique* (1657), p. 165. Hobbes, *The Art of Rhetoric* (Molesworth), p. 517.

IV.B. *Using any kind of contrary expression*

This often involved using a pleasant or good name for an unpleasant or bad thing.

CLASSICAL PRECEDENTS: Quintilian *Institutio* VII.vi.54-58.

John Smith, *Rhetorique* (1657), pp. 45-48:

English Examples of an Irony

. . . . So when the Persian army was at variance among themselves, *Philip* of Macedon (their utter enemy) said, He would send his army to make them friends.

Also: Charles Leslie, *Best Answer Ever was Made* (1709), p. 8 [?].

Pope, *Dunciad* (Sutherland), pp. 62-63:

> O thou! whatever Title please thine ear,
> Dean, Drapier, Bickerstaff, or Gulliver!
> Whether thou chuse Cervantes' serious air,
> Or laugh and shake in Rab'lais' easy Chair,
> Or praise the Court, or magnify Mankind,
> Or thy griev'd Country's copper chains unbind;

Or praise the Court, &c.] *Ironicè*, alluding to *Gulliver*'s Representations of both—. . . .

Also: Ibid., pp. 201-6, note beginning *"There is certainly nothing in his style,"* quoted on p. 86 below.

Swift, *Correspondence* (Ball), II, 323:

If Mr. Bolton apprehends I do him a kindness, and will give me any ironical thanks on that score, I shall either bear them or return them as well as I am able.

Also: John Lawson, *Lectures Concerning Oratory* (1760), pp. 257-68.

v. *IRONY* AS UNDERSTATEMENT

The word *understatement* is here used to indicate a sense of *irony* distinct from the verbal irony of self-depreciation.[54] Whatever else Socrates' pose of ignorance may be thought to have been, it was at times a clever kind of mock praise for his antagonist. He did not mean what he said; he meant nearly the opposite. Understatement does mean what it says, but it says only part of what it means. Self-depreciation as a form of blame-by-praise (Dict. III) ostensibly leads in the wrong direction. Understatement leads in the right direction but does not go far along the way.

[54] Sedgewick uses the terms as roughly synonomous. See, for instance, G. G. Sedgewick, "Dramatic Irony" (1913), pp. 72-73.

Despite a real difference in method, understatement and the ironies of blame-by-praise and praise-by-blame frequently have a like effect, perhaps because both work by implication, requiring the audience to keep a sharp eye out for the whole or the hidden meaning. The varieties of understatement were ensconced in sixteenth-century rhetoric before John Hoskins wrote, but apparently he was the first English rhetorician to identify litotes and meiosis as ironic. By the early eighteenth century understatement seems to have been accepted as a standard ironic device.

v.a. *Denial of the contrary*

This sense differs from Dict. III and Dict. IV in that an idea contrary to or different from what is meant is not asserted but denied, producing an effect of extreme restraint conveniently called understatement. In English rhetoric this device appeared regularly from the sixteenth century into the eighteenth as *litotes*,[55] but beginning with Hoskins some writers identified it as ironic.

John Hoskins, *Directions for Speech and Style* (Hudson), pp. 25-26:

> The fourth way of amplifying is by *Intimation*, that leaves the collection of greatness to our understanding, by expressing some mark of it. It exceedeth speech in silence, and makes our meaning more palpable by a touch than by a direct handling.... This may be done with *ironia*, or denial:
>
> He was no notorious malefactor, but he had been twice on the pillory and once burnt in the hand for trifling oversights.

What is denied here is not the opposite but the superlative. In the phrase "trifling oversights" the second type of understatement (Dict. v.B) is operating.

Thomas Blount, *Academie of Eloquence* (1645), p. 31:

> ...the former fashion of *Diminution* sometimes in Ironious sort goes for *Amplification*, As speaking of a great personage, *No mean man*....

[55] Puttenham, *Arte of English Poesie* (Willcock-Walker), p. 184. Peacham, *Garden of Eloquence* (1593), pp. 150-51. Angel Day, *English Secretorie* (1595), Part II, pp. 84-85. Thomas Hall, *The Schools Guarded* (1655), pp. 163-70. *Art of Speaking* (1708), p. 62. John Harris, *Lexicon Technicum* (1704) and (1726) under "litotes." Bailey, *Dictionarium Britannicum* (1730) under "litotes."

ALSO: John Smith, *Rhetorique* (1657), pp. 45-48.   Edward Phillips, *New World of Words* (1671), (1678), (1706).

Gentleman's Magazine, XIV (Jan., 1744), 9:

... it is, in my Opinion, no Faculty of great Use to Mankind, to prepare palatable Poyson. ...

ALSO: *Ibid.,* p. 11.   On page 14 of the same issue the speech in which the above passage shines is excoriated as full of the "Language ... of Irony and Burlesque."

Francis Hare, *New Defence of Bangor* (1720), pp. 14-15:

Had his L——p meant this as a Reflection on Popish Countries only, 'tis not to be imagined he would not have said so.

Anthony Collins, *Discourse concerning Ridicule and Irony* (1729), p. 46, refers to the above pamphlet as *ironic.*   The passage quoted is not atypical.

V.B. *Intimation*

Assume a scale of comparison:

oldest   older   old   young   younger   youngest

If the object under fire is *youngest,* ironies III and IV would approach it through *oldest, older,* or *old,* but irony of understatement V.B approaches through *young.*   This device was usually called *diminution* or *meiosis,*[56] but beginning with Hoskins it was sometimes identified as ironic.

John Hoskins, *Directions for Speech and Style* (Hudson), pp. 29-30:

Here are figures that make a fair offer to set forth a matter better than it is.

[He discusses hyperbole and correctio and then:]

There are two contrary ways to these former, and both lead to amplification, but in dissembling sort.   The first is *Ironia,* which expresseth a thing by contrary, by show of exhortation when indeed it dehorteth, as

Yet a while, sleep a while, fold thine arms a while, etc., and so shall necessity overtake thee like a traveller, and poverty set upon thee like an armed man.

[56] Thomas Wilson, *Rhetorique* (G. H. Mair), pp. 120-21.   Peacham, *Garden of Eloquence* (1593), pp. 168-69.   Thomas Hall, *The Schools Guarded* (1655), pp. 163-70.   Hobbes, *The Art of Rhetoric* (Molesworth), p. 518.

Or as if a man should say:

It is simple credit that a diligent man shall come to, when he shall stand before princes.

It was but small charge of idle money that the Egyptians bestowed upon the erecting of a *pyramis* of brick, when the expense in onions and garlic for workmen's diet in the building of it came to above 238,000 pounds of money.

Milo had but a slender strength, that carried an ox a furlong on his back and then killed him with his fist and ate him to his breakfast.

Titormus had a reasonable good arm, that could hold two bulls by the tail, the one in one hand, the other in the other, and never be stirred out of the place by their violent pulling.

Here *small, slender, reasonable* amplify as much as if you had said *great, exceeding, incredible.*

Hoskins does not seem to be aware that his examples slide from illustrating one method to illustrating another, but there can be no question that his last example exhibits an irony of understatement quite different in method, if not in tone, from the blame-by-praise irony of the first. Thomas Blount, *Academie of Eloquence* (1654), pp. 25-26, repeats Hoskins verbatim, and John Smith, *Rhetorique* (1657), pp. 45-48 repeats the "Milo had but a slender strength..." example under "English Examples of an Irony."

Pope, *Iliad* (1756), IV, 119-22:

> The dropping head first tumbled to the plain.
> So just the stroke, that yet the body stood
> Erect, then roll'd along the sands in blood.
>   Here, proud *Polydamas,* here turn thy eyes!
> (The tow'ring *Ajax* loud-insulting cries)
> Say, is this chief extended on the plain
> A worthy vengeance for *Prothaenor* slain?
> Mark well his port! his figure and his face
> Nor speak him vulgar, nor of vulgar race;
> Some lines, methinks, may make his lineage known,
> *Antenor's* brother, or perhaps his son.
>   He spake, and smil'd severe, for well he knew
> The bleeding youth: *Troy* sadden'd at the view.

In Pope's index "Speeches or Orations" the above is listed as "In the irony, or sarcasm." The ninth line illustrates understatement v.A, and the next two lines, mockingly tentative—but not misleading—about an obvious identification, show how v.B may be manipulated.

Anthony Collins, *Discourse concerning Ridicule and Irony* (1729), p. 10:

"Religion then, it seems, must be left to the Scholars and Gentlefolks, and to them 'tis to be of no other use, but as a Subject of Disputation to improve their Parts and Learning; but methinks the Vulgar might be indulged a little of it now and then, upon Sundays and Holidays, instead of Bull-baiting and Foot-ball."

On page 30 Collins refers to the above as *irony;* the second clause demonstrates mild understatement of the ironist's own attitude.

On page 46 Collins refers to Francis Hare's *New Defence of Bangor* (1720) as ironic. In that pamphlet Hare indulges in understatement such as "... there is one very material thing, which he seems to have forgot. .." (p.8), and referring to something he thinks quite contradictory and ridiculous as "very strange" (p. 7). This type of wide-eyed understatement was common in the pamphlet warfare of the time.

On page 47 Collins refers to the pamphlet *D–n of W—r still the same* (1720) as ironic. One passage therein (p. 13) shows how circumlocution may achieve the effect of understatement:

... ridiculous *Questions* are here ask'd, which only put one in Mind of Something which is inseparable from the Disease of *Cavilling*.

VI. *IRONY* AS INDIRECTION

VI.A. *Statement of a corollary of one's criticism without statement of the criticism itself*

This sense is derived from a traditional type of satiric jest which was sometimes identified as ironic, probably because, like understatement, it makes explicit only part of its meaning, the context acting to complete the meaning for an alert audience. This strategy, of course, falls easily under the definition "saying one thing and meaning another."

CLASSICAL PRECEDENTS: Cicero *On Oratory* II.67ff., Scaevola's jest. Quintilian *Institutio* VI.iii.68. Cf. Hoby, *Courtier* (Everyman), pp. 159-61, 165, 166-67.

Richard Sherry, *Rhetorike* (1555), fol. xxvi:

Myctirismus [a kind of irony], a counterfayted laughter, but yet suche one as may be perceyved. Persius. I care not, to be as Arcesilas is.

ALSO: Foxe, *Monuments* (1596), p. 329, col. 2.

Puttenham, *Arte of English Poesie* (Willcock-Walker), pp. 186-91:

...by the figure *Ironia,* which we call the *drye mock....* And as *Alphonso* king of Naples, said to one that profered to take his ring when he washt before dinner, this will serve another well: meaning that the Gentlemã had anõther time takē thē, & because the king forgot to aske for them, never restored his ring againe.

ALSO: John Smith, *Rhetorique* (1657), p. 77. Fielding, *Covent-Garden Journal* (Jensen), II, 114-15[?]. William Guthrie, *Cicero De Oratore* (1822), pp. 197-200, Scaevola's jest. William Guthrie, *Quinctilianus His Institutes* (1756), II, 56.

John Lawson, *Lectures Concerning Oratory* (1760), pp. 257-68:

Or lastly, Ironies are made to turn upon Subjects foreign, and are improperly bitter; as in this of the Orator to Antony,
"In one Place you also aimed at Pleasantry; Good Gods how little did it become you! In which you are faulty; for you might have derived some Wit *from your Wife, an Actress.*"

vi.b. *Meaningful reply to a submerged meaning of a remark*

Like vi.a this sense is derived from a traditional type of jest analyzed and illustrated by Cicero and Quintilian. Through Cicero[57] particularly it entered English rhetoric, but Cicero's designedly casual progression from one type of jest to another left terminology vague, so that this one, although clearly identifiable, appears in English under a variety of denominations.[58] For instance, in a

[57] Cicero *On Oratory* II.67 ff.
[58] Thomas Wilson, *Rhetorique* (G. H. Mair), p. 139, and further on, the jests of Maximus to Salinator and of Diogenes on wine ("dissembling"). Hoby, *Courtier* (Everyman), p. 161, the jest of the Duke to the Captain who had lost Saint Leo. North, *Plutarch* (1595), p. 461 ("Marius"), ("mock"). Puttenham, *Arte of English Poesie* (Willcock-Walker), pp. 186-91 ("asteismus" or the "civill jest").

note to Cicero's discussion William Guthrie remarks: "The species mentioned here is precisely what we in England call *bulls*."[59] Nevertheless, Cicero had discussed this type of jest directly after irony, and Quintilian calls an example of it irony.   On occasion the English did likewise.

CLASSICAL PRECEDENTS: Quintilian *Institutio* VI.iii.89-92.   Plutarch *Lives*, "Marius" 24, "Lucullus" 27.   Plutarch *Moralia* 199 *ef.*

Puttenham, *Arte of English Poesie* (Willcock-Walker), pp. 186-91:
. . . by the figure *Ironia*, which we call the *drye mock* . . . as it was said by/a French king, to one that praide his reward, shewing how he had beene cut in the face at a certain battell fought in his service: ye may see, quoth the king, what it is to runne away & looke backwards.

John Smith, *Rhetorique* (1657), pp. 77-79:
Astismus . . . a kind of civil jest without prejudice or anger. . . .

It is a kinde of an Irony consisting of a pleasant and harmlesse jest: it is taken for any mirth or pleasant speech void of rusticall simplicity and rudenesse.

2. The occasion of mirth may be taken from a fallacy in sophistry, that is, when a saying is captiously taken and turned to another sense, contrary or much different from the speakers meaning: as,

To one demanding of *Diogenes* what he would take for a knock upon his pate, he made this answer, that he would take an helmet.

Now he that made the demand, meant what hire, and not what defence.

ALSO: William Guthrie, *Quinctilianus His Institutes* (1756), II, 62.

VII. *IRONY* AS THE GRAVE ELABORATION OF A FICTION FOR THE PURPOSE OF CASUAL SATIRE OR AIMLESS MYSTIFICATION

This sense differs from blame-by-praise (Dict. III.B.ii) in that the elaborated fiction is not in itself intended as blame-by-praise; it is simply mystification, or the framework into which satire may be built, or both.   Although this sense is very close to *irony* as any

Peacham, *Garden of Eloquence* (1593), pp. 33-35 ("asteismus").   Philemon Holland, *Plutarch's Morals* (1603), p. 433 ("mock").   *Plutarch's Morals* (1691), I, 281 ("jeering").
   [59] William Guthrie, *Cicero De Oratore* (1822), pp. 197-200.

discourse not meant to be taken seriously (Dict. viii), it seems to have been independent in referring to an identifiable technique and a more positive intention. The variety and pervasiveness of elaborate ironies in the Augustan age, the fact that irony in sense vii says "something other than it means," and the similarity in surface structure and often motive to blame-by-praise—all these factors probably produced this extension of meaning, which is synonymous with some senses of *banter*.

CLASSICAL PRECEDENTS: Plato *Apology* 37e [?] (see comment on Dacier translation below).

Dacier, *Plato* (1701), II, 41:

...if *I* tell you that my silence would be disobedience to God, and upon that account I cannot hold my peace; you will not believe me, you'll look upon the whole Story as a mysterious Irony.

The possible irony alluded to here by Socrates, though a mockery, is not in his usual style. Socrates' symbol, God, was a recurrent one which stood in a constant and complicated relationship to him; it was not an instrument of sarcastic praise. If his excuse was to be construed as a mockery, it must have been as a sort of mystifying fiction. And this seems to be how André Dacier or his English translator took it: "you'll look upon *the whole story* as a *mysterious* Irony"[60]—a translation which probably reflects a consciousness of like methods in Augustan writing more than an accurate understanding of Plato.

Pope, *Dunciad* (Sutherland), pp. 201-6:

Preface prefix'd to the five imperfect Editions of the Dunciad, printed at Dublin and London, in Octavo & Duod.

(a) The Publisher to the Reader

... every week for these two Months past, the town has been persecuted with Pamphlets, Advertisements, Letters, and weekly Essays, not only against the Wit and Writings, but against the Character and Person of Mr. *Pope.* And that of all those men who have received pleasure from his Writings (which by modest computation may be about a hundred thousand in these Kingdoms of *England* and *Ireland,* not to mention

---

[60] Cf. *Plato his Apology of Socrates* (1675), p. 60: "ye will not believe me, as if dissembling the matter in jest." The Loeb translation: "you will think I am jesting and will not believe me."

Jersey, Guernsey, the *Orcades,* those in the *New world,* and *Foreigners* who have translated him into their languages) of all this number, not a man hath stood up to say one word in his defence.

The only exception is the Author of the following Poem, who doubtless had either a better insight into the grounds of this clamour, or a better opinion of Mr. *Pope's* integrity, join'd with a greater personal love for him, than any other of his numerous friends and admirers.

Further, that he was in his peculiar intimacy, appears from the knowledge he manifests of the most *private* Authors of all the *anonymous* pieces against him, and from his having in this Poem attacked no man living, who had not before printed or published some scandal against this particular Gentlemen [*sic*].

How I became possest of it, is of no concern to the Reader; but it would have been a wrong to him, had I detain'd this publication: since those *Names* which are its chief ornaments die off daily so fast, as must render it too soon unintelligible. If it provoke the Author to give us a more perfect edition, I have my end.

Who he is, I cannot say, and (which is great pity) there is certainly nothing in his style and manner of writing, which can distinguish, or discover him. For if it bears any resemblance to that of Mr. *P.* 'tis not improbable but it might be done on purpose, with a view to have it pass for his. But by the frequency of his allusions to *Virgil,* and a labor'd (not to say *affected*) *shortness* in imitation of him, I should think him more an admirer of the *Roman* Poet than of the *Grecian,* and in that not of the same taste with his Friend.

I have been well inform'd, that this work was the labour of full *six* years of his life, and that he retired himself entirely from all the avocations and pleasures of the world, to attend diligently to its correction and perfection; and six years more he intended to bestow upon it, as it should seem by this verse of *Statius,* which was cited at the head of his manuscript.

Oh mihi bissenos multum vigilata per annos, Duncia!

Hence also we learn the true *Title* of the Poem. . . .

> *About a hundred thousand*] It is surprizing with what stupidity this Preface, which is almost a continued Irony, was taken by these Authors. This passage among others they understood to be serious. . . . [1729 note]
> *The Author of the following Poem,* &c.] A very plain Irony, speaking of Mr. *Pope* himself. [1729 note]
> *There is certainly nothing in his Style,* &c.] This Irony had small effect in concealing the Author. The Dunciad . . . had not been publish'd two days, but the whole Town gave it to Mr. *Pope.* [1729 note]
> *The Labour of full* six *years,* &c.] This also was honestly and seriously believ'd by divers of the Gentlemen of the Dunciad. . . . [1729 note]
> [*Duncia*] The same learned Prefacer took this word to be really in *Statius.* [1729 note]

The first irony explicitly noted here (*"About a hundred thousand"*) has the sound of the much later Romantic ironist Tieck making fun of his own efforts through exaggerated self-congratulation,[61] but though such may have been Pope's intention, it is likely that he used the word "Irony" in reference to this particular passage to mean only the opposite of literal (Dict. VIII).

The "continued Irony" is the fiction of the innocent publisher discussing an unknown poet and the circumstances of composition. Pope uses this fiction to say certain things he could not say gracefully in his own person and to mount a few glancing attacks on his enemies, but the fictional structure itself has no function other than mystification, and the ironies explicitly pointed to in the notes are not satiric shafts but simply false statements used to elaborate the fiction.

Anthony Collins, *Discourse concerning Ridicule and Irony* (1729), p. 47:

... he took the true and proper Method, by publishing an *Answer* to the said *Irony,* compos'd in the same *ironical Strain,* intitled, *The Dean of* Worcester *still the same* ... Which Answer does, in my Opinion, as much Honour to the Bishop, by its Excellency in the *ironical Way....*

D–n of W—r still the same (1720), pp. 3-6:

It has been observ'd long ago, upon a like Occasion to the present, that when *Cardinals* appear abroad without the Ensigns of their Dignity, it is in order to avoid the Trouble of giving or receiving any Compliments. But then it ought to be remark'd at the same time, that They never *give,* nor *receive,* any *Affronts* or *Rudenesses.* There is something in this Manner of Appearing that is agreeable and innocent, without being indecent. It avoids the Uneasiness of *Ceremony* to ones self, without giving the Uneasiness of *Rude Treatment* to Others. But some Spirits cannot be content with this Common Manner of being *incognito,* in which a Man is allowed to pass as *Unknown;* and in which he will be always respected as long as he preserves a *Decorum,* and does not break in upon the Rules either of *Society,* or of *Good Manners.*

[61] *Selbstparodie* was one of the definitions of Romantic irony given by the German Romantics themselves (see G. G. Sedgewick, *Of Irony* [1948], p. 15), and it is certainly a frequent component of the irony of manner (Dict. III.A). Such blame-by-praise irony as Pope's here, turned back upon the author or mock-author, was not infrequent in Augustan satiric and humorous writing. For another example of the use of *irony* to name such self-mockery, see pp. 172-73 below.

There is Another Sort of *Mock-appearance,* now too much in fashion. It is this. Many have found that the *Characters* They are obliged to sustain in their daily Appearance and ordinary Life, are too great a Confinement to the Freedom of their Souls; that they chain up the natural Bent and Vigour of their Minds; and give too close a Restraint to the Passions and Dispositions They feel within. And therefore, They have invented a way of remedying so great an Evil. They have resolved, at some certain times, to throw off these *Common Appearances,* which are in truth the Restraints of a *Real Disguise,* in which They should otherwise pass their whole Life; and assume Their own *Real Characters* by way of a *Disguise,* which is indeed only Nominal. For the *Real* Disguise is changed for the *Seeming* One; and the *Seeming* Disguise is indeed the *Real Man,* whose *Inside* and *Outside* have by this means only changed their Situation.

This succeeds very well with Those who have preserved their External *Characters* or *Persons* uniformly in ordinary Life; and know how to vary from Them, with Address, whenever they change the Appearance. But when an Unskilful Actor mixes himself in such a *Scene;* not knowing himself enough to be sensible that He has, in his ordinary Character, been exactly the same that He is now going to apear; nothing is received and entertained with more *Ridicule.* As soon as He comes upon the *Stage,* He *betrays* Himself. Either his *Aukward Gate,* or some other Peculiarity in his *Manner,* makes him known. Or, if not, as soon as He *speaks,* his *Words* reveal him. Perhaps the *Rudeness* of his *Freedoms,* which He mistakes for *Wit;* Or the *Affectation* of Something more than ordinary, which He mistakes for a Superiority of *Genius;* Or some other *Propriety,* which He cannot separate from Himself, immediately discover Him. The only Reason why He *attempts* to appear in *Disguise,* is to display more freely the same Dispositions which He has not been able to hide in his ordinary Habit. And He is treated accordingly. In such Assemblies, every One who enters is upon an Equality: And He who uses *Freedoms,* must be content to accept them in return.

It is just thus in the *Disguises* of Writers. There are Those who can assume a *Character* differing from their own in their ordinary Life, and are able to keep up to it with Regularity and Uniformity. There are Those who assume One with the same View; but are not able to stir a Step in it without shewing Themselves too plainly to be the very reverse to what They would *personate.* And some chuse to *imagine* themselves in *Disguise,* merely to give themselves a loose, and to shew more of *Themselves,* and their own True *Natural Tempers,* than They are willing to hope They do, in their ordinary *Persons.*

There is no one, I confess, who had ever less Occasion, or less Temptation, to take this Method than the *D--n of W---r.* He has shewn as much *Contempt* of the *Bishop* of *Bangor;* has treated him with as much Rudeness, and as keen Reproach; whilst He calls Himself by *his own* Name; and *owns* Himself to be Himself; as any one need wish to do. And then for the display of his *Learning* and *Criticism;* there is still less need of his going out of his proper ordinary Character. But I know not what it is. He has judg'd this a very narrow Sphere of *Action:* And has chosen *Another,* in which he seems to think the *Licentiousness* of Words to be the True *Freedom* of *Conversation.* Here he hopes, He may *wanton* in Abuse, in Misrepresentation, and in personal Reproaches, entirely foreign to the Cause into which He has unfortunately thrust Himself.

ALSO: *Ibid.,* pp. 6-7. Here the fiction is not a dramatic situation but a fabrication of motive within an elaborately forced context of values.

Smollett, *Don Quixote* (1755), I, xv-xvi:

He has, upon other occasions, made severe remarks upon the scarcity of patrons among the nobility of Spain, and even aimed the shafts of his satire at the throne itself. In his dedication of the second part of Don Quixote, to the count de Lemos, he proceeds in this ironical strain: "But, no person expresses a greater desire of seeing my Don Quixote, than the mighty emperor of China, who, about a month ago sent me a letter by an express, desiring, or rather beseeching, me to supply him with a copy of that performance, as he intended to build and endow a college for teaching the Spanish language from my book, and was resolved to make me rector or principal teacher." I asked if his majesty had sent me any thing towards defraying the charges; and, when he answered in the negative, "Why then, friend, said I, you may return to China as soon as you please; for my own part, I am not in a state of health to undertake such a long journey; besides, I am not only weak in body, but still weaker in purse, and so I am the emperor's most humble servant. In short, emperor for emperor, and monarch for monarch, to take one with the other, and set the hare's head against the goose giblets, there is the noble count de Lemos, at Naples, who, without any rectorships, supports, protects, and favours me to my heart's content."

This facetious paragraph certainly alludes to some unsubstantial promise he had received from the court.

Although this irony may be viewed as blame-by-praise through burlesque exaggeration, the dominant intention seems to be to use the fiction as a springboard for direct attack.

VIII. *IRONY* AS ANY DISCOURSE NOT MEANT TO BE TAKEN SERIOUSLY

This sense was a peripheral extension of meaning which probably gained a foothold as the word became current and the thing confusingly pervasive. Blame-by-praise, the commonest type of irony in the Augustan age, always involved language not meant to be taken at its face value, and a stock definition of the word was that *irony* is "saying something other than one means" (see pp. 31-33 above). It was natural, though not very discriminating, for people to use *ironic* loosely as antithetic to *serious, direct, sincere, literal. The Shortest-Way with the Dissenters . . . Consider'd* (1703), p. 5:

[The author of this pamphlet thought that if Defoe had meant the irony of his *Shortest-Way* seriously he would only have been stating the truth; Defoe's defense that his pamphlet had been all irony was exasperating.]

Yet it is all a Banter, nothing but an *Irony* to the Minutest Syllable, that *Synagogues have been put up at our Church-Doors* is meer Illusion, that Dissenters ran away with Places of Trust, and were chosen for Magistrates and Governours, nothing but Fancy, and We have no manner of Reason to look out for Posterity, and secure the Exercise of the True Religion, which we happily Enjoy under the best of Queens to succeeding Ages.

ALSO: *Ibid.*, pp. 15, 16, 18; *The Fox with his Fire-brand Unkennell'd* (1703), pp. 6 [?], 23 [?]. John Oldmixon, *Logick and Rhetorick* (1728), pp. 21-28 (there is an element of blame-by-praise in Oldmixon's use of *irony* in this passage, quoted on pp. 158-59 below, but the dominant sense seems to be transparently unserious language). Orrery, *Remarks on Swift* (1752), p. 262. Johnson, *Lives* (Birkbeck Hill), III, 63-64, quoting Dr. Delany.

IX. *IRONY* AS ANY KIND OF DERISIVE ATTACK

This is also a peripheral extension of meaning, roughly synonymous with *ridicule, mockery,* and *scoffing.* It is present, side by side with the traditional rhetorical sense, in some of the stock definitions (see p. 34 above) and in actual use.

A briefe examination (1566), sig. ***2:

... for want of matter, thorow your spirite of ironie, you must (as you do to the Prince, the Counsayle, the Byshops, the learned men & wise) geve also to the advertisementes theyr gyrde and nip. ...

The example of this spirit of irony given two paragraphs later seems to be straightforward derision.

ALSO: Burton, *Anatomy of Melancholy* (1621), pp. 20-27[?] (see Dict. x).

John Bulwer, *Chirologia and Chironomia* (1644), p. 183:

To locke the Thumbe betweene the next two Fingers, is an ironicall vulgarisme of the *Hand* used by Plebeians when they are contumeliously provoked thereunto, and see that they cannot prevaile by vieing words, their spleene appealing to their *Fingers* for aid, who thus armed for a dumbe retort, by this taunting gesture seem to say avant. This position of the *Fingers* with the Ancients was called *Higa,* and the moderne Spaniards by objecting the *Hand* formed to this reproachfull expression, imply as much as if they should say *padicavite,* with us it is usually their garbe who mocke little children.

ALSO: *Ibid.,* pp. 170 [?], 177-78, 181-83 [?]. It should be noted that Bulwer's involved and ingenious analysis of the meaning of his rhetorical gestures makes it difficult to know how he would have explained what seems obviously to be direct scoffing.

Anthony Collins, *Discourse concerning Ridicule and Irony* (1729), p. 21:

... If it be a Fault in those reverend Divines, mention'd in the foregoing Article, to use *Irony, Drollery, Ridicule,* and *Satire,* in any Case; or if the Fault lies in an exorbitant Use thereof, or in any particular Species of *Drollery* ... it is fit some Remedy should be employ'd for the Cure of this Evil.

Ibid., p. 26:

IV. Let me here add, that I am apt to think, that when you draw up your Law, you will find it so very difficult to settle the Point of *Decency* in Writing, in respect to all the various kinds of *Irony* and *Ridicule,* that you will be ready to lay aside your Project; ... if our Lawmakers were, out of a rational Principle, disposed to give Liberty by Law to a *serious* Opposition to publickly receiv'd Notions, they would not think it of much Importance to make a Law about a Method of *Irony.*

Ibid., p. 30:

It will probably be a Motive with you to be against abolishing *Drollery,* when you reflect that the Men of *Irony,* the *Droles* and *Satirists,* have been and always will be very numerous on your side. . . .

ALSO: *Ibid.,* passim, especially pp. 21-30, 54, 74, 77. Collins also uses *irony* in the traditional rhetorical senses. Two tendencies can be guessed from his use of the word: people were so conscious of the spate of ironic writing that when they discussed any ridicule they felt irony had to be mentioned; this awareness also led people to extend the reference of *irony* to any writing of similar tone or intent, regardless of rhetorical structure.

ALSO: "An Essay on Gibing" (1727), pp. 5-10 [?], 20 [?]. *Gentleman's Magazine* (Jan., 1731), I, 12.

Female Spectator (1755), III, 319-20:

A genteel raillery, which cannot give offence, yet if play'd on a person of wit, will make them asham'd of saying anything to incur it; and though I am no friend to what they call banter, ridicule, or irony, in any other case, yet when it is made use of to cure the faults of those persons we have no authority to reprove, I think it highly laudable.

x. DRAMATIC IRONY

In a situation involving *dramatic irony* as that term is understood by David Worcester, there are two characters. There is first of all the "dupe," who stubbornly pursues a course leading to disaster while oblivious of warning signposts, if any. There is second the "audience" (including a backward-looking dupe after disaster has struck), which sees disaster approaching and interprets any signposts properly. When dramatic irony is one component of a piece of literary art, the author takes the same point of view as the audience, he creating what it enjoys. When dramatic irony appears in real life distinct from literature, the author may be called Fate, and there may be no signposts. The irony in dramatic irony inheres in the fact that the words, circumstances, or events which seem to the dupe to be leading to a favorable conclusion produce an unfavorable one. The frame of mind which leads an author to create dramatic irony and which dramatic irony may produce in an audience is one of philosophic detachment from the interests and involvements of life. This frame of mind Sedgewick calls the irony of detachment.

Dramatic irony differs from the irony of manner (Dict. iii.a) in that the irony of manner is a particular kind of behavior in the author of the irony; whereas the author of dramatic irony is either totally self-effacing or nonhuman. Dramatic irony differs from the verbal ironies (Dict. iii.b, iv through ix) in two ways: the misleading factors need not be verbal; there must be a dupe and an audience (whereas the effect of verbal irony depends on the object's not being duped and no audience to his deception is necessary). Of course, though, if a man is fooled by ironical encomiums the audience is free to enjoy dramatic irony. It is highly questionable that anyone during the English classical period consciously used the word *irony* to refer to the dramatic situation defined above. The *N.E.D.* offers an illustration, dated 1649, in which *irony* seems to mean our irony of Fate, but as Sedgewick remarks, "it is based on a complete misunderstanding of the passage quoted."[62] I have, however, encountered three passages which seem to suggest this sense of the word, whether accidentally or not, and I discuss them below.

Thomas Nashe, "To the Gentleman Students" (G.G. Smith), pp. 309-10:

> But the hunger of our unsatiate humorists, beeing such as it is, readie to swallowe all draffe without indifference, that insinuates it selfe to their senses under the name of delight, imployes oft times manie thred bare witts to emptie their invention of their Apish devices, and talke most superficiallie of Pollicie, as those that never ware gowne in the Universitie; wherein they revive the olde saide Adage, *Sus Minervam,* & cause the wiser to quippe them with *Asinus ad Lyram.* Would Gentlemen & riper judgements admit my motion of moderation in a matter of follie, I wold perswade them to phisicke their faculties of seeing & hearing, as the *Sabaeans* doo their dulled senses with smelling; who (as *Strabo* reporteth), over-cloyed with such odoriferous savours as the naturall encrease of their Countrey (Balsamum, Amomum, with Myrrhe and Frankencense) sends foorth, refresh their nosthrills with the unsavorie sent of the pitchie slime that *Euphrates* casts up, and the contagious fumes of Goates beardes burnt; so woulde I have them, beeing surfetted unawares with the sweete

---

[62] G. G. Sedgewick, *Of Irony* (1948), p. 21.

satietie of eloquence which the lavish of our copious Language maie procure, to use the remedie of contraries, and recreate their rebated witts
not, as they did, with the senting of slyme or Goates beardes burnt, but
with the over-seeing of that *sublime dicendi genus,* which walkes abroad
for wast paper in each serving mans pocket, and the otherwhile perusing
of our Gothamists barbarisme; so shoulde the opposite comparison of
Puritie expell the infection of absurditie, and their over-rackte Rhetorique
bee the Ironicall recreation of the Reader.

The element of blame-by-praise in the act of reading a piece of bad
writing in order to refresh one's appreciation of good writing, and
the fillip to association in the phrase "the remedie of contraries,"
no doubt led Nashe to his use of the word "Ironicall" here. But
his use is—probably unintentionally—suggestive. *Irony* here refers not to a verbal device but to the mental attitude of an audience
as it watches a fool labor for a good effect all the while the very
tools he is laboring with are producing a bad one. The effect of
this sight on the audience is to detach it from its allegiances and
reawaken its sense of proportion.

Thomas Nashe, *Works* (McKerrow), II, 246-50:

At the verie pointe of our enterance into Wittenberg, we were
spectators of a verie solemne scholasticall entertainment of the Duke of
Saxonie thether.

At the townes end met him the burgers and dunsticall incorporationers
of *Wittenberg* in their distinguished liveries, their distinguished liverie
faces, I meane, for they were most of them hot livered dronkards. . . .

A bursten belly inkhorne oratour called *Vanderhulke,* they pickt out
to present him with an oration, one that had a sulpherous big swolne
large face, like a Saracen, eyes lyke two kentish oysters, a mouth that
opened as wide every time he spake, as one of those old knit trap doores,
a beard as though it had ben made of a birds neast pluckt in peeces,
which consisteth of strawe, haire, and durt mixt together. He was ap-
parelled in blacke leather new licourd, & a short gowne without anie
gathering in the backe, faced before and behinde with a boistrous beare
skin, and a red night-cap on his head. To this purport and effect was
this broccing duble beere oration.

Right noble Duke (*ideo nobilis quasi no bilis,* for you have no bile
or colar in you), know that our present incorporation of Wittenberg, by
me the tongue man of their thankfulnes, a townesman by birth, a free
Germane by nature, an oratour by arte, and a scrivener by education,
in all obedience & chastity, most bountifully bid you welcome to Witen-

berg: welcome, sayd I? O orificiall rethorike, wipe thy everlasting mouth, and affoord me a more Indian metaphor than that, for the brave princely bloud of a Saxon. Oratorie, uncaske the bard hutch of thy complements, and with the triumphantest troupe in thy treasurie doe tre-wage unto him. What impotent speech with his eight partes may not specifie, this unestimable gift, holding his peace, shall as it were (with teares I speak it) do wherby as it may seeme or appeare to manifest or declare, and yet it is, and yet it is not, and yet it may be a diminutive oblation meritorious to your high pusilanimitie and indignitie. Why should I goe gadding and fisgigging after firking flantado amfibologies? wit is wit, and good will is good will. With all the wit I have, I here, according to the premises, offer up unto you the cities generall good will, which is a gilded Can, in manner and forme folowing, for you and the heirs of your bodie lawfully begotten to drinke healths in. The scho-lasticall squitter bookes clout you up cannopies and foot-clothes of verses. We that are good fellowes, and live as merry as cup and can, will not verse upon you as they doe, but must do as we can, and entertaine you if it bee but with a plaine emptie Canne. He hath learning inough that hath learnde to drinke to his first man. Mechanicall men they call us, and not amisse, for most of us being *Maechi,* that is, cuckoldes and whoore-masters, fetch our antiquitie from the temple of *Maecha,* where Mahomet was hung up. Three partes of the worlde, America, Affrike, and Asia, are of this our mechanike religion. *Nero,* when he crid, *O quantus artifex pereo,* profest himselfe of our freedome, insomuch as *Artifex* is a citizen or craftes man, as well as *Carnifex* a scholler or hangman. Passe on by leave into the precincts of our abhomination. Bonie Duke, frolike in our boure, and perswade thy selfe that even as garlike hath three prop-erties, to make a man winke, drinke, and stinke, so we will winke on thy imperfections, drinke to thy favorites, and al thy foes shall stinke be-fore us. So be it. Farewell.

The Duke laught not a little at this ridiculous oration, but that verie night as great an ironicall occasion was ministered, for he was bidden to one of the chiefe schooles to a Comedie handled by scollers. *Acolastus,* the prodigal child, was the name of it, which was so filthily acted, so leathernly set forth, as would have moved laughter in *Heraclitus.* One, as if he had been playning a clay floore, stampingly trode the stage so harde with his feete that I thought verily he had resolved to do the Car-penter that set it up some utter shame. Another flong his armes lyke cudgels at a peare tree, insomuch as it was mightily dreaded that he wold strike the candles that hung above their heades out of their sockettes, and leave them all darke. Another did nothing but winke and make faces.

Nashe's "ironicall occasion" may be taken as parallel to "ridiculous oration," the word "ironicall" being simply a stylistic substitute for "ridiculous." But this was not a common extension of *irony*'s meaning. What seems to have suggested it to Nashe is the nature of the ridiculousness. In attempting to praise the Duke, Wittenberg's orator unwittingly insults him. The night's entertainment too is so bad as to be insulting. Again, in attempting to bring credit to themselves through their welcoming speech and a play, the natives behave so preposterously as unintentionally to burlesque themselves. Today we might use "ironical" in this situation because under the eye of an astute audience a labored effort has unintentionally produced exactly the result least desired, thus using the word to mean the irony of Fate or dramatic irony. But Nashe may have used "ironicall" only to mean that praise conveyed blame, unintentional though this result was.

Burton, *Anatomy of Melancholy* (1621), pp. 20-27:

   Charon in *Lucian,* as hee wittily faines, was conducted by *Mercurie* to such a place, where hee might see all the world at once, and after hee had sufficiently vewed and looked about, *Mercurie* would needs know of him, what he had observed, hee told him that hee saw a vast multitude and a promiscuous, *hee could discerne cities like so many Hives of Bees, wherein every Bee had a sting, and they did naught else but sting one another, some dominering like Hornets bigger then the rest, some like filching wasps, others as Drones.* Over their head were hovering a confused company of perturbations, hope, feare, anger, avarice, ignorance, &c and a multitude of diseases hanging over, which they still pulled on their heads. Some were brawling, some fighting, riding, running, for toyes and trifles, and such momentary things. In conclusion he condemned them all, for madmen, fooles, idiots, asses. *O stulti quanam haec est amentia?* O fools o madmen he exclaimes, *insana studia, insani labores, &c* mad indeavours, mad actions, mad, mad, mad. *Heraclitus* the Philosopher, out of a serious meditation of mens actions fell a weeping, and with continuall teares bewailed their miseries, madnesse, and folly. *Democritus* on the other side fel a laughing, their whole life to him seem'd so ridiculous, and hee was so far caried with this Ironicall passion, that the cittizens of *Abdera* tooke him to be mad, and sent therefore Embassadours to *Hippocrates* the Physitian, that hee would exercise his skill upon him. But the story is set down at large by *Hippocrates* himselfe, in his Epistle to *Damogetus....*

Hippocrates asking the reason why he laughed: he told him at the vanities and fopperies of the time. To see men so empty of all vertuous actions, to hunt so farre after gold, having no end of ambition, to take such infinite paines for a little glory, and to be favored of men, to make such deepe mines into the earth for gold, & many times to find nothing, with losse of their lives and fortunes. Some to love dogges, others horses, some to desire to be obeyed in many provinces and yet themselves will knowe no obedience. Some to love their wives dearely at first, and after a while to forsake and hate them, begetting children, with much care and cost for their education, yet when they growe to mans estate, to despise them, neglect and leave them naked to the worlds mercy. Doe not these behaviours expresse their intolerable folly? ... O wise Hippocrates, I laugh at such things being done, but much more when no good comes of them, and when they are done to so ill purpose.

O most worthy *Hippocrates,* you should not reprehend my laughing, perceaving so many fooleries in men: for no man will mocke his owne folly, but that which he seeth in another, and so they justly mocke one another.

When *Hippocrates* heard these words, so readily uttered without premeditation to declare the worlds vanity, full of ridiculous contrariety, hee made answer that necessity compelled men to many such actions, and diverse wills ensuing from divine permission, that we might not be idle, being nothing is so odious to them as sloth and negligence. Besides men cannot foresee future events, in this uncertainty of humane affaires, they would not so marry, if they could foresee the causes of their dislike and separation, or parents if they knew the houre of their childs death, so tenderly provide for them: or an husbandman sowe, if he thought there would be no increase; or a marchant adventure to sea, if hee foresawe shipwracke; or be a magistrate, if presently to bee deposed. Alas, worthy *Democritus,* every man hopes the best, and to that end he doth it, and therefore no such cause to laughter.

Democritus hearing this excuse, laughed againe alowd, perceaving he did not well understand what he had said concerning perturbations and tranquillity of the minde. Insomuch, that if men would governe their actions by discretion & providence, they would not declare themselves fooles, as now they doe, and he should have no such cause of laughter, but, quoth he, they swel in this life as if they were immortall, for want of understanding. It were enough to make thē wise, if they would but consider the mutability of this world, and how it wheeles about, nothing firm and sure, he that is now above, tomorrow is beneath, he that sate on this side to day, to morrow is hurled on the other: and not considering these things they fall into many inconveniences and troubles, coveting thinges of no profit, and thirsting after them, tumbling headlong into many calamities. So that if men would attempt no more then what they can beare, they should lead contented lives, & learning to know themselves would limit their ambition.... Seeing men are so fickle, so sottish, so intemperate, why should I not laugh at those to whom folly seemes wisdome, and will not bee cured, and perceave it not?

No doubt the key to "this Ironicall passion" lies in Democritus' saying "he should have no such cause of laughter, but ... they swel in this life as if they were immortall, for want of understanding." Seeing the self-absorbed, pompous folly of man, Democritus laughs, as Socrates and Lucian and Erasmus had laughed. The fact that they had been called ironists perhaps led Burton to apply the word to the laughter of Democritus, although Democritus had only the motive of an ironist—his discourse was straightforward and he sought no audience. Since his only expression was derisive laughter, Burton probably means by *irony* here only "mockery, derision" (Dict. ix). Yet one wonders whether there was in Burton's mind, as there must have been in the minds of many of the *Anatomy*'s modern readers, any application of the "Ironicall passion" of Democritus to his free play of mind over all the world and the ironies of Fate which beset it. It is not impossible that the conjunction of this attitude with the laughter which reminded Burton of ironical laughter and thence perhaps of the ironist Socrates' wide-ranging detachment should produce such an extension of the word's reference. But the scant evidence is not helpful. In the sixth edition Burton added Socrates to the catalogue of authorities for the total foolishness of man:

Burton, *Anatomy of Melancholy* (Dell), p. 37:

When Socrates had taken great pains to find out a wise man, and to that purpose had consulted with philosophers, poets, artificers, he concludes all men were fools; and though it procured him both anger and much envy, yet in all companies he would openly profess it.

There is no hint here of anything more than agreement between Socrates and Democritus that all men are fools, deserving of derision.

THREE

THE METHODS OF BLAME-BY-PRAISE
ASSOCIATED WITH *IRONY*

It would be difficult to believe that any technique of blame-by-praise was not clearly understood by the great Augustan satirists. Swift stands in undisputed pre-eminence as the virtuoso of the prose irony of controversy; the poetic burlesques of Pope are the best in the language; certain characters of Fielding fused irony and the illusion of fiction in a way that permanently influenced both the world of satire and the world of the novel. From our own age of explicit, polite, and neutral prose we go to the Augustan masters to learn how these other, more artful things were done. The great Augustans too learned their techniques from masters and apprentices who wrote long before them. Although these earlier ironies did not attract to themselves the word *irony* so frequently as did those of the Augustans, we do find that most, though apparently not quite all, of the techniques developed during the Augustan age had been associated with the word *irony* in Classical times and during the Renaissance, limited though such recognition often was.

i. *Socratic self-depreciation*

As we have observed,[1] the method of blame-by-praise that has been attached to the word *irony* for the longest time is that notorious irony of Socrates, "who was called an *ironist* because he assumed the rôle of an ignorant man lost in wonder at the wisdom

[1] Pp. 3-6 above.

of others."[2]   It should be noted that self-depreciation may function
in several ways.   It may be joined to explicit praise of another
object and the audience be meant to reverse both judgments, thereby
elevating the ironist and depressing his object; or the explicit praise
may disappear, the audience being expected to find it implicit in
the comparison suggested by the ironist's self-depreciation, both explicit and implicit judgments still to be reversed; or the ironist's
self-depreciation may not be reversed to his credit at all, the audience taking his modesty as nothing more than a device of the irony.
Thus the *Rhetoric to Alexander*[3] and Cicero[4] refer to instances of
ironic self-depreciation joined to ironic praise in which both judgments are explicit and both are meant to be reversed by the audience, but Lucian offers a delightful example of the completely
explicit pattern in which one feels that the self-depreciation of
the ironist is meant only as support for the undeserved praise, not
as enhancement of himself.[5]   In speaking of "the employment of
irony in making apologies or asking questions"[6] Quintilian is thinking of the kinds of ironic self-depreciation which often only imply
ironic praise, and elsewhere he follows an example of the completely
explicit pattern with one which depends on implication:

It is also *irony* when . . . we concede to our opponents qualities which we
are unwilling that they should seem to possess.   This is specially effective when we possess these qualities and they do not, as in the following
passage,

> "Brand *me* as coward, Drances, since thy sword
> Has slain such hosts of Trojans."

A like result is produced by reversing this method when we pretend to
own to faults which are not ours or which even recoil upon the heads of
our opponents, as for example,

> " 'Twas I that led the Dardan gallant on
> To storm the bridal bed of Sparta's queen!"[7]

The earliest English association of self-depreciation with the
word *irony* that I have found is John Hooper's (1548):

[2] Quintilian *Institutio* IX. ii. 44-53.
[3] *Aristotle's Rhetoric* (1686), p. 257.
[4] Cicero *Letters to Quintus* III. iv. 4.   Cicero *Brutus* 85-87.
[5] Lucian *Anacharsus* 17-18.
[6] Quintilian *Institutio* VI. ii. 15-16.
[7] *Ibid.,* IX. ii. 44-53.

Here doth Moses speak *ironice,* and seemeth to deny the thing he would affirm.   As Aristotle or Cicero might say, when they have applied all their labour, and done the best they can to make their scholars learned, yet profiteth nothing, then depart out of the school, and say unto their audience, "I never opened unto you the science that I taught you;"— not that the fault was in them, but in the auditors that neglected their diligence and doctrine. . . .[8]

Cicero's audience here is meant to reverse his self-depreciation by recognizing that he has taught very well, but in addition the self-depreciation acts as a pointer to his real opinion that the students have not learned anything, so that his audience is led also to reverse Cicero's implied praise of his students' attentiveness.   Another type of self-depreciation, the pose of innocent ignorance in the face of an indisputable conclusion, is connected to *irony* by Angel Day, who, after describing minutely a dishonest servant boy who would obviously steal anything he could lay his hands on, comments: "In the ende (by whose theft God knowes) the man had a chest broken up, and a little coyne and plate stolne. . . ."[9]   Day's parenthesis implies that he cannot imagine the boy as a thief, but his preparatory description is so obvious the audience automatically takes Day's remark as not very subtle irony.   A far nicer use of assumed innocence occurs in an irony pointed out by Richard Baxter: St. Paul, reprimanded by the bystanders for reviling the high priest Ananias, replies, "I wist not, brethren, that he was the high priest: For it is written, Thou shalt not speak evil of the ruler of thy people."[10]   Paul's innocence here acts simply as the vehicle of unmerited praise, praise which only someone sympathetic with Paul's view of the usurper Ananias would see to be ironic, for there is no overt indication of his real opinion in the statement itself.   The very opposite of innocent ignorance is utilized in the "very *majestic Irony*" which Anthony Blackwall attributes to Milton's God upon the revolt of Lucifer:

> Son! Thou in whom my Glory I behold
> In full Resplendence, Heir of all my Might,

[8] John Hooper, *Early Writings* (Parker Soc.), p. 420.
[9] Angel Day, *English Secretorie* (1595), Part I, pp. 44-45.
[10] Richard Baxter, *A Paraphrase on the New Testament* (1701), Acts 23:5.

> Nearly it now concerns Us to be sure
> Of our Omnipotence![11]

Here the ironist first aggrandizes himself and then, assuming all this glory, depreciates himself in relation to the object of his irony, as though Lucifer were a respectable foe. John Smith gives an example from the Bible which makes the whole pattern explicit in its simplest form: "We are fools, ye are wise, we nothing, ye all, &c."[12] A subtler form of the complete pattern is explained by Anthony Blackwall: St. Paul has been pleading his cause before Agrippa, who finally answers:

You almost persuade me to become a Christian.

Some commentators make *Agrippa*'s answer to be an irony and ridicule upon the apostle; as if he had said, *Do you think me so weak as easily to be persuaded out of the religion of my ancestors, or become your proselyte by a short harangue, and a few words of insinuation?* But this is forced and unnatural, against the stream of the generality of the ablest critics and commentators; and not very agreeable to the context.[13]

In the delightful correspondence between Gay and the Duchess of Queensberry in England, and Swift in Ireland, there occurs a bit of playfully ironic self-depreciation which the Duchess carries to an extreme of exaggeration. Gay and his Duchess have been writing joint letters, many of them importuning Swift to visit Amesbury, which Swift has answered by making all sorts of impossible conditions to be met before he will accept the invitation. His most recent letter has rebuked the Duchess with mock severity for not joining Gay in writing the last letter from Amesbury. The Duchess' answer is, in part:

Dear Sir, —Mr. Gay tells me I must write upon his line, for fear of taking up too much room. It was his fault that I omitted my duty in his last letter; for he never told me one word of writing to you till he had sent away his letter. However, as a mark of my great humility, I shall be ready and glad to ask your pardon upon my knees as soon as ever you come, though not in fault. I own this is a little mean-spirited, which I hope will not make a bad impression, considering you are the occasion. I submit to all your conditions, so pray come; for I have not only prom-

---

[11] Anthony Blackwall, *Introduction to the Classics* (1728), pp. 176-79.

[12] John Smith, *Rhetorique* (1657), pp. 45-48. See also Fynes Moryson, *Itenerary* (1617), p. 160.

[13] Anthony Blackwall, *Sacred Classics Defended* II (1731), p. 81.

ised myself, but Mr. Gay also, the satisfaction to hear you talk as much nonsense as you can possibly utter.[14]

Swift answers:

... madam, understand one thing, that I take all your ironical civilities in a literal sense. . . .[15]

It is of course the Duchess' exaggeration which turns her sincere respect into playful irony of the sort Swift loved.

In "A Letter Written by the Reverend Mr. John Hales of Eaton, to Arch-Bishop Laud, upon Occasion of his Tract concerning Schism," Anthony Collins thinks Hales "shews himself to have been another *Socrates,* one of the greatest Masters of *true Wit* and *just Irony.* . . ."[16] The following excerpt gives us a sample of Hales' style:

I have much marvelled, whence a Scribbled Paper, dropt from so worthless and inconsiderable a Hand as mine, should recover so much Strength, as to be able to give *Offence.*. But I confess it to be most true, that *Bellum inchoant inertes, fortes finiunt;* And a weak Hand often kindles that Fire, which the Concourse of the whole Vicinity cannot quench. If therefore any Fire can arise out of so poor a Spark, (which I can hardly conceive,) I am my Self here at hand to pour on Water, to prevent a farther Mischief.

Whosoever hath the Misfortune to read it, shall find in it, for Stile, some things *over-familiar* and *Sub-rustick;* some things more *pleasant* than needed; some thing more *Sour* and *Satyrical.* For these, my Apology is but this, that *Your Grace* would be pleased to take in consideration, *first,* what the *Liberty of a Letter* might entice me to. *Secondly,* I am, by Genius, *Open* and *Uncantelous;* and therefore some Pardon might be afforded to harmless *Freedom,* and *Gayety of Spirit,* utterly devoid of all Distemper and *Malignity.*

... whereas I did too *plainly* deliver my Self *De Origine Dominii,* and denied it to be founded either in *Nature* or in *Religion,* I am very well content to put off the decision of this point till *Elias* comes. In the mean time, whether it be true or false, let it pass for my Mistake; for 'tis but a point of mere Speculation, which we fall upon when we study *Aristotle's Politicks;* and in common Life and Use, hath no place at all. For *Authority* is not wont to *dispute;* and it goes but lazily on, when it must defend it self by *Argument* in the Schools.[17]

[14] Pope, *Works* (Elwin-Courthope), VII, 236.
[15] *Ibid.,* VII, 249.
[16] Anthony Collins, *Discourse concerning Ridicule and Irony* (1729), p. 46.
[17] Francis Hare, *Difficulties and Discouragements* (1716), pp. 40-45.

Hales does achieve something very like the true Socratic tone; moreover, he uses it not for a passing gibe but as a pose to be maintained through the whole course of his letter. Collins' attention to this pose as irony is indicative of the Augustans' increasing critical awareness of irony as something more than clever repartee.

ii. *Direct praise*

Because it is the simplest, no doubt, direct praise has been the most frequently recognized method of ironic praise ever since Socrates was called *eiron* when he employed it to supplement and emphasize his subtler method of self-depreciation.[18]   As we have observed above, when self-depreciation is used as a method of blame-by-praise the ironist often points up implied praise of his antagonist by making an explicit statement of it. The *Rhetoric to Alexander,* which includes the earliest extant formulation of blame-by-praise irony, offers in illustration precisely this combination.

An Irony is, when we know one thing and dissemble another. *We must not say, that these men, who boast they have done us so much good, have been the People that have done us all this mischeif.* But when we call things by contrary names, then thus. *These good men were they that did the mischeif to our Confederates;* but we wicked People, they that did 'em all the kindness.[19]

But direct ironic praise, "when anything disgraceful is designated by an honourable term,"[20] has pursued most of its career apart from Socratic self-depreciation.   Cicero[21] and Quintilian[22] both recommend it, and Plutarch[23] and Lucian[24] refer to instances of it as *irony.*

The earliest appearance of *irony* in English is accompanied by an elementary example of direct praise,[25] and later (1533) Thomas

[18] G. G. Sedgewick, "Dramatic Irony" (1913), pp. 92-93, and Plato *Gorgias* 489*de.*
[19] *Aristotle's Rhetoric* (1686), p. 257. The "Rhetoric to Alexander" is attributed to Aristotle and included in the translation as Book IV.
[20] Cicero *On Oratory* II. 67 ff.
[21] *Ibid.*
[22] Quintilian *Institutio* VIII. vi. 54-58; IX. ii. 44-53.
[23] Plutarch *Lives,* "Timoleon" 15. Plutarch *Moralia* 44*d.*
[24] Lucian *A Literary Prometheus* 1; *Lexiphanes* 1.
[25] See Dict. III.B.ii above.

More explains how this method works:

> But then that I cal them [heretics] again good names: this thing lo thys good man rekeneth a veri môstrous maner, to make them both good and badde. But thys is a monster lo of every mãs making. For so call not I theym alone, but the whole people to, in such maner of speaking as every man useth, whẽ he calleth one self noughty lad, both a shreud boy and a good sonne, the tone in ye proper simple spech, the tother by the fygure of ironye or antiphrasis. And by a lyke maner fygure saint Hierome against the olde heretike Vigilanti, calleth him somtime Vigilantius, & somtyme agayne Dormitantius, and so he calleth that heretike two contrarye names, as wel a I do these.[26]

More is talking about the most elementary kind of direct ironic praise, in which the ironist vents his real opinion quite openly and then uses a sudden reversal of terms as rhetorical ornamentation. By mid-century Thomas Wilson, inspired by Cicero and Quintilian, was offering models for more extended and exaggerated though far from subtle praise of an unworthy object, but he calls the method *dissembling* rather than *irony*,[27] as does Hoby.[28] Abraham Fraunce, however, instances several *ironies* in Philip Sidney which are both elaborated and polished, among them this one:

> *Sir Philip Sid. a continued Ironia between Pas and Nico.*

Nico. Who doubts but *Pas* fine pipe againe will bring
         The auncient praise to Arcade shepheards skill?
         Pan is not dead, since *Pas* begins to sing.
Pas.   Who evermore will love Apolloes quill,
         Since *Nico* doth to sing so widely gape?
         Nico his place farre better furnish will.
Nico. Was this not he who for *Cyringaes* scape
         Raging in woes, first Pastors taught to plaine?
         Doo you not heare his voyce and see his shape?
Pas.   This is not he, that failed her to gaine
         Which made a bay, made bay a holy tree:
         But this is one that doth his musicke staine.[29]

Sidney sustains the ironic battle between Pas and Nico with a series of flattering allusions, and the real attitudes of the two shepherds

---

[26] Thomas More, *Works* (1557), "The debellacion of Salem and Byzance," chap. v, p. 939. Miles Coverdale repeats More's illustration in *Remains* (Parker Soc.), II, 333.

[27] Thomas Wilson, *Rhetorique* (G. H. Mair), pp. 134-56.

[28] Hoby, *Courtier* (Everyman), pp. 159-61.

[29] Abraham Fraunce, *Arcadian Rhetorike* (1588), Book I, chap. vi.

are not at all blatant, although in the fifth line and the last Pas is blunter than Nico, who reveals his irony only in the laughable exaggeration of his praises. The sort of ironic allusion Sidney uses here was later remarked upon by the Earl of Chesterfield: "it would be a manifest irony to call a very ugly fellow an Adonis..., or to call a cowardly fellow an Alexander, or an ignorant fellow Polyglot...."[30] But allusion may be used not only to carry the ironic praise but also to reveal the ironist's real meaning, as it was in the "Ironicall message"[31] sent July 6, 1714, from Bolingbroke in London to Swift in Ireland through John Barber.

My Lord bid me tell you this morning, that he will write to you, and let you know that as great a philosopher as you are, you have had the pip; that the public affairs are carried on with the same zeal and quick dispatch as when you was here; nay, that they are improved in several particulars; that the same good understanding continues; that he hopes the world will be better for your retirement; that your inimitable pen was never more wanted than now; and more, which I cannot remember.[32]

It is of course the standard of comparison Bolingbroke alludes to, that stage of paralysis and cross-purposes at which the government of Oxford and Bolingbroke had arrived, which furnishes clues to the real import of the irony here.

Another means of varying direct praise was illustrated by Angel Day:

Ironia, a scoffe or flout, as when we say, *Alas good man*, or to one that hath set debate or contention, *you have spun a fair threed* or to him that hath made a long speech to no purpose, *you have brought foorth a mightie molle-hil....*[33]

An amusing example of the metaphoric technique is labeled *irony* by Smollett:

"She is ... a tight, good humoured sensible wench, who knows very well how to box her compass; well trimmed aloft, and well sheathed alow, with a good cargo under her hatches." The commodore at first imagined this commendation was ironical....[34]

[30] Chesterfield, *Letters to His Son* (Strachey-Calthrop), I, 61.
[31] Swift, *Letters to Ford* (Nichol Smith), p. 29.
[32] Swift, *Correspondence* (Ball), II, 172-73.
[33] Angel Day, *English Secretorie* (1595), Part II, pp. 79-80.
[34] Smollett, *Peregrine Pickle* (Shakespeare Head), II, 43-44.

Here the metaphors not only carry the ironic praise but also reveal the ironist's real meaning through his incongruous object of comparison.

The use of ambiguity in direct praise was illustrated nicely by Plutarch:

> Another, on going to Athens, saw that the Athenians were hawking salt fish and dainties, collecting taxes, keeping public brothels, and following other unseemly pursuits, and holding none of them to be shameful. When he returned to his own country, his fellow-citizens asked how things were in Athens, and he said, "Everything fair and lovely," speaking ironically and conveying the idea that among the Athenians everything is considered fair and lovely, and nothing shameful.[35]

The ironic praise and the meant blame are both explicitly stated in one and the same phrase. A popular piece of irony in the English classical period makes use of two phases of meaning which, although they are the sting on the whip, are only one part of the whole irony.

> Then, said the Lord, with holy ironie
> Whence man the folly of his pride might see,
> The earthy man like one of us is grown,
> To whom, as God, both good and ill is known,
> . . . .[36]

Here is the double sense "to know evil by observation" and "to know evil by participation."

Thomas Herbert pointed out an irony in which direct ironic praise is conveyed through the effect of its object on the ironist:

> This Isle is hard to be ascended; not that the passage is craggy, but that it is so Precipitous. The Sailors have an Ironick Proverb, The way is such, as a man may chuse whether he will break his heart going up, or his neck coming down. . . .[37]

In the phrase "a man may chuse" the sailors praise the Isle for its charity, but with a slight indirection, and they state their real views immediately following. A similar way of putting direct praise in

[35] Plutarch *Moralia* 236c.
[36] Allen Apsley, *Order and Disorder* (1679), pp. 65-66. See also Peacham, *Garden of Eloquence* (1593), pp. 35-36; Anthony Collins, *Discourse concerning Ridicule and Irony* (1729), pp. 22-23.
[37] Thomas Herbert, *Travels* (1677), p. 392. Cf. Anthony Blackwall, *Sacred Classics Defended* II (1731), p. 81.

a slightly indirect way was discussed by both John Gilbert Cooper[38] and the *Monthly:*

Translation from the French *of a letter of* Racine *the younger, to his brother, on his poem on* Religion, *in which the saying of* Socrates, *in his last minutes, of his owing a cock to* Esculapius, *is accounted for.*

Socrates does not tell *Crito* to sacrifice a cock, but says simply, and without more, "Crito, *we owe a cock to* Esculapius". . . . Do not you plainly discern that this is raillery? And that *Plato,* who supports his characters with an *Homerical* exactness, makes him die, as he had lived, with irony in his mouth? It was a proverbial saying, when any one who had escaped a dangerous disorder, for another to tell him, that, *for that bout, he owed a cock to* Esculapius. . . . This is all the mystery: *Socrates* meant without doubt, *It is now that we owe a fine cock to* Esculapius; *for I am certainly got over all my ills.* A thought too . . . perfectly conformable to the idea he had of death.[39]

There is no doubt that Socrates meant his remark as some sort of praise for Esculapius; the problem is that he maintained his ironic pose and left his real meaning to an audience's understanding of the whole situation.

The great difficulty of not stating one's real views, of maintaining ironic praise to the end, is evident in an irony pointed out by William Gurnall:

That friar was . . . sound in his judgment in this point, who, preaching at Rome one Lent, when some cardinals and many other great ones were present, began his sermon thus abruptly and ironically. Saint Peter was a fool, Saint Paul was a fool, and all the primitive Christians were fools; for they thought the way to heaven was by prayers and tears, watchings and fastings, severities of mortification, and denying the pomp and glory of this world; whereas you here in Rome spend your time in balls and masks, live in pomp and pride, lust and luxury, and yet count yourselves good Christians, and hope to be saved; but at last you will prove the fools, and they will be found to have been the wise men.[40]

By the time he arrives at the point of bestowing his ironic praises the unfortunate friar has lost his desire to be ironic and can only berate. That art which is the very antithesis of such shilly-shallying is evident in a passage from *Gulliver's Travels* singled out by a commentator on that book:

[38] John G. Cooper, *Socrates* (1750), p. 186 n.
[39] *Monthly Review,* I (July, 1749), 172.
[40] C. H. Spurgeon, *Treasury of David* (1885), p. 420.

As also Pages 108, 109, &c. where an Account is given of the Lords and Commons, the Bishops and Judges; of which this is most remarkable, viz.

THAT the first are the Ornament, &c. of the Kingdom—worthy Followers of their renowned Ancestors, whose Honour had been the Reward of their Virtue, from which their Posterity were never once known to degenerate, &c. There are some who will needs have this Passage to be Ironical but with what Grounds, we leave it to the Reader to determine.[41]

It is only the absolute thoroughness of the praise which in its impossible perfection gives the irony away, but of course the audience must be on the ironist's side. Otherwise he is met by a response like that elicited from one of Defoe's antagonists: *"the Purest, and most Flourishing Church in the World.* They are his own Words, ... and must never pass for an Irony with Honest Men, though his brief *Explication* affirms 'em for such with him. . . ."[42]

In a pamphlet Collins called ironic[43] the author gives us a rather different sort of direct ironic praise. The Dean has accused the Bishop of being applauded by *Nazarenus* and *Independent Whig:*

The D--n, I must acknowledge, has this peculiar Happiness in the present *Reproach,* almost unknown to Him in Any other; *viz.* that he is very secure from having it retorted upon Him; being One of those very few *Writers,* whose *Reputation* in the *Controversy* now on Foot, No Sort of Men *Injure* by their *Applauses.*[44]

Instead of beating about the bush by praising the Dean because everyone applauds him and then having to introduce his real opinion in some fashion, the author goes directly to the point and praises him for his failure. The extended use of this tack is illustrated in the speech of a senator of Lilliput on the government's methods of regulating the gin traffic.

This Bill therefore appears to be designed only to thin the Ranks of Mankind, and to disburthen the World, of the Multitudes that inhabit it, and is perhaps the strongest Proof of political Sagacity that our new Ministers have yet exhibited. They well know, my Lords, that they are

[41] *Gulliver Decypher'd* (1726?), pp. 33-34.
[42] *The Shortest-Way with the Dissenters ... Consider'd* (1703), p. 3.
[43] Anthony Collins, *Discourse concerning Ridicule and Irony* (1729), p. 47.
[44] *D--n of W---r still the same* (1720), pp. 100-101.

universally detested, and that wherever a *Lilliputian* is destroyed, they
are freed from an Enemy; they have therefore opened the Flood-gates
of Gin upon the Nation, that when it is less numerous, it may be more
easily governed.

Other Ministers, my Lords, who had not attained to so great a
Knowledge in the Art of making War upon their Country, when they
found their Enemies clamerous and bold used to awe them with Prosecutions and Penalties, or destroy them like Burglars with Prisons and with
Gibbets.   But every Age, my Lords, produces some improvement, and
every Nation, however degenerate, gives both [*sic*] at some happy
Period of Time to Men of great and interprising Genius.   It is our
Fortune to be Witnesses of a new Discovery in Politics, and may con-
gratulate ourselves upon being Contemporaries with those Men, who
have shewn that Hangmen and Halters are unnecessary in a State, and
that Ministers may escape the Reproach of destroying their Enemies, by
inciting them to destroy themselves.[45]

Here the speaker, all the while he is exaggerating the government's
viciousness, is praising that viciousness in terms of direct value judgment.

No doubt the elaboration by Pope and Swift[46] of direct ironic
praise into extended and sustained pieces of satire encouraged the
popular recognition of the technique.   It was also inescapable in
the controversial pamphlets and other occasional prose of the time.
Thus there was rather more awareness in the second quarter of the
eighteenth century than earlier, of the long piece of direct ironic
praise.   Evidence of this awareness appears, among other places, in
"A Proposal humbly offered to the Senate of Great Lilliput," in
the *Gentleman's Magazine* for November, 1740:

What the Proposer has to offer . . . nearly concerns their own Interest,
and therefore will probably meet with a favourable Attention.   It is
nothing less than the entire Demolition . . . of what has been, and continues still to be a greater Thorn in their Sides, that ill-contriv'd Figure
of Rhetorick, called *Irony* (in plain English *Sneer*) a mischievous Figure,
that has done more Damage to the honourable M---y and Senate, than
the Enemies of our Nation have sustain'd by 100 Men of War and
40000 hand Forces. . . .   'Tis by the Means of this Figure (ill betide
the first Inventer and the Propagaters of it!) that the Views of Ministers
are exposed to the inconsiderate Multitude.   If a few honest Members of
the House of Clinabs for their unsullied Fidelity and Attachment to the

---

[45] *Gentleman's Magazine*, XIV (Jan., 1744), 12.
[46] *Gulliver Decypher'd* (1726?), pp. 33-34.

M---ry, instead of promoting the Good of those that sent them thither, are rewarded with a small Pension, or accept of a Place from him of some Emolument to themselves, tho' of no Manner of Use to the Publick: Why presently these Ironists let all the World know it by extolling their Integrity, Disinterestedness, and Independency. If the Administration squanders away the publick Money, and increases their own, these Sneerers take Occasion to expose them, by magnifying their Frugality and good Oeconomy. If great Fleets are mann'd at Sea, which (for strange Reasons of State) have done nothing; and if a large Body of Land Forces have been kept up at a vast Expence, whose utmost Exploits have been the Robbing of a Hen-roost, or stealing of a Sheep, or some such Feats of War, this they ridicule by calling it a vigorous Prosecution of the War. If a Legate be bamboozled and outwitted, effecting nothing for Years together, they will blast him with their Sneering Commendations of his Sagacity, Penetration, and Address.[47]

iii. *Simple concession*

In its most blatant form the technique of ironic concession is demonstrated perfectly by Sancho Panza. He and Don Quixote having discovered that the dread noises heard during the night were only six fulling-mill hammers, Sancho bursts into raucous laughter:

Four times he ceased, and four times he returned to his laughter with the same impetuosity as at first. Whereat *Don Quixote* gave himself to the devil, especially when he heard him say, by way of irony; 'You must know, friend *Sancho*, that I was born by the will of heaven in this our age of iron, to revive in it the golden, or that of gold. I am he, for whom are reserved dangers, great exploits, and valorous atchievements.' And so he went on, repeating most or all of the expressions, which *Don Quixote* had used at the first hearing those dreadful strokes.[48]

Sancho's method of praising the Don is not direct but is the simple parroting of the Don's earlier statements, now ridiculous in a changed situation. Occasionally an irony can be analyzed as both direct praise and concession. If a fool thinks he is a fine fellow, to call him a fine fellow is both to praise him directly for what he is not and to concede a foolish point of view. This double action is

---

[47] X, 547-48.
[48] Charles Jarvis, *Don Quixote* (1742), I, 105. Jarvis' is the first English translation to use *irony* in this passage; earlier ones, and the contemporary Wilmot translation, used the usual rough synonyms.

illustrated in a biblical irony used by Hall and Smith. Here it is a slight exaggeration of the conceded opinion which reveals the ironist's real meaning:

Job 12.2. Thus he taunts at his false friends: No doubt but ye are the people, and wisdome shall die with you: as if he had said, in your own conceits there are none wise but your selves. No doubt but reason hath left us, and is gone wholly unto you; yea wisdome is so tyed to your persons, that her conversation and ruine depends upon yours.[49]

Puttenham's first example of "Ironia" gives us a direct value judgment which is not reversible, however, but is concession: "as he that said to a bragging Ruffian, that threatened he would kill and slay, no doubt you are a good man of your hands. . . ."[50] And no doubt he was. But by conceding the ruffian's claim within a wider context of values, the ironist has him beating the air. When the ironist leaves the area of direct value judgment to concede an opinion, argument, or point of view, the technique is of course easier to distinguish. Although it may develop into the ironic defense, or ironic advice, these will be considered distinct devices—"complicated concession," if one likes.

Quintilian notes the irony of concession and illustrates it, first with a piece of ironic advice, second with simple concession in combination with self-depreciation,[51] and later Lucian calls a somewhat exaggerated concession irony.[52] The earliest English reference to concession as *irony* appears in Miles Coverdale about 1541. Before being burned at the stake for heresy D. Barnes had made a "Protestation" which was answered by John Standish. In his answer to Standish, Coverdale first quotes Barnes, then Standish, and then makes his attack.

Barnes.

I am come hither to be burned as an heretic, and you shall hear my belief; whereby ye shall perceive what erroneous opinions I hold.

Standish.

Mark here, how he useth ironia, *etc.*

[49] John Smith, *Rhetorique* (1657), pp. 45-48. See also Thomas Hall, *The Schools Guarded* (1655), pp. 163-70.
[50] Puttenham, *Arte of English Poesie* (Willcock-Walker), pp. 186-91.
[51] See p. 100 above.
[52] Lucian *Zeus Tragoedus* 52.

Coverdale.

Ye confess that D. Barnes in his foresaid words doth use *ironia*; . . . it is evident, that when he said these words . . . his meaning was, how that the people should know, that he held no erroneous opinions, as it appeareth by these his words following.[53]

In his irony here Barnes concedes the total point of view of his persecutors on why he has come to the stake, on what he will say, on what his audience will understand by what he says. He does not exaggerate their point of view nor underline the irony with verbal posturings. He relies entirely on his statements that follow to re- veal the ironic import of his opening concession. Stephen Gardiner points out a similar concession in an attack made by Thomas Cranmer.[54] A nice bit of concession from the Bible is adduced by Thomas Granger:

Thus our Saviour Christ answereth the proude, covetous Hypocrites, the Pharisees contemptibly reproaching him for keeping company with Publicanes and sinners.

He answereth them, *Vers.* 12.13. The whole neede not the Phisitian, but the sicke, I came not to call the righteous, but sinners to repentance.

Here hee confuteth, and reproveth their ignorance and their pride by ironicall concession.[55]

The phrase "ironical concession," referring to ironic advice and de- fense as well as to simple concession, seems to have become familiar rhetorical terminology in the seventeenth century.[56] In relating such contrary opinions, Obadiah Walker suggests, the ironist should be sure "there is a sufficient prejudice of them," and should intro- duce them with an ironical "It is obvious" or "I believe" or "Unless I err."[57] But it is just such posturing that makes the following passage of Augustan concession too obvious:

. . . 'tis easy to shew from almost every one of his L---p's Books, that his Adversaries are strange Creatures, Men of Avarice and Ambition, gov-

---

[53] Miles Coverdale, *Remains* (Parker Soc.), II, 331, 333.

[54] Thomas Cranmer, *Answer unto ... Gardiner* (1551), p. 69.

[55] Thomas Granger, *Divine Logike* (1620), pp. 381-82.

[56] *Ibid.*; Thomas Hall, *The Schools Guarded* (1655), pp. 163-70; John Smith, *Rhetorique* (1657), pp. 203-4; Anthony Blackwall, *Introduction to the Classics* (1728), pp. 207-8, 212, and *Sacred Classics Defended* (1727), pp. 254, 256.

[57] Obadiah Walker, *Art of Oratory* (1659), p. 93.

erned by Interest and Passion, without Charity, Learning or Judgment; which last Characters need no other Proof, than that they dare to differ from him, which they never do, but at the same time they differ from themselves, and *run into perpetual Contradictions.*[58]

A subtler manner is implied by Eliza Haywood in the *Female Specta-tor*. The beautiful Sabina had an irrational prejudice against Welsh-men so strong that she absolutely refused even to see the lovelorn Luellin until his friend her brother interceded for him. Having accomplished his intercession, her brother "took his leave, with thanking her in an ironical way, though gravely, for the considera-tion she testified to have for him, in resolving to use a *Welchman* well, because he had a value for him."[59]

Another technique of pointing up an ironic concession is to concede rather more than the immediate argument so that the ad-ditional concession, by emphasizing the nature of the conceded thing in a larger or more detailed or simply different context, acts to underline its ridiculousness. An obvious form of this device was illustrated by Richard Sherry:

> Astysmus, whan a thyng is polished with some mery conceit, as Virgil speaking of twoo foolishe Poetes, Mavius and Bavius sayde: He that hateth not Bavius, lette hym love thy verses, O Mevi, joyne foxes, and mylke he goates.[60]

Here Virgil concedes the possibility of a certain pastime and then goes on to concede the possibility of two other foolish pastimes, which act as metaphoric expressions of his real opinion. Danett's *Comines* gives us a different type of extension:

> After the K. had reposed himselfe a few daies at Pisa, he departed to Florence, where they had declared unto him the great wrong he had done their estate, by restoring the Pisans to libertie contrarie to his promise. Those that were appointed to make answer heereunto excused the fact: saying, that the King had not well understood with what conditions Pisa

[58] Francis Hare, *New Defence of Bangor* (1720), pp. 64-65. This pamphlet is referred to as ironic by Anthony Collins, *Discourse concerning Ridicule and Irony* (1729), p. 46.
[59] *Female Spectator* (1755), IV, 122-23.
[60] Richard Sherry, *Rhetorike* (1555), fol. xxvi.

was delivered unto him, neither understood he another treatie he made with the Florentines:*

* This is *Ironicè* spoken because the King brake this second treatie also, mentioned in the very next chapter, notwithstanding that he understood it wel ynough.[61]

That irony so often quoted during the sixteenth and seventeenth centuries seems to be of the same nature: "As the Jewes said to Christ: now let him come down from the crosse, and save hymselfe, that saved other."[62] And Anthony Collins offers us another instance of this technique:

"On the Day of the Dissolution of the last Parliament of King *James the First* . . . at Dinner . . . His Majesty ask'd the Bishops, *My Lords, cannot I take my Subjects Money when I want it, without all this Formality in Parliament?* The Bishop of *Durham* readily answer'd, *God forbid, Sir, but you should; you are the Breath of our Nostrils.* Whereupon the King turn'd and said to the Bishop of *Winchester, Well, my Lord, what say you? Sir,* replied the Bishop, *I have no Skill to judge of Parliamentary Cases.* The King answer'd, *No Put-offs, my Lord; answer me presently. Then, Sir,* said he, *I think it is lawful for you to take my Brother* Neal's *Money, for he offers it.*[63]

The method of concession can be made the ground of a substantial satire, although it of course tends toward complication. John Stephens carried it to considerable length in Essay I of his *Essayes and Characters Ironicall*[64] by assuming throughout the false point of view toward virtue held by his antagonists, but his concession is so ostentatious and his real attitude so obvious that the Essay seems as much a hostile description of the point of view as a concession of it, yet as description it is nearly enough literal not to be burlesque. Defoe's *The Shortest Way with the Dissenters* was irrevocably far more successful in using this extended technique, and the word *irony* was widely associated with his pamphlet.[65] He himself insisted that simple concession was what the entire pamphlet was: "Thus a poor author has ventured to have all mankind call him villain and traitor to his country and friends, for making other people's thoughts speak in his words."[66]

---

[61] Thomas Danett, *Comines* (Whibley), II, 200.

[62] Richard Sherry, *Rhetorike* (1555), fol. xxvi.

[63] Anthony Collins, *Discourse concerning Ridicule and Irony* (1729), p. 26.

[64] See Dict. III.B.ii, pp. 65-67 ff., above.

[65] *The Fox with his Fire-brand Unkennell'd* (1703), *The Shortest-Way with the Dissenters . . . Consider'd* (1703), and Defoe, *Explanation of the Shortest Way* (Trevelyan), p. 57.

[66] *Ibid.*, p. 57.

iv. *Ironic advice*

This technique, which is fundamentally a dramatizing of simple concession, is defined for us by Anthony Blackwall:

False and unmerited Praise lashes an Offender with double Severity, and sets his Crimes in a *glaring Light*. A lively and agreeable kind of this *Trope* is *ironical Exhortation*: By this when a Man has largely reckon'd up the Inconveniencies and Mischiefs that attend any Practice or way of Living, he concludes with feign'd Encouragement and Advice to act after that Manner, and pursue that very Course of Life.[67]

Such irony as Blackwall recommends here is by its very nature obvious, the ironical exhortation acting merely as a frame for what the ironist really thinks.

An instance of ironic advice had been given by Quintilian[68] and John Lawson repeats "this spirited Irony of *Dido:*"

> Go follow *Italy* thro' Tempests, haste,
> Seek flying Kingdoms o'er the watry Waste.[69]

The earliest English reference to ironic advice produces a rather confused point of view in which statement of the actual "Inconveniencies and Mischiefs" hinders the "feign'd Encouragement." Catholic proscriptions connected with meat or drink are the object of John Philpott's attack:

. . . what else, I pray thee, do their decrees contain, than a certain new Jewish fashion? Whom Paul for these words, and for that imitation, ironeously doth scorn: "Touch not, taste not, handle not, which all perish with the abusing [i.e., *using*] of them, and are after the commandments and doctrines of men; which things have the similitude of wisdom in chosen holiness and humbleness in words only," when indeed they be mere madness and superstition.[70]

During the next two centuries a stock example of ironic advice was Christ's statement, "Sleepe on and take your rest. This saying Christ speaketh in a contrary sense, meaning that trouble was nigh at hand to waken them out of their securitie."[71] The rhetorics of Peacham, Hoskins, Blount, Hall, and Smith all use it and it is

---

[67] Anthony Blackwall, *Introduction to the Classics* (1728), pp. 176-79.
[68] Quintilian *Institutio* IX. ii. 44-53.
[69] John Lawson, *Lectures Concerning Oratory* (1760), pp. 257-68.
[70] John Philpott, *Writings* (Parker Soc.), pp. 418-19.
[71] Peacham, *Garden of Eloquence* (1593), pp. 35-36.

discussed in the *Gentleman's Magazine* for October, 1751.[72]   A correspondent is puzzled by this passage in the account of Christ's passion, for when Christ returns from praying the first and second times, he rebukes his disciples for sleeping, but the third time

he is made to act a part quite contrary to the former; to recommend to them a profound and quiet rest: *Sleep on now and take your rest. . . .* in the next words he adds a quite contrary order; "Arise, let us be going: behold, he is at hand that doth betray me."   What can this inconsistency mean? . . . Does he speak ironically to his disciples in the first part, and mean thus, "Sleep on now and take your rest if you can?"   This cannot be; an irony includes in it that laughing sneer, which was too light for any part of our Saviour's life, much more so, when his soul was sorrowful unto death.

Solomon's advice in Ecclesiastes 11:9, "*Rejoice O young Man, and let thy Heart chear thee in the Days of thy Youth...*"[73] was another popular illustration of irony.   Such advice could upon occasion rise to prophetic scope and fervor, as in Jeremiah's prophecy to Egypt that the King of Babylon would invade and lay it waste:

3. Prepare ye shield, & buckler, and goe forth to battel.   4. Yoke horses, & mount ye horsemen: stand in helmets, furbish the speares, put on coates of maile.   5. What then?   I saw them feareful, and turning their backs, their valiants slaine: they fled in hast, neither looked they backe: terrour on everie side, saith our Lord.   6. Let not the swift fly, nor the strong thinke that he is safe: Toward the North by the river Euphrates they were overcome, and fel downe.   7. Who is this that riseth up as a floud: and as it were of rivers, so his streames doe swel?   8. Aegypt riseth up like a floud, & the waves thereof shal be moved as rivers, & shall say: Rysing up I wil cover the earth: I wil destroy citie, and the inhabitants thereof.   9. Get ye up on horses, & in chariots, & let the valiants come forth, AEthiopia, and the Lybians holding the shield, and the Lydeans taking, and shooting arrowes.   10. And that day of our Lord the God of hosts, is a day of revenge, that they may take vengeance of his enemies: the sword shal devour, and be filled, and shal be drunken with their bloud: for the victime of our Lord the God of hosts is in the Land of the North by the river Euphrates.   11. Goe up into Galaad, & take refine (c) ô virgin the daughter of AEgypt: thou doest in vaine multiplie medecines, there shal not be health to thee.

(c) AEgypt accounted it-self invincible: and so the Prophet ironiously calleth it the virgin daughter, as in this whole passage he speaketh by the same figure *ironia,*

[72] XXI, 456.
[73] Blackmore, *Essays* I (1716), p. 149.

willing them to doe those things which should nothing help nor profite thē, as appeareth by the next words: *Thou doest in vaine multiplie medicines, or remedies, and v. 5. 10. 16.*[74]

All these pieces of advice are aimed directly at the persons whose views are being ironically conceded. But the pattern can be varied. Smollett describes the fluttering of hearts which Peregrine Pickle excited among two groups of ladies at Bath, the youthful flirts and the old-maid moralizers.

> If our hero, in the long-room, chanced to quit one of the moralists, with whom he had been engaged in conversation, he was immediately accosted by a number of the opposite faction, who, with ironical smiles, upbraiding him with cruelty to the poor lady he had left, exhorted him to have compassion on her sufferings; and turning their eyes towards the object of their intercession, broke forth into an universal peal of laughter.[75]

Here the moralizers' views are ironically conceded by means of mocking advice offered to Peregrine, and Pope notes a passage in the *Iliad* in which Juno ironically concedes Jupiter's omnipotence by advising the other gods to submit.[76]

Ironic advice sustained and elaborated into a substantial satire was first clearly associated with the word *irony* in Swift's latter days. The "directions to servants" type of thing seems particularly to have elicited use of the word. An editorial comment in the 1755 edition of Swift's *Works* points with interest to the entertaining irony of his *Directions*,[77] and Orrery comments with distaste that Swift should have been "ironical upon useful subjects."[78] The translation of Dedekind's *Grobianus* published in 1739 is called "An Ironical Poem" on the title page and dedicated to Swift, "Who first Introduc'd into these Kingdoms...an Ironical Manner of Writing." The poem is, of course, parallel in technique to Swift's *Directions*, as the following sample demonstrates:

> No Garters use; but let your whole Undress
> The native Charms of Negligence confess.

[74] *Douay Bible* (1635), Jeremiah 46: 3-16. A similar instance is analyzed in Stephen Marshall, *Emanuel* (1648), pp. 1, 7-8.
[75] Smollett, *Peregrine Pickle* (Shakespeare Head), II, 253.
[76] Pope, *Iliad* (1756), VI, Index under "In the Irony, or sarcasm" and IV, 137.
[77] Swift, *Prose Works* (Temple Scott), XI, 360.
[78] Orrery, *Remarks on Swift* (1752), pp. 282-85.

> Let dangling Stockings, with becoming Air,
> Leave to the Sight your brace of Mill-posts bare:
> So shall each Girl admire thee to her Cost;
> While thy blue Veins, and Muscles well-imbost,
> And brawny Limbs, with Bristles overgrown,
> Make the fond Maiden wish thee for her own.[79]

The ironical cast of a rather different kind of advice, "a Persuasive to people to eat their own Children," is pointed out in the *Memoirs of Scriblerus*.[80]

Ironical exhortation need not be so obvious as Blackwall suggested. Unless the advice is patently foolish, it is up to the ironist how foolish it is made to appear. However, in most of the ironical exhortations quoted above the ironists have made their real view of the advice offered almost obtrusively explicit.

v. *Ironic defense*

J. A. K. Thomson points out that after Lucian had learned the technique of comic irony from Plato he invented the "Ironical *defence*," which became the "favourite and the deadliest weapon of Swift,"[81] but Lucian himself does not use the word *irony* to refer to any instances of this device. In the seventeenth century, however, a very popular biblical illustration of irony does employ it.

> . . . elevating or extenuating of the objection is made by an acute Ironie; or severe derision, including both a confutation, and a sharpe reproofe of a wilfull, and proud adversarie.
>
> Thus *Elias* answereth the Priests, and people of *Baal*, who held *Baal* to be a God. For in seeming to consent to them irronically, he both confuteth, and reproveth their madnesse. *Eliah* mocked them and saide, cry aloud, for he is a God, either he is talking, or he is pursuing, or he is in a journey, or peradventure he sleepeth, and must be awaked. . . .[82]

As Granger says, the irony begins with a concession, thrown into the form of advice; it is in elaborating the concession that Elijah

---

[79] Friedrich Dedekind, *Grobianus* (1739), p. vi.
[80] Pope, *Works* (1751), VI, 192.
[81] J. A. K. Thomson, *Irony* (1927), pp. 204-5.
[82] Thomas Granger, *Divine Logike* (1620), pp. 381-82. See also Thomas Hall, *The Schools Guarded* (1655), pp. 163-70; John Smith, *Rhetorique* (1657), pp. 45-48; *Art of Speaking* (1708), pp. 305-11; Blackmore, *Essays* I (1716), p. 149.

picks up the tools of ironic defense quite naturally in obedience to
the situation and the genius of the ironic impulse. What reveals
his intended meaning, of course, is the premise of the defense.
Gods are not supposed to be hindered from hearing prayers by
travel and conversation. Thus Elijah's defense of Baal proceeds,
in actuality, by praising Baal's hollow godship. Most ironic defense does work in this way, although the simplest form of it,
straightforward rejection by the ironist of what he himself says and
really means, does not. This elementary ironic defense is utilized
by the Iago-like Rui Gomez of Otway's *Don Carlos*. Has the
Queen been unfaithful with her own stepson?

> *R. Go.* Good Heaven forbid that I should ever dare
> To Question Virtue in a Queen so fair.
> Though she her Eyes cast on her Glorious Sun,
> Men oft see Treasures and yet covet none.
> *King.* Think not to blind me with dark Ironies,
> The Truth disguis'd in Obscure Contraries.[83]

The numerous elaborations of ironic defense into substantial
satires for early eighteenth-century pamphlet warfare naturally at-
tracted attention to the fact that here was *irony*. Such awareness
is evident in a letter to the *Grub-street Journal*:

Gentlemen,
      Though you profess your selves Members of *Grub-street*, and ad-
vocates for that ancient Society, I have some reason to suspect that you
are false Brethren, and have a wicked design of exposing the Grubean
Art to contempt, under a specious pretence of defending it, by the modern
Jesuitical method of ironies and *innuendos*.[84]

The ironical "Defence..." became almost a controversial genre.
In the *Tale of a Tub* Swift announced his intention of writing *A
Modest Defence of the Proceedings of the Rabble in all Ages*, and
Anthony Collins called attention to several pamphlets[85] of the sort.
Francis Hare's *New Defence of the Lord Bishop of Bangor's Ser-
mon ... Considered as it is the Performance of a Man of Letters*

[83] Otway, *Works* (Summers), Act II, scene 1, pp. 89-90. A parallel use of
the technique occurs in Cambridge, *Scribleriad* (1752), Book III, note to line 11,
p. 45, called irony by Cambridge on pp. xiii-xv.
      [84] *Grub-street Journal*, Nov. 26, 1730.
      [85] Anthony Collins, *Discourse concerning Ridicule and Irony* (1729), p. 61,
and the pamphlets discussed below.

(1720) "is an ingenious *Irony*,"[86] he remarks.   The groundplan is laid down in the first few pages:

So many Pieces having been writ in Vindication of the Bishop of *Bangor*'s famous Sermon, that 'tis not easy to know so much as the Names or Number of them; I have often wonder'd, that neither his L---p nor any of his Friends have ever once pleaded, what, in my humble Opinion, is the very best Defence that can be made for it; the *great Haste and Hurry*, in which it was composed; of which there appear in every part the most visible Marks, which plainly shew it not to be the Result of his L---p's maturer Judgment, but a Heap of loose, general Thoughts, huddled up in a tumultary manner, and thrown together for want of Time, without Art or Order.   *Sermons*, in the Nature of them, are not expected to be exact and labour'd Compositions, much less to be just Discourses or complete Treatises, especially when upon difficult and nice Subjects.

Hence it is that *Preachers* often perform in a manner much below themselves, as well as below the Subject they have undertaken.

And this appears to have been so much the Bishop of *Bangor*'s Case in his late Sermon, so far as one can judge by the Composition it self, compared with his L---p's known Character; that I can truly say, I very much expected his Lordship would have made this one part at least of his Defence. . . .

. . . so much am I a Friend to the *Liberty of the Understanding*, and to free Enquiries, and think so much Indulgence due to all ingenuous Attempts of that Kind, that I cannot deny my self the Pleasure of offering to the World this new Argument in his L---p's Defence, even against his Will, and hope to convince others, if not himself, that when his L---p composed this Sermon, which has given so much Offence, he had a very good Right to this Plea, however he may have since forfeited it.   With this View I have reconsider'd his L---p's Sermon, and find my Sentiments just the same they were upon the first reading of it.

His Lordship having something *extraordinary* to offer about the Nature of the *Church*, prepares his Hearers for it by a *pompous Introduction*, which makes about a fourth part of the whole Sermon.[87]

Unfortunately Hare proceeds with the kind of attack into which his opening irony has already, by page 3, degenerated.   Although he picks up the main irony occasionally thereafter, it serves chiefly as framework rather than vehicle.   The same fault besets Charles

---

[86] *Ibid.*, p. 46.
[87] Francis Hare, *New Defence of Bangor* (1720), pp. 3-5.

Leslie's pamphlet published in 1704, the first page of which is quoted by Collins:

The same Author attacks Bishop *Burnet's Speech upon the Bill against Occasional Conformity,* by a Pamphlet intitled, *The Bishop of* Salisbury's *proper Defence from a Speech cry'd about the Streets in his Name, and said to have been spoken by him in the House of Lords upon the Bill against Occasional Conformity;* which is one perpetual *Irony* on the Bishop, and gives the Author occasion to throw all manner of Satire and Abuse on the Bishop. The beginning of this Pamphlet, which is as follows, will let the Reader into the full Knowledge of the Design of the Irony, and the manner of Execution.

"The License of this Age and of the Press is so great, that no Rank or Quality of Men is free from the Insults of loose and extravagant Wits.

"The good Bishop of *Salisbury* has had a plentiful Share in this sort of Treatment: And now at last, some or other has presum'd to burlesque his Lordship in printing a Speech for him, which none that knows his Lordship can believe ever came from him.

"But because it may go down with others who are too apt to take Slander upon trust, and that his Lordship has already been pelted with several Answers to his Speech, I have presum'd to offer the following Considerations, to clear his Lordship from the Suspicion of having vented (in such an august Assembly) those crude and undigested Matters which are set forth in that Speech, and which so highly reflect on his Lordship's self."

He has taken the same Method of Irony to attack the said Bishop for his *Speech* on the *Trial* of *Sacheverel,* and for a *Sermon.* . . .[88]

Fog's *Weekly Journal* for June 2, 1733,[89] made a great fuss about "Mr. *Walsingham's* Irony" in the *Free Briton* of a few weeks before. Walsingham had disliked a speech on the recent riots in the City which the Lord Mayor had delivered to the Grand Jury. Walsingham's method in his paper is quite simple. He denies that the Lord Mayor had made the speech because it is misleading and contains an *"illegal* and *absurd Distinction."*[90] Such ironies as these, popular as they were, are child's play when set beside Swift's *Argument against Abolishing Christianity,* called ironic by Deane Swift.[91] Swift's *Argument* is extraordinarily intricate: it will be said here only that he attacks the unscrupulous agnostics who sup-

---

[88] Anthony Collins, *Discourse concerning Ridicule and Irony* (1729), pp. 58-59.
[89] No. 239.
[90] *London Magazine,* II (June, 1733), [266-67].
[91] Deane Swift, *Essay upon Swift* (1755), pp. 135-36.

ported the Establishment with the Gospel left out, by ostentatiously defending their point of view in an exceedingly unwelcome way.

vi. *The fallacious argument*

A popular device among Augustan ironists was the patently false enthymeme, which they used frequently to support the main design of advice, concession, defense, or direct praise.[92]   The chief function of this device was to introduce the ironist's real sentiment without breaking the ice—usually thin—of mock praise.   The way it operates is evident in an early illustration used by Abraham Fraunce:

O notable affection, for the love of the father, to kill the wife, and disinherite the children.   O single minded modestie, to aspire to no lesse, than to the princelie Diademe.[93]

Here each argument offered ostensibly in support of the praise destroys it, but insofar as the arguments are introduced as though they were valid, they participate in the ironic pose.   The device could be carried to some length, as it was in the *Gentleman's Magazine* for January, 1744.   A member of the Senate of Lilliput arose to attack a bill for the sale and consumption of gin:

My Lords,

Though the noble Lord who has been pleased to incite us to an unanimous Concurrence with himself and his Associates of the Ministry in passing this excellent and wonder-working Bill, this Bill which is to lessen the Consumption of Spirits, without lessening the Quantity which is distilled, which is to restrain Drunkards from drinking, by setting their favourite Liquor always before their Eyes, to conquer Habits by continuing them, and correct Vice by indulging it according to the lowest Reckoning, for at least another Year. . . .[94]

The ironist's design here begins with direct praise, upon which he elaborates with a sequence of concessions supported by obviously

---

[92] An interesting analysis of the methods of ridiculously fallacious logic is made by John M. Bullitt, *Swift and Satire* (1953), pp. 92-122.

[93] Abraham Fraunce, *Arcadian Rhetorike* (1588), Book I, chap. vi.

[94] XIV, 6-15.   On p. 14 the Hurgo Yali says that this speech is full of "Irony and Burlesque."   Cf. Francis Hare, *New Defence of Bangor* (1720), pp. 64-65—Collins calls this pamphlet "An ingenious *Irony.*"

fallacious and contradictory arguments each of which expresses his real view of the facts. A simpler passage is explained by Fielding in a note to his translation of *Plutus*:

Poverty. Well then, I proceed now to the Purity of Mens Manners, and I shall convince you, that Good-Manners dwell entirely with me; for all Abuse belongs to Riches.

Chrem. O certainly! for to steal, and to break open Houses, is, no Doubt, a very mannerly thing.

Blepsid. Yes, by *Jove:* it must be certainly very reputable,* if the Thief be obliged to conceal himself.

*... the Meaning, if it wants Explanation, is, that it must be a very reputable Thing indeed, which a Man is obliged to hide himself for having done. We need not observe that this is spoke ironically.[95]

The difficulty of maintaining even as convenient an ironic pose as fallacious argument is demonstrated in the following attack on the first Earl of Shaftesbury, the author of which felt it necessary to explain why his fallacious arguments were fallacious.

His Obedience to the Government is sufficiently evident, insomuch, that That never chang'd, but He did: His endeavours for public Peace are eminently notorious: For in the late Civil War (in spight of all Obligations of Honour and Loyalty to the contrary) he forsook the King, and carry'd over his Regiment to the Parliament, on Purpose (as much as in him lay) to weaken the Royal Cause, and by the Ruin of that, to bring that War to an End, that no more Rebel Blood might be shed, though the great Martyr's Veins were drained afterwards without Mercy.[96]

A famous irony contained in *The History of John Bull* conveys mock praise through concession of an opposing opinion—i.e., that a nation may dismiss its king at will—and supports this concession with what at the time seemed an obviously fallacious argument by analogy: as a wife may renounce her husband at will. Then the ironist further complicates his irony by pretending to argue in the opposite direction: i.e., that a wife may renounce her husband just as a nation may dismiss its king. Allan Ramsay, writing early the kind of analysis which was to become more common as the century progressed, dissected this fallacious argument:

[95] Fielding, *Plutus* (1742), pp. 55-57. Cf. Smollett, *Peregrine Pickle* (Shakespeare Head), IV, 109-10.
[96] *Somers Tracts* (1748), I, 153-54. The editor notes "The ironical Vein which runs thro' this Piece."

This waggery has for title, *Mrs.* Bull's *vindication of the indefeasible right of Cuckoldom incumbent upon wives, in case of the tyranny, infidelity, or insufficiency of their husband's; being a full answer to the Doctor's sermon against Adultery.* And it is introduced into that excellent piece of allegorical humour, *The History of John Bull,* of which it makes a part; as a wen makes a part of the fair body that is disgraced by it.

To detect the fallacy of this pretended piece of Ridicule, let us follow the advice of Aristotle, and reduce it to the formality of a syllogism or two. As thus: First, the author ironically informs you, that

A wife is to her husband, what a nation is to its king:
Now, it being lawful for a nation to shake off its king whenever it is displeased with him, and to take another in his room:
Ergo, it is lawful for a wife to renounce her husband, whenever he incurs her displeasure, and to confer her favors upon anyone she likes better.

To make this ironical syllogism serve the purpose of the party, the faithful reader is charitably supposed to resolve it into the following...

It is contrary to all order and the common sense of mankind, that a wife should, upon any occasion, think herself authorized to abjure her fidelity to her husband.
And a nation being exactly to its king, what a wife is to her husband:
Ergo, it is contrary to common sense to believe, that any failure in a king can ever absolve his subjects from their allegiance. *Quod erat demonstrandum.*[97]

vii. *Burlesque*

In his *English Burlesque Poetry, 1700-1750,* Richmond P. Bond presents abundant evidence that the early eighteenth century arrived at a critical conception of two burlesque techniques: "the first represents mean Persons in the Accoutrements of Heroes, the other describes great Persons acting and speaking like the basest among the People. *Don Quixote* is an Instance of the first, and *Lucian's* Gods of the second."[98] Imitation, then, and caricature, are the identifying characteristics of burlesque: "all distortions and exaggerations

[97] Allan Ramsay, *Essay on Ridicule* (1762), pp. 34-37.
[98] Addison in *Spectator* No. 249 (Dec. 15, 1711), quoted by Richmond P. Bond, *English Burlesque Poetry* (1932), p. 40.

whatever are within its proper province," Fielding remarks.[99]   As this popular formula was usually expressed, burlesque would seem to have been limited to the imitation of character, but there are indications that the Augustans also included caricature of logical argument—the *reductio ad absurdum*—under the burlesque heading. Their simplified scheme may be considered unhistorically, simply as a critical tool, or it may be considered as an historical conception of burlesque.   Taking the latter view, we find that the word *irony* and the words *burlesque* and *mock-heroic* and *parody* came into not infrequent association in the second quarter of the eighteenth century as Augustans gave explicit recognition to one of the tactics of irony.   But the word itself, in specific references, had before then been associated with the techniques of burlesque understood simply as methods of satiric attack.   Nor is this surprising.   When we review the devices of irony already distinguished, we see that they contain within themselves the potentials of burlesque.   Direct praise sometimes tempts the ironist to description.   Simple concession is already imitation; it is a brief step to exaggerated concession and burlesque.   Ironic advice, ironic defense, and the fallacious argument frequently work through exaggerated concession, advising, defending and arguing by utilizing the objects' own views exaggerated to ridiculous extremes.   Burlesque is, then, a quite natural flowering of simpler methods of ironic praise.   Its advantages for the ironist are not hard to see.   The imitation inherent in burlesque gives him an opportunity to depict and explain what it is he is attacking, and the exaggeration of burlesque forces the audience to grasp his real meaning.

The way in which the burlesque of an idea functions was explained by John Dennis.   After quoting the *Spectator*'s praise of Sidney's panegyric on "*the old Song of* Piercy *and* Douglas," Dennis comments:

. . . instead of affirming that Sir *Philip Sidney* has gone too far, he pretends to insinuate that he falls too short; for the *Spectator* vindicates the very Expression of *Chevy Chase*, in which one thing, I must confess, he does seem to me to come something near to a Jest, and to make a fine ironical Ridicule upon Sir *Philip Sidney*.[100]

[99] Fielding, *Joseph Andrews* (Mod. Lib.), p. xxvi.
[100] Dennis, *Critical Works* (Hooker), II, 33-34.

Not everyone would agree with Dennis' reading of this passage, but he does expose a popular method of irony. The technique of accepting an opponent's point of view and then, with apparent approval, of carrying it to a ridiculous extreme which forces the audience to recognize the irony, was one of Swift's favorites:

> I do affirm, [says he, severely, but with exquisite irony indeed, in the Dedication of the *Tale of a Tub* to Prince Posterity,] upon the word of a sincere man, that there is now actually in being a certain poet, called *John Dryden*, whose translation of Virgil was lately printed in a large folio, well-bound, and, if diligent search were made, for aught I know, is yet to be seen.[101]

In *A Modest Proposal*[102] Swift uses both the fictitious character of the projector and the objective tone of fallacious argument to convey his ironic approval of a shocking exaggeration of English policy toward Ireland. In *An Argument against Abolishing Christianity*[103] he uses the ironic defense to praise a somewhat less extreme exaggeration of certain current ideas.

Anthony Collins calls attention to a pamphlet which is "wholly an *Irony*" and a fine one, executed with "Learning, Sense, and Wit,"[104] Francis Hare's *The Difficulties and Discouragements Which attend the Study of the Scriptures in the Way of Private Judgment*, first published in 1714. The pamphlet is ostensibly a letter to a young clergyman in explanation of the rather startling advice its author had offered. To begin with, the study of the Scriptures is very difficult because you must understand the Old Testament, the Apocryphal Books, Oriental languages, Greek, Latin, and Jewish civilization. Second, even if you accomplish this understanding it will do you no good, for Orthodox Faith is founded not on the Scriptures but on the Catholic Tradition handed down from one Bishop to another, and the early Fathers and Councils had a very poor knowledge of the Scriptures. Nor is an understanding of this Tradition difficult to come by, for the established Church is orthodox in all essential points, which any noodlehead can find in the

---

[101] Joseph Warton, *Essay on Pope* (1806), II, 242.

[102] Dict. III.B.ii, p. 73, above.

[103] Johnson, *Lives* (Birkbeck Hill), III, 12, speaks of this "happy and judicious irony."

[104] Anthony Collins, *Discourse concerning Ridicule and Irony* (1729), p. 45.

Liturgy and Articles. Following this course is not only easy but also safe. Moreover, it is accepted among Protestants that whatever is necessary to be believed is plainly and clearly revealed in the Scriptures; therefore you have no reason to study the obscure passages. Third, close study of the Scriptures will do a great deal of harm to you and the public, for it is independent discoveries which have caused all the disputes in the Church and destroyed its peace. These discoveries may be wrong, and even if not wrong, will be condemned because they are different or new. You yourself will be judged a heretic: everyone will turn against you, you will have no influence over your parishioners, you may even be excommunicated or imprisoned while your family starves. If you observe the clergymen noted for learning, you will find they spent their time on classical authors and any other pursuit rather than on study of the Bible. Therefore, don't, at all costs, study the Bible.

Throughout his argument Hare maintains his ironic innocence very carefully, never falling into a frank statement of his real point of view. (He saves that for an appended "Conclusion.") His method is simply to set down with ostensible approval a series of ideas each of which had been seriously advanced by one group and another, and then to draw from each the quite logical though extreme conclusion which neither any of the groups nor his audience could accept.

Some of the mid-century Augustans recognized, judging by their casual comments, that such irony uses what is fundamentally a burlesque method. We find this awareness in the *Monthly Review* for July, 1753,[105] in a review of "The pernicious Effects of the Christian Religion considered; *and its nature proved to be subversive of the common Good. To which is added, in the Conclusion, a brief, but clear Vindication of Free-thinking.*"

'The author, in no very high-wrought irony, endeavours to ridicule infidelity and free-thinking. His burlesque of the proposition, that 'private vices are public benefits,' may be given as a specimen of his humour.

'Since private vices, says he, are found to be public benefits, christianity, which is the inveterate enemy of vice, is an enemy also to the public, that would be benefited thereby. Thus, for instance, theft and robbery, those

---

[105] IX, 67-68.

crimes for which so many suffer continually in a christian nation; in an entire community of free-thinkers, on the contrary, would be mightily encouraged and promoted. For, were all men honest, what a number of smiths, carpenters, and other artificers, with their families, must starve, as, upon this supposition, there would be no demand for locks, bolts, bars, and doors, with the like useful contrivances to guard against the dishonest? It would therefore be a good stroke in politics, if instead of transporting malefactors to our colonies, we should send for them all back again: for though some may think, that we have already thieves (and free-thinkers) enough in the nation, to answer all the purposes of trade (and infidelity) which is the chief glory of these kingdoms; yet we cannot, methinks, encourage too much those useful members of society, though we should exchange religion and honesty for them; since if private vices be really and truly beneficial, the public will be most effectually served by promoting their growth; and then we need proceed but one step farther, that is, to hang up all the honest men for the good of their country.

Our author here has carried his opponents' supposed premise to a logical extreme all good men would prefer not to accept, but in a pamphlet called *irony* by Collins, Francis Hare does not bother with logical extensions. He simply exaggerates his opponent's attitude in a crass and obvious way:

Very tragical Effects are to be imputed to this *Change of the Sense* affixed to certain Sounds: *It has Invaded the most sacred and important Subjects, touches the very Vitals of all that is good, and is just going to take from Mens Eyes the Boundaries of right and wrong.* Direful Scene! Impending Danger! Ruin, certain Ruin! Here is the justest Cause for *Resistance* in the World; it *ought in Duty to be resisted with a more open and undisguised Zeal.* What room for *Passive Obedience* in so desperate a Case? Who can be angry at his L---p's resisting Zeal, when it is so very necessary? When the very *Vitals of all that is good* are invaded, and preserved, if not now bravely defended.[106]

Hare's use of burlesque in reducing an idea to absurdity is childish and gauche by comparison with that of the member of the Senate of Lilliput who arose to attack the government's methods of regulating the gin traffic:

Thus, my Lords, they conceived, that they had reformed the common People without infringing the Pleasures of others, and applauded the happy Contrivance by which Spirits were to be made dear only to the Poor, while every Man who could afford to purchase two Gallons

[106] Francis Hare, *New Defence of Bangor* (1720), p. 6.

was at Liberty to riot at his Ease, and over a full flowing Bumper look down with Contempt upon his former Companions, now ruthlessly condemned to disconsolate Sobriety, or obliged to regale themselves with Liquor which did no speedy Execution upon their Cares, but held them for many tedious Hours in a languishing Possession of their Senses and their Limbs.

If I, my Lords, might presume to recommend to our Ministers the most probable Method of raising a large Sum for the Payment of the Troops of the Electorate, I should, instead of the Tax and Lottery now proposed, advise them to establish a certain Number of licensed Wheelbarrows, on which the laudable Trade of Thimble and Button might be carried on for the Support of the War, and Shoe-Boys might contribute to the Defence of the House of *Aurista*, by raffling for Apples.[107]

A few pages later an opponent of this senator of Lilliput excoriates him for not being able to discuss a serious subject "in any other Language than that of Irony and Burlesque."

Low burlesque, as distinct from the burlesque of ideas, imitates people instead of conceding arguments, and it degrades its people by caricature downward of action and manners and social status, instead of extending argument to a logical extreme. It is interesting to observe how cleverly the author of the speech quoted immediately above has used low burlesque to dramatize his *reductio ad absurdum*. Having carried the government's principles to an extreme of caste distinction and selfish sybaritism, he proceeds to paint a little picture after the manner of Hogarth, a picture in which those who benefit by the government's laws are drawn as maudlin drunks around a table loaded with overflowing bumpers. Not content with this exaggeration, our author proceeds to an even more absurd extreme and dramatizes it in a like manner. Such low burlesque was a technique in itself occasionally associated with *irony*. Angel Day gives us an illustration in which the attitude of an opponent is caricatured in precisely this way:

You complaine that I have done you injurie, if I have, whie then doe you not content your selfe to pursue the revengement thereof, either with manlike or lawful extremitie? whie take you for a refuge these canckred foolish upbraidings, womannish encountrings, unseemlie lyings, & childish threatnings. If we follow the rule you begin, we must straight waies be children, and then I must wrangle whie you stole awaie *Toms*

[107] *Gentleman's Magazine*, XIV (Jan., 1744), 8, 11.

bread & butter, and you must threaten if I tell of that, you wil then complaine of me for eating up the firmĕtie that was kept for the childs breakfast, or how I drunk up my grandams Ale & toste, or lickt bread in the dripping pan, or some such like waightie causes.[108]

The childish comparisons Day labels "Ironia." So too the "indecent likenesse and imitation of man" which led Topsell to call the ape "a subtill, ironicall, ridiculous and unprofitable Beast"[109] could be only low burlesque. In even the most patently insulting of low burlesques ironic praise is to be found in the very fact of imitation, that highest of compliments.

In high burlesque the element of ironic praise is much more strongly felt, for the elevated language of high burlesque keeps constantly before the audience an atmosphere of admiration and praise. Thus high burlesque is usually less blatantly antagonistic than low. It is worth noting, however, that the manners and morals depicted in high burlesques are often as thoroughly degraded by caricature as are those depicted in low burlesque. And this exaggeration need not surprise us, for unless his audience already shares his contempt for his characters the ironist must supply a picture which will arouse that contempt. The only distinguishing characteristic of high burlesque, then, is the elevated language in which it is couched.

Such elevated diction was recommended to the ironist by Aristotle,[110] and Thomas Gordon offered similar advice to the Augustan wits:

... The *Ironical Stile* may be of Service to you on the greatest Occasions, and serve to ridicule the most solemn Things, and notorious Truths, if you do but put some fantastical Expressions into the pompous Eulogium, or print some ambiguous Words in significant *Italick* Characters.[111]

The *London Journal* commented on the use of this style in the mock-heroic:

[108] Angel Day, *English Secretorie* (1595), Part II, pp. 45-47.
[109] See Dict. III.B.ii, p. 64, above.
[110] Aristotle *Rhetoric* III. vii. 11. See G. G. Sedgewick, "Dramatic Irony" (1913), pp. 123-24. See also Theodore Goulston, *Aristotelis de Rhetorica* (1619), p. 195; Hobbes, *A Briefe of the Arte of Rhetorique* (1637?), pp. 163-64; *Aristotle's Rhetoric* (1686), pp. 182-83.
[111] *Humourist* II (1725), pp. 99-102.

To use Epithets, Metaphors, and Comparisons, in describing a Horse Race, or relating what passed on a Bowling-Green, is, if I may use Mr. *Bays's* Expression, to *transverse the Splendid Shilling, and to introduce a kind of* Miltonick *Burlesque in Prose:* If this be done ironically, it will undoubtedly raise a Smile; if seriously, a Horse Laugh....[112]

Such appearances cheek by jowl of *irony* and *mock-heroic* or (high) *burlesque* were common in the second quarter of the eighteenth century,[113] and the *Grub-street Journal* gives us a conjunction of *irony* and *parody:*

> From the Pegasus in Grub-street.
> Sir,
> Having lately read a collection of entertaining and agreeable poems, I found a beautiful burlesque, or parody, of a very unmeaning copy of verses, wrote by A. P--ps Esq; which I send you to publish in your Journal. I do not doubt but the public will be pleased with the humorous ridicule of such sort of poetical productions, as are only sound without sense.

> *The* Flea. *Inscribed to* Namby Pamby.

> Little hind'rer of my rest,
> Thus I tear thee from my breast:
> Bosom traytor! pinching harm!
> Wounding me, who kept thee warm!
> Through my skin thou scatter'st pains,
> Crimson'd o'er with circling stains.
>   Skipping mischief! swift as thought!
> Sanguine insect—? art thou caught—!
> Nought avail thy nimble springs,
> Caus'd perhaps by viewless wings:
> Those thy teeth that cheat our sight,
> Cease their titillating bite:
> I, from all thy vengeance freed,
> Safe shall sleep, and cease to bleed.

> Your humble servant,
> Ironicus.[114]

An early instance of the technique of high burlesque to which the word *irony* was applied seems to occur in Ben Jonson's *Cynthia's Revells.* A pack of foolish, affected courtiers having planned an

[112] *London Journal*, No. 938 (July 9, 1737).
[113] See chap. IV, pp. 166-71, below.
[114] *Grub-street Journal*, June 28, 1733.

evening of revels at which two of their group will meet in a challenge of courtship, demonstrating their skill in all the punctilios of courtly behavior, Mercury and Crites decide to join the group to mock it. Mercury challenges one of the courtiers and imitates their affectations so well that they, unaware of the mockery, award him the victory. Crites is impatient. He himself challenges a courtier and imitates the manner with such exaggeration that the whole group, now understanding the burlesque satire, disperses. It is this project which Mercury and Crites discuss beforehand:

> *Mer.* . . . .
> It is our purpose, Crites, to correct,
> And punish, with our laughter, this nights sport
> Which our court-*Dors* so heartily intend:
> And by that worthy scorne, to make them know
> How farre beneath the dignitie of man
> Their serious, and most practis'd actions are.
>   *Cri.* I, but though Mercurie can warrant out
> His under-takings, and make all things good,
> Out of the powers of his *divinitie*,
> Th'offence will be return'd with weight on me,
> That am a creature so despisde, and poore;
> When the whole Court shall take it selfe abusde
> By our *ironicall* confederacie.[115]

It is perhaps not quite accurate to call the working out of this confederacy high burlesque, since no elevated language is involved. Instead mock praise is implicit in the apparent approval with which Mercury and Crites join in the proceedings. What turns their irony into burlesque at all is that Crites, finding Mercury's veritable imitation too subtle for the audience, himself moves on to exaggerated imitation—and thus reveals the real intent of their mockery.

Mercury and Crites were able, apparently, to maintain their mask of approving participation to the end. The author of "A modest Vindication of the Earl of Shaftesbury: In a Letter to a Friend concerning his being Elected King of Poland" was not so skilled. The editor of the *Somers Tracts* points out the "ironical Vein which runs thro' this Piece...."[116] The irony is no doubt

---

[115] Jonson, *Works* (Herford-Simpson), IV, 130-32.
[116] *Somers Tracts* (1748), I, 153.

meant to consist in a pompous narrative style joined to low caricature of Shaftesbury and his cohorts, and the author certainly man-
ages to supply low caricature. He does not, however, manage to
keep up the style but instead falls into vulgar language and blunt
statements of his real view. During the "late *Inter-regnum* in
Poland," he begins, "there had been many illustrious candidates
for election, Sobieski among them, since he had kept the Turk from
encroaching farther on the Polish frontier. After surveying all the
kingdoms of Europe, the Polish Diet settled on Shaftesbury. The
crown was sent over for him to try it on, narrowly escaped being
stolen, and was sent

back again by a trusty Messenger, concealed in the Hulk or Shell of a
Holland Cheese, taken asunder merely for that Purpose, and cemented
together again by an Art, fit for no Man to know, but a King presump-
tive of *Poland*.

All things thus prepared; his Election being carryed in the Diet so
unanimously and so *nemine contradicente*, that no Man to this Hour
ever heard of it but himself; it is not to be imagined how this little
Grigg was transported with the Thoughts of growing into a *Leviathan*;
he fancied himself the Picture before *Hobb*'s Commonwealth already;
nay, he stopt up his *Tap* (as I am told) on purpose that his Dropsy might
swell him big enough for his Majesty, and of a sudden grew so utter an
Enemy to all Republics and Antimonarchical Constitutions, that from
that Hour he premeditated, and laid the Foundation of a worse Speech,
than that famous one, which he uttered once in our *English* Senate,
entituled *Delenda est Carthago*.[117]

Upon reflection the King-elect decided that the Great Turk must
not only be subdued but also converted, and not to the Catholic
but to the Protestant church, a step which involved converting the
Polish nation to Protestantism as well. He resolved therefore to
take a number of ministers to Poland with him, thirty of whom are
listed each one in this fashion: "*Jean Drydenurtzitz*, Our Poet
Laureat, for writing Panegyrics upon *Oliver Cromwel*, and Libels
against his present Master King *Charles* II. of *England*."[118] Then
one night he had a vision of the Popish plot which led him to give
up the whole venture.

[117] *Ibid.*, I, 155.
[118] *Ibid.*, I, 157.

The same double action of elevated language and low caricature is evident through much of the *Dunciad*, and is explicitly noted
in a footnote to Book II, line 149 of the 1729 quarto:

Our good Poet, (by the whole cast of his work being obliged not to
take off the Irony) where he cou'd not show his Indignation, hath shewn
his Contempt as much as possible: having here drawn as vile a picture,
as could be represented in the colours of Epic poesy.   Scriblerus.[119]

The vileness of some of the pictures is not in doubt, nor Pope's skill
in sustained elevation of language in painting them.   The *Daily
Journal* of March 29, 1728, describes another irony of this kind:

Looking over the Discourse prefix'd to the Third Volume of *Miscellanies* lately publish'd, I observ'd it to conclude with an ironical Project
for the Advancement of the Stage: . . . the ingenious Authors have, with
a good deal of labour'd Dulness, described a ridiculous Society, govern'd
by a Board of Six super-annuated Criticks, who are to meet in a
Privileged Place, for fear of Arrests; who are to be provided at the
*Publick Expence, with Diet-Drink, Spitting-Pots, and all other Neces-
saries of Life.* . . .[120]

viii. *The fictitious character*

A good many burlesques, as we have just now observed, work
through exaggerated imitation of real people who are familiar to
the ironist's audience.   When the ironist sets out on the satiric imitation of a group of faceless people or a complex of nonhuman ideas,
he has before him the problem of giving his irony both focus and
interest.   A popular solution to this problem in the Augustan age
was the fictitious character, the embodiment of all the qualities,
habits, and ideas the satirist was aiming at.   Perhaps because the
ironist must work to create precisely the representative character he
wants, perhaps because the method itself verges on prose fiction, the
ironic character usually tended toward more subtlety, even when it
was used in high or low burlesque, than did burlesque of familiar
people and things.[121]

[119] Pope, *Dunciad* (Sutherland), p. 119.   See also *ibid.*, Book III, ll. 315-28
and note.
[120] *Gulliveriana* (1728), pp. 285-86.
[121] The allegory was another much-noticed technique.   Thomas Gordon in

In 1615 George Sandys referred to the "ironicall personating of a father following the exequies of his sonne, introduced by Lucian...,"[122] and the *Praise of Folly* furnished throughout the English classical period one type of model for the use of the fictitious character. Anthony Collins praised both the book and Erasmus, noting his *"pleasant* and *ironical* manner."[123] A complimentary poem preceding Bishop Kennett's translation sketches the design nicely:

> Satyr and Panegyrick, distant be,
> Yet jointly here they both in one agree.
>
> . . . .
>
> Folly by Irony's commended here,
> Sooth'd, that her Weakness may the more appear.
> Thus Fools, who trick'd, in Red and Yellow shine,
> Are made believe that they are wondrous fine,
> When all's a Plot t'expose them by design.
>
> . . . .
>
> Though Folly Speaker be, and Argument,
> Wit guides the Tongue, Wisdom's the Lecture meant.[124]

the *Humourist* II (1725), pp. 96-105, suggests it as an ancient and successful mode of scandal. The "Ambiguity or *double Entendre* of a Fable" arouses curiosity and gives the reader the satisfaction of solving a puzzle. It is easy to turn a minister of state into a fox and the people into sheep. A less trite method personifies the virtues, vices, and passions in such a way that they resemble great men, Ambition resembling a famous minister of state, etc. He notes that "in our own Country, *Hudibras, Atalantis,* and *John Bull,* are Instances" of allegory. Gordon classifies the ironical mode, however, quite separately from allegory. Pope remarks in "A Key to the Lock" (Pope, *Prose Works* [Ault], p. 182), speaking of party writers, "it has been their Custom of late to vent their Political Spleen in Allegory and Fable. If an honest believing Nation is to be made a Jest of, we have a Story of *John Bull* and his Wife; if a Treasurer is to be glanced at, an *Ant* with a *white Straw* is introduced; if a Treaty of Commerce is to be ridiculed, 'tis immediately metamorphosed into a Tale of Count *Tariff*." An anonymous critic in the *Publick Register* for Jan. 17, 1741 (No. 3), speaking of Swift's "Dedication to Prince *Posterity*," points out that "He gives a Newness to his Subject by Allegory. . . ." The subject to which Swift's method gives newness is sneering praise of his contemporaries, and thus allegory becomes subservient to ironic panegyric, but the critic here does not identify the two methods with each other in any way. Allan Ramsay calls *John Bull* an allegory and notes an "ironical syllogism" which makes a part of it (see pp. 124-25 above), but he does not equate the two methods either. Thus there was apparently no identification of *irony* with allegory such as there had been in the sixteenth century (see pp. 10-11 above).

[122] Sandys, *Relation of a Journey* (1615), p. 83.
[123] Anthony Collins, *Discourse concerning Ridicule and Irony* (1729), pp. 10-13.
[124] White Kennett, *A Panegyrick upon Folly* (1709), pp. xiv-xvi.

Although in his Dedication to More, Erasmus remarks of his character Folly that "having brought her in speaking, it was but fit that I kept up the character of the person,"[125] it is only fair to say that Folly is more a personified vice than a living character. Erasmus uses her to focus his ironical arguments and leaves her at that. The same observation can be made of Swift's use of the ironical character, although both he and Erasmus do maintain each character's logical point of view consistently. The *Argument against Abolishing Christianity,* for instance, is primarily an ironic defense supported by fallacious argument. Although the defense is made by a fictitious character who does project a distinct personality, he is not the center of the audience's attention.[126] Nor are the three heroes of the *Tale of a Tub,* of which Swift himself observed "there generally runs an Irony through the Thread of the whole Book,"[127] very lively human creations. Nevertheless the *Tale* helped alert people to this method of attack, as is evident in Allan Ramsay's explanation of it:

The Tale of the Tub, like *Don Quixote,* is of the argumentative kind of Ridicule, whose business is to oppose false opinions; and operates by raising up fictitious characters to act in familiar occurrences in life, upon principles false and chimerical, and by representing the obvious consequences of such a proceeding, convincing the reader of the falshood and absurdity of such principles and opinions.[128]

In a marginal note[129] Swift punctured an "irony" of fallacious argument in *"The Memoirs of a Preston Rebel. A Ludicrous Account of the Principles of the Northumberland Insurgents, and the Causes of their taking Arms,"* published in the *Free-Holder* for December 30, 1715. Although Swift does not refer *irony* to the device of the fictitious character, the enthymeme he reverses is stated by the supposed author of the piece, a Preston rebel Addison created as the exaggerated representative of all those luckless reactionaries. Thirty

---

[125] Erasmus, *Folly* (Allen), pp. 1-6.

[126] John M. Bullitt, *Swift and Satire* (1953), pp. 56-67, offers an interesting analysis of Swift's "ironic masks," the fictitious authors who are the vehicles of many of his ironies.

[127] Swift, *Tale of a Tub* (Davis), p. 4.

[128] Allan Ramsay, *Essay on Ridicule* (1762), pp. 53-54 n. See also *Publick Register* (Jan. 24, 1741), No. 4.

[129] Swift, *Prose Works* (Temple Scott), X, 371-72.

years later, after another uprising, Henry Fielding adopted a similar character as the mainspring of his *Jacobite's Journal*. Squire Trott-Plaid maintains himself through sixteen issues. Here is an example of his style from the first:

To say the Truth, our Party hath been very unfairly accused of having formerly concealed themselves from deep political Principles: whereas those who know us thoroughly, must know we have not any such Principles among us: For we scorn to regulate our Conduct by the low Documents of Art and Science, like the Whigs; we are governed by those higher and nobler Truths which Nature dictates alike to all Men, and to all Ages; for which Reason very low Clowns, and young Children, are as good and hearty Jacobites as the wisest among us: For it may be said of our Party as it is of Poets;

Jacobita nascitur, non fit.

In Reality, the Party hath so long chose to lay dormant, and have hitherto disavowed their Principles, from one or more of the following Reasons:

First, many have been afraid to reveal their Opinions, not from the Apprehension of Danger to their Persons, or of any Persecution on that Account; for I scorn to lay more to the Charge of the Whigs than is honestly their Due; but they have suspected that it might be some Objection to them in their Pursuit of Court-Favours, or Preferment, that they were desirous of removing the present King and his Family, and of placing another on the Throne in their stead. Moreover, they conceived, and that without the Help of any deep Politics, that Outcries against Ministers, on Pretence of their attempting to undermine the Liberty of the Subject, would not come with so proper a Weight from Men who profest the Tenets of indefeasible, hereditary Right, arbitrary Power, and prostrate Non Resistance. Again, they apprehended that Republicans, who are an artful kind of People, might decline any Union with Men who wanted to exchange a limited for an absolute Monarch. And lastly, that the Dissenters would be extremely timorous on account of their Religion, and would rather chuse to tolerate a Church which tolerates them, than to run the Venture of being extirpated by the Popish-Christian Methods of Fire and Faggot.[130]

In Number 17 Fielding threw off the impersonation:

In plain Fact, I am weary of personating a Character for which I have so solemn a Contempt; nor do I believe that the elder *Brutus* was more uneasy under that Idiot Appearance which he assumed for the

[130] Fielding, *Jacobite's Journal*, No. 1 (Dec. 5, 1747).

Sake of his Country, than I have been in the Masque of Jacobitism, which I have so long worn for the same amiable and honest Purpose; in order, if possible, to laugh Men out of their Follies, and to make them ashamed of owning or acting by Principles no less inconsistent with Common Sense, than detrimental to the Society.

Here then I shall pull off the Masque, and openly avow that I *John Trott-Plaid*, Esq; notwithstanding my Name, do, from my Heart, abhor and despise all the Principles of a Jacobite, as being founded on certain absurd, exploded Tenets, beneath the lowest Degree of a human Understanding.

Many Reasons, besides my great Abhorrence to this Character, have urged me to lay it down for the future.

First, I have observed that tho' Irony is. . . .[131]

Here, in the hands of an accomplished novelist, the fictitious character really comes alive, even though Fielding is using him for exactly the same purpose as had Swift and Erasmus, to speak in ridiculous form the opinions the ironist is attacking. But by giving his characters a name and a place—Squire Trott-Plaid has a wife and an ass—Fielding gives body to the ironic praise implied by his approving presentation of these characters.

Fielding may very well have learned the usefulness of giving life to his ironic character from *Don Quixote*, for in that burlesque so real is the Don we nearly forget the asininity he represents— or, to put it more accurately, we come very close to sympathizing with his obsession. This can hardly be said of the hero of Cambridge's *Scribleriad*; nevertheless Cambridge does try to give Scriblerus more life than Swift had given the heroes of the *Tale*. The ironic aspect of such mock-heroics as *Don Quixote* and the *Scribleriad* was recognized frequently toward the middle of the eighteenth century, as we have noted before, and in the conjunction of these two planets *irony* and *burlesque* we see the influences which could lead to a realization of the rôle the ironic attitude might play in prose fiction of a less openly satiric kind. Only Fielding, in our period, seems to have speculated on this relationship. In his Preface to Sarah Fielding's *David Simple*, after classing the novel as a comic epic poem along with *Le Lutrin*, the *Dunciad*, Butler and Cervantes, he says of Sarah's novel:

[131] *Ibid.*, No. 17 (March 26, 1748).

This fable hath in it these three difficult ingredients, which will be found on consideration to be always necessary to works of this kind, viz., that the main end or scope be at once amiable, ridiculous, and natural.

If it be said that some of the comic performances I have above mentioned differ in the first of these, and set before us the odious instead of the amiable; I answer, that is far from being one of their perfections; and of this the authors themselves seem so sensible, that they endeavour to deceive the reader by false glosses and colours, and by the help of irony at least to represent the aim and design of their heroes in a favourable and agreeable light.[132]

We note that Fielding is not now concerned with burlesque character as an effective vehicle for satire. He is concerned with character in itself, and the function of irony in the presentation of it; and his remarks arise out of his thoughts about a novel.

[132] Fielding, *Works* (Stephen), VII, 274-75.

FOUR

CRITICISM OF THE ART OF IRONY

During the English classical period a good deal of social and moral criticism concerned itself with that whole range of discourse variously called satire, ridicule, raillery, humor, irony, and banter. But the art of irony received far less critical attention. It is probably accurate to say that throughout our entire period there appeared not a single full-dress, serious critical essay on the artistic principles involved in irony considered by that name. The sort of criticism we do find is casual and fleeting, at least until the second quarter of the eighteenth century. Then a few people did stop to pay more than perfunctory attention to this art which had been practiced so well. Out of this practice were slowly evolved certain standards and principles which we now take for granted—they seem utterly obvious. But we should remember that they were not obvious then.

i. *The glaring light of contrary comparison*

The theory of "surprising incongruity" which has had a long history in explanations of wit, humor, laughter, burlesque, and ridicule,[1] not surprisingly also explained irony for the English classical age on the few occasions when that device was theorized about by name. Cicero had remarked that "dissimulation" "steals into the minds of men in a peculiar manner,"[2] but he did not analyze the source of its efficacy. Nor did Quintilian, being primarily attentive

[1] See John W. Draper, "Theory of the Comic in Eighteenth-Century England" (1938), pp. 219-20; Richmond P. Bond, *English Burlesque Poetry* (1932), *passim.*
[2] Cicero *On Oratory* III. 53.

to the relation of an irony to its author rather than to its audience. The theory which was to be accepted in the English classical period was, so far as I have found, first expressed in English by Henry Peacham:[3]

> The especiall use of this figure [Antiphrasis] is to reprehend vice, and mock folly: for by expressing a vertue, and signifying a vice, it striketh the mind of the offender with the sharpe edge of contrarie comparison, whereby he is compelled to see the great differēce betweene what he is, and what he ought to be, between what he hath done, and what he ought to have done, and so by looking in the cleare glasse he may be ashamed of his foule face, I meane his foule fact.[4]

The idea cropped up again during the Restoration in the *Art of Speaking,* translated from the French of the "Messieurs Du Port Royal,"[5] and Anthony Blackwall, discussing *irony* for the early eighteenth century, repeated the doctrine:

> This Way of Expression has great Force in correcting Vice and Hypocrisy, and dashing Vanity and Impudence out of Countenance. To dress up a scandalous Wretch in all the Virtues and amiable Qualities that are directly contrary to the vicious and ugly Dispositions which have render'd him infamous, only makes him excessively ridiculous in those Mock-Ornaments; and more effectually exposes him for a publick Mark of Derision. False and unmerited Praise lashes an Offender with double Severity, and sets his Crimes in a *glaring Light.*[6]

ii. *The two strategies of irony*

In saying that irony dresses up a "scandalous Wretch in all the Virtues ... that are directly contrary to the vicious ... Dispositions which have render'd him infamous" Blackwall was defining that strategy of irony which praises an object for being what it is not. This conception of the ironic method was expressed frequently during the second quarter of the eighteenth century.[7] Perhaps the best

---

[3] W. G. Crane says that the *Garden of Eloquence* was derived largely from John Susenbrot's *Epitome troporum ac schematum.* See Crane's *Wit and Rhetoric in the Renaissance* (Columbia Univ. Stud. in Eng. and Comp. Lit., 1937).

[4] Peacham, *Garden of Eloquence* (1593), pp. 24-25.

[5] *Art of Speaking* (1708), pp. 305-11.

[6] Anthony Blackwall, *Introduction to the Classics* (1728), pp. 176-79.

[7] *Craftsman* (1731), I, 102-4 (No. 18, Feb. 7, 1727). *Gentleman's Magazine,* X (Nov., 1740), 547-48 (quoted on pp. 110-11 above); XV (April, 1745), 207-8.

statement of it was made by Thomas Gordon in his essay "Of Libels," a piece of ironic advice on how to "Bastinado great Men with Prudence and Discretion." Gordon recommends, along with allegory, the historical parallel, and other modes of "Scandal," the ironical method:

Another Mode of *Political Satire* is the *Ironical* or *Mock Panegyrick*. This too is of very ancient Date, but not so commonly used as it has been of late. Several of the *Roman* and *Grecian* Orators made use of it in their publick Harangues to the People. . . .

I need not quote any *English Railers* who have followed this Method; we have for this Year or two past abounded in this sort of State-Panegyrick; I will therefore, under this Head, content myself with prescribing a Rule or two proper to be observed by all *Ironical Defamers*.

First, As there is no Man in the World, how good soever, who has not some Faults; and as, on the other Hand, every Man, how bad soever, has some Virtues; take a particular Care that you do not in any of your Mock-Applauses, praise any one for good Qualities which he is thought to *possess*, but dwell entirely upon those which he is known to *want*. By this Means you cannot fail of having your Grimace understood, and raising the malignant Grin of your Readers.

The same Rule will hold, if you would lash the Times under any King or Government whatsoever; if the Nation is engaged in a *War*, extoll the general *Peace* and *Tranquillity* which reigns in it; if Money or Provisions are scarce, thank God and the Government for the *Plenty* which it enjoys; if any other Nation outwits it in a Treaty, commend the Policy of its Ministers; or if they lose a Battel, cry up the Conduct of its Generals. In short, whatever be the State of the Publick, always make that the Subject of your Panegyrick which other People complain of; for at all Seasons, and in all Governments, there will be Matter of Complaint to those whose Constitution or Interest inclines them to be discontented.

The *Lying* Mode, which is somewhat like the *Ironical*, and consists (after having set forth the Blackness of Corruption, and the Punishment which it deserves) in a positive Affirmation, that our present Ministers are guilty of none of the Crimes before-mentioned; and in a solemn Thanksgiving for our Happiness under a wise and honest Administration.[8]

Memoirs of Grub-street (1737), I, viii-x. Chesterfield, *Letters to His Son* (Strachey-Calthrop), I, 36, 61.

[8] *Humourist* II (1725), 96-105.

That the strategy of irony which Gordon describes should have been uppermost in people's minds is understandable when we recall the most popular stock definition of the rhetorics and dictionaries: *irony* is saying the contrary, or opposite, of what one means. Most of the illustrations of this definition were uncomplicated examples of praising an object for being what it was not. However, when we consider certain of the tactics of irony popular in the Augustan age and before, we realize that they did not, in fact, praise an object for being what it was not; they praised it for being what it really was. Thus ironic concession simply holds an opponent's views up to a clear light by echoing them with mock approval. Ironic advice recommends that its object continue to pursue precisely those foolish or vicious or vulgar courses it is already pursuing. The burlesque of ideas accepts its object's point of view and then, with apparent approval, carries it to a ridiculous extreme; or as "low" burlesque, it accepts the character of its object and then, with approval implied in the very fact of imitation, degrades its object into caricature; or as "high" burlesque, it often describes exaggeratedly degraded people and actions in elevated language. This language and its associations keep constantly before the audience the atmosphere of praise, but like low burlesque high burlesque too offers an exaggerated version of what the object really is. In the fictitious character the ironist can represent in summary and often exaggerated form what his object is, at the same time projecting ironic approval through his role as creator of that character. Even the direct value judgment can be used to say, quite simply, that it is a fine thing to be a thief—not, it is a fine thing to be so honest.

The difference between the two strategies of irony is, of course, one of emphasis. The ironist who emphasizes what his object is not takes it for granted that the audience already sympathizes with his point of view, or he utilizes an obvious situation, or he scatters clues to reveal his intended meaning. He may use metaphors, allusions, self-depreciation which is meant to be transferred to the object of comparison, or fallacious arguments as clues; or he may exaggerate his praise to such a degree of fulsomeness that his audience must boggle at it. The other ironist chooses to emphasize the terrible thing that his object really is, framing that picture in mock praise of some kind. Thus the second strategy of irony does indeed bestow unmerited praise upon its object, but that praise is only the frame for an accurate or exaggerated delineation of the object; whereas the first strategy is primarily concerned with elaborating unmerited praise.[9]

The second strategy had of course been implicit in some of the rhetorical discussions of irony and comments on individual ironies from Cicero and Quintilian on, but the Restoration and Augustan periods developed the idea into a minor doctrine, although they never defined it quite so clearly as they did the first. The *Art of Speaking* noted that "by making every one speak according to the principles he follows, thereby we make them their own Informers, and publish whatever in them is either ridiculous or mean,"[10] and Wolseley elaborated the same idea:

nothing requires less skill than to baffle and expose to universal Contempt those slight and trivial Notions, which others, who seem *given over to believe a Lye,* cry up for Master-pieces of Wit and Reason; to name 'em for Arguments is to ridicule 'em, and but to state 'em right is to confute 'em.[11]

It was this perception that furnished Defoe with his defense of the *Shortest Way:*

[9] The underlying relationships here can be put into the schematic form of variations on an ironic proposition. Praise of what an object is not may take these forms:

A1 This despicable person is a good man.
A2   X is a good man.
A3   X is a paragon of virtue.

In the first the ironist puts into words both meant blame and ironic praise; in the second, he utilizes nonverbal factors in the situation to supply the blame; in the third he activates those nonverbal factors by exaggerating his praise. Praise of the object for being what it is may take these forms:

B1   This (despicable) person is a bad man.
B2   This (despicable) person is X.
B3 This (unspeakably vicious) person is X.

Throughout *B* the subject is described with a sympathy which implies praise, but the description itself depicts a despicable person. In *B1* the meaning of the description is spelled out; in *B2* the audience is expected to derive the meaning of the description for itself; in *B3* the description is exaggerated in such a way that the audience cannot miss its import.

[10] *Art of Speaking* (1708), p. 311.
[11] Robert Wolseley, *Valentinian* (Spingarn), pp. 4-5.

The paper has its immediate original from the virulent spirits of some men who have thought fit to express themselves to the same effect in their printed books, though not in words so plain, and at length, and by an irony not unusual, stands as a fair answer to several books published in this liberty of the press. . . .

The sermon preached at Oxford, 'The New Association,' 'The Poetical Observator,' with numberless others, have said the same thing, in terms very little darker, and this book stands fair to let those gentlemen know that what they design can no further take with mankind than as their real meaning stands disguised by artifice of words; but that when the persecution and destruction of the dissenters, the very thing they drive at, is put into plain English, the whole nation will start at the notion, and condemn the author to be hanged for his impudence.[12]

A much blunter use of the second strategy was remarked by Sir Richard Blackmore, who implored writers engaged in controversy to "cease by ironical Compassion, insultingly to commiserate the Weakness and Ignorance of the Opponent. . . ."[13] In the irony Blackmore is thinking of here, mock sympathy and defense are used to create an atmosphere of praise in which the most flatly insulting direct value judgments are made. The ironist is in effect praising his object for being a fool. The ironic advice of *Grobianus; or the Compleat Booby. An Ironical Poem* was explained by its English translator: "the Author's Design, is to laugh Men out of the Error of their Ways; recommending most Virtues by a Representation of the contrary Vices. . . ."[14] Such casual recognition of the second strategy of irony was not uncommon.

iii. *Clues to meaning*

It is evident from the above discussion and our analyses in the preceding chapter that one of the chief problems an ironist must face up to is the extent to which he can count on his audience to grasp his real meaning. His job is to put before his audience a false point of view and to present it as though he really accepts it; yet his audience must recognize both that the point of view is false

[12] Defoe, *Explanation of the Shortest Way* (Trevelyan), p. 56.
[13] Blackmore, *Essays* II (1717), pp. 252-53.
[14] Friedrich Dedekind, *Grobianus* (1739), p. vi.

and that he is not accepting but attacking. His problem is "the double dissimulation, or dissembling of dissimulation, necessary in this species of ridicule...."[15] Unlike the criminal, he wants to get caught. If he is not caught the object of his attack escapes unharmed while the ironist remains the sole and sterile audience to his own cleverness. Thus he must dissemble the fact that his praise is insincere, but he must not dissemble so well that ultimately he deceives anyone. As Swift complained in "Cadenus and Vanessa,"

... those who aim at Ridicule
Shou'd fix upon some certain Rule,
Which fairly hints they are in jest,
Else he must enter his Protest:
For, let a Man be ne'er so wise,
He may be caught with sober Lies....[16]

In the preceding chapter we noticed a number of the ways in which an irony may reveal itself, and most of these ways were pointed out in the critical comments of the English classical period. Three types of clue by which an audience may discover an irony had been named by Quintilian:

that class of allegory in which the meaning is contrary to that suggested by the words, involves an element of irony, or, as our rhetoricians call it, *illusio*. This is made evident to the understanding either by the delivery, the character of the speaker or the nature of the subject. For if any one of these three is out of keeping with the words, it at once becomes clear that the intention of the speaker is other than what he actually says.[17]

This trichotomy, in complete or truncated form, was repeated automatically by the rhetorics of the English classical age,[18] and we see it at the back of Defoe's mind in his *Explanation of the Shortest Way:*

The Author professes he thought, when he wrote the book, he should never need to come to an explanation, and wonders to find there should be any reason for it.

[15] *World* (Chalmers), XXVI, i-iv (Preface).
[16] Swift, *Poems* (Williams), II, 707-8.
[17] Quintilian *Institutio* VIII. vi. 54-58.
[18] Thomas Wilson, *Rhetorique* (G. H. Mair), pp. 184-85. Richard Sherry, *Rhetorike* (1555), fol. xxvi. Abraham Fraunce, *Arcadian Rhetorike* (1588), Book I, chap. vi. Peacham, *Garden of Eloquence* (1593), pp. 35-36. John Smith, *Rhetorique* (1657), pp. 45-48. *Art of Speaking* (1708), p. 63. Anthony Blackwall, *Introduction to the Classics* (1728), pp. 176-79. Ephraim Chambers, *Cyclopaedia* (1728), Vol. II, "Irony."

If any man takes the pains seriously to reflect upon the contents, the nature of the thing, and the manner of the style, it seems impossible to imagine it should pass for anything but a banter upon the high-flying churchmen.[19]

In less automatic analyses of the kind of clue available to irony one or another of Quintilian's three kinds often achieved independent prominence. The "delivery" was always felt to be important. Thus Abraham Fraunce, taking a sour view of the capacities of audiences, pointed out that

In the particular applying of the voyce to severall words, wee make tropes that bee most excellent plainly appeare.   For without this change of voyce, neither anie *Ironia*, nor lively *Metaphore* can well bee discerned.[20]

John Bulwer specified several gestures which were appropriate to the ironist[21] and Nathan Bailey made delivery the most important sign of an irony: "The chief Sign of this Trope is generally the Tone of the Voice in pronouncing Ironies."[22]   The second kind named by Quintilian, the "nature of the subject," was given special importance by the Augustans, thinking, as many of them in the wake of Shaftesbury did, that the ridicule inheres in the object rather than in the eye of the beholder so that it will not take but will recoil on the satirist if the object is not really in itself ridiculous. This point of view emphasized an obvious aspect of irony.   Thus as we have seen Thomas Gordon advised the ironist that if he dwells entirely upon the good qualities which the object of his satire "is known to *want*" he cannot fail of having his "Grimace" understood.[23]   The *Craftsman* expressed the accepted theory in detail:

when a common Strumpet is extoll'd for her Chastity; a Debauchee for his Temperance; or a corrupt Minister of State for his disinterested Love of his Country; the *Irony* holds good, and every Body understands the Author's meaning as well as if it had been express'd in the plainest Terms. But where would be the *Irony*, or the *Satire*, in calling *Lucretia* chaste, *Caesar* valiant, or *Cato* just? —Would not the World believe such a Man *in earnest*; or laugh at his *Folly* and *Impotence*? —It could not therefore

---

[19] Defoe, *Explanation of the Shortest Way* (Trevelyan), p. 55.

[20] Abraham Fraunce, *Arcadian Rhetorike* (1588), Book II, chap. i.

[21] See pp. 70 above, 163 below.

[22] Bailey, *Universal Etymological English Dictionary* II (1727), "Irony." See also Bailey, *Dictionarium Britannicum* (1730), "Irony"; Ephraim Chambers, *Cyclopaedia* (1741, 1743), Vol. I, "Irony."

[23] See p. 143 above for full quotation.

be my Design, in any of the preceding Papers, to asperse the *present Administration*, in an ironical Manner, without being guilty of so great a Weakness as to imagine, that I could impose Characters upon the World, of which *Those Gentlemen* are a living and exemplary Confutation.[24]

Both Gordon and the *Craftsman* take for granted that the ironist can be sure of his audience's attitude, but in more ticklish situations, Obadiah Walker had warned, the ironist is warranted in "Relating contrary opinions" only "when there is a sufficient prejudice of them. . . ."[25] Chesterfield advised his son always to consider fairly whether he deserved the compliments that were paid him, for if he did not, the compliments were likely to be meant ironically.[26] The Earl did not take into account, as our own age dazzled by the vision of two sides to every question almost invariably would, the possibility that his son's opinion of his own virtues might differ from an antagonist's. As the *Craftsman* remarked, "If a person, against whom *irony* is level'd, is so arrogant and self-sufficient as to be persuaded that he is possessed of all the virtues and great good qualities to which he is entirely a stranger, he will be, like the man in the almanack, insensible of a smart, though all his beholders see him stuck full of darts."[27] "The character of the speaker," third of Quintilian's kinds, did not achieve any emphasis in independent criticism, although having experienced Butler and Marvell, the Augustans were on constant lookout for drolls.

In his formal classification of clues to an irony Quintilian does not call attention to internal inconsistency. In a later passage he does:

Irony involving a *figure* does not differ from the *irony* which is a *trope*, as far as its *genus* is concerned, since in both cases we understand something which is the opposite of what is actually said; on the other hand, a careful consideration of the *species* of *irony* will soon reveal the fact that they differ. In the first place, the *trope* is franker in its meaning, and, despite the fact that it implies something other than it says, makes no pretence about it. For the context as a rule is perfectly clear, as, for example, in the following passage from the Catilinarian orations. "Re-

[24] *Craftsman* (1731), I, 102-4.
[25] Obadiah Walker, *Art of Oratory* (1659), p. 93.
[26] Chesterfield, *Letters to His Son* (Strachey-Calthrop), I, 36 (XXIX, July 15, 1739).
[27] *Gentleman's Magazine*, XV (April, 1745), 207-8.

jected by him, you migrated to your boon-companion, that excellent gentleman Metellus." In this case the irony lies in two words, and is therefore a specially concise form of *trope*. But in the *figurative* form of irony the speaker disguises his entire meaning, the disguise being apparent rather than confessed. For in the *trope* the conflict is purely verbal, while in the *figure* the meaning, and sometimes the whole aspect of our case, conflicts with the language and the tone of voice adopted. . . .[28]

The sort of inconsistency which Quintilian notes first here, in which the verbal context of the irony openly indicates how the irony is to be taken, is recognized by John Smith's *Rhetorique* in discussing "Synchoresis" or "Concession":

A figure when an argument is ironically or mockingly yeelded unto, and then marred with a stinging retort upon the objector.

.   .   .   .

Here first you have an Ironical concession, but after this, a stinging [but] which mars all.[29]

Robert Ferguson seems to have internal inconsistency in mind when he says that an irony "may be easily discerned either by the thing it self which is spoken, or by some circumstance or other in the Oration."[30] Swift's *Reasons . . . for repealing the Sacramental Test in favour of the Catholics* elicited a pertinent comment from Orrery:

The greatest art, and the keenest strokes of irony display themselves throughout the whole composition: and the conclusion of it is drawn up with a mixture of serious and ironical arguments that seem to defy all kinds of refutation.[31]

Unspecified by Quintilian, another type of clue within the context of the irony itself is recognized by the Preface to *Grobianus*. As the Preface points out, the poem ostensibly recommends the practices which in reality it is condemning. How is the audience to know that these practices are vicious? The poem gives us, says the Preface: "Vice depicted in her proper Colours," "an exact Picture of Iniquity and Imprudence"; "Here every Imprudence and Indecency is set in the most conspicuous Light. . . ." *Don Quixote,*

---

[28] Quintilian *Institutio* IX. ii. 44-53.
[29] John Smith, *Rhetorique* (1657), pp. 203-4.
[30] Robert Ferguson, *The Interest of Reason in Religion* (1675), pp. 299-300.
[31] Orrery, *Remarks on Swift* (1752), p. 288.

says the writer, does the same thing.[32] *Grobianus* uses ironic advice to convey a satiric picture which by its nature reveals the irony;[33] Fielding's *Jacobite's Journal* uses the fictitious character:

it is impossible for any Man to unite the contradictory Doctrines of a Protestant and a Jacobite, without being guilty of all the glaring and monstrous Absurdities which I have endeavoured to assign to that motley Character.[34]

The object itself, then, if properly displayed, reveals its own absurdity. A somewhat subtler instance of the same type of clue is analyzed by Richard Owen Cambridge in discussing his *Scribleriad:*

By Irony is generally understood the saying one thing and meaning another. Then how shall it be known whether a burlesque writer means the thing he says or the contrary? This is only to be found by attention and a comparison of passages. Let us endeavor to see this by an instance. *Scriblerus* is promis'd the grand Elixir, it is frequently insinuated that he is to possess this secret of transmuting metals and prolonging life, and the work concludes without explaining directly that he is disappointed in his expectations. But will it not appear that these expectations are ironically given, when we find all preceding ones to have been so? For of all the many prophecies delivered to him, the only one fulfill'd is that of his being reduced to a state of Beggary in his pursuit of Alchymy.[35]

In the Augustan period, as we have seen, burlesque stood in a somewhat ambiguous but nonetheless important relation to irony. In our discussion in the preceding chapter of the burlesque methods of writing called *irony* in the English classical period, we have already observed the large part which exaggeration and caricature played in conveying the ironist's real meaning. Augustan criticism was very much aware of this literary technique both in burlesque and in writing that was not primarily burlesque. Shadwell, talking about "wilde Romantic *Tales*," complains that "they strein Love and Honour to that Ridiculous height that it becomes Burlesque."[36] Addison thinks that burlesque "ridicules Persons" "by drawing them quite unlike themselves."[37] Shaftesbury attacks the mental

---

[32] Friedrich Dedekind, *Grobianus* (1739), pp. viii-xi.
[33] Cf. Anthony Blackwall's explanation of the method of ironic advice quoted on p. 116 above.
[34] Fielding, *Jacobite's Journal*, No. 17 (March 26, 1748).
[35] R. O. Cambridge, *Scribleriad* (1752), pp. xiii-xv.
[36] Thomas Shadwell, *Sullen Lovers* (Spingarn), II, 150.
[37] Quoted by Richmond P. Bond, *English Burlesque Poetry* (1932), p. 40.

habit of buffoons because love of diversion leads them to distort and travesty everything they see.[38]   John Brown utilizes the same idea to show—in Shaftesbury's teeth—that ridicule succeeds against the good, the true, and the beautiful precisely because it does depict them falsely, "through the oblique Mediums of Ridicule...."[39] Deane Swift attacks Orrery's *Remarks* as one entire "burlesque upon Swift's character, representing his life and writings in a thousand caricaturas."[40]   But the conventional Augustan analyses of burlesque, which Richmond P. Bond excerpts so thoroughly, never came to a clear-cut decision as to exactly what is exaggerated.   In applying elevated praise to mean objects, does the mock-heroic exaggerate in its mock praises or does it exaggerate the meanness of the object, or both?   Only Fielding seems to have attacked this problem head on. He is not, as Mr. Bond rightly says, representative; he is better than that.   Fielding tells us in the Preface to *Joseph Andrews* that he has included certain "parodies or burlesque imitations."

But though we have sometimes admitted this in our diction, we have carefully excluded it from our sentiments and characters; for these it is never properly introduced, unless in writings of the burlesque kind, which this is not intended to be.

He goes on to argue that the comic, as distinguished from burlesque, confines itself "strictly to nature."

I have hinted this little concerning burlesque, because I have often heard that name given to performances which have been truly of the comic kind, from the author's having sometimes admitted it in his diction only; ... but surely, a certain drollery in stile, where characters and sentiments are perfectly natural, no more constitutes the burlesque, than an empty pomp and dignity of words, where everything else is mean and low, can entitle any performance to the appellation of the true sublime.

But to illustrate all this by another science, in which, perhaps, we shall see the distinction more clearly and plainly, let us examine the works of a comic history painter, with those performances which the Italians call Caricatura, where we shall find the true excellence of the former to exist in the exactest copying of nature; insomuch that a judicious eye instantly rejects anything *outré*, any liberty which the painter hath taken

[38] Shaftesbury, *Life, Letters, Regimen* (Rand), pp. 171-72.
[39] John Brown, *Essays on Characteristics* (1751), pp. 56-57.
[40] Deane Swift, *Essay upon Swift* (1755), pp. 70-72.

with the features of that *alma mater*; whereas in the Caricatura we allow all license—its aim is to exhibit monsters, not men; and all distortions and exaggerations whatever are within its proper province.

Now, what Caricatura is in painting, Burlesque is in writing; and in the same manner the comic writer and painter correlate to each other.[41]

High burlesque, Fielding is saying, is unjustified praise applied to people and sentiments whose characteristics are distorted and exaggerated into caricature. This is a more precise description of most high burlesque than the conventional criticism of the time was able to furnish, but as Fielding admits, the word *burlesque* often referred to writing that would not fall under his definition.

However, the quality of exaggeration as a clue to irony was brought nearer to irony so called than through the link of burlesque. To Quintilian's trichotomy of clues, Anthony Blackwall added a fourth: "the Exorbitance of the Commendations."[42] A critique of *Female Taste* in the *Monthly Review* for June, 1755,[43] evidences a consciousness of the other type of exaggeration. Like that of *Grobianus*, the satire of *Female Taste* consists in its ironical advice to commit the very faults it sets out to reform. In one place the poem suggests that in order to buy fine clothes a lady is justified in selling her pictures, silver, jewels, wedding ring, and dishes. We think, the *Monthly* remarks, "our author aggravates too much."

Such an hyperbole must inconsistently suppose this vain lady to preserve no state nor shew at home, to have nothing to eat off; as a very little more exaggeration must render the dishes indeed superfluous, by supposing her to have nothing to eat.

It is not exaggeration of praise, but caricature of the object of attack which the critic is here noticing, and condemning an excess of. Thomas Gordon had already outlined this ironic technique in his essay "Of Libels" partially quoted above:[44]

Secondly, if you find it necessary to banter any Publick Proceeding, which is generally applauded, and reasonably set on Foot; never forget in your ludicrous Approbation to give it another Turn, and insist upon such Topicks as will create Jealousy in the Minds of Men, and disgust them against those who undertake it. In case of a *War*, though ever

[41] Fielding, *Joseph Andrews* (Mod. Lib.), pp. xxiv-xxvii.
[42] Anthony Blackwall, *Introduction to the Classics* (1728), pp. 176-79.
[43] XII, 510.
[44] See p. 143 above.

so necessary or unavoidable, represent it as the Effect of a noble Spirit that delights in Danger and *Knight-Errantry*, in quelling Foreign Tyrants, and freeing *Foreign* Nations, without any *Selfish* Regard to *Domestick* Considerations. Extol the disinterested Merit of a Prince, who exhausts his own Blood and Treasure in Defence of his unhappy Neighbours, and the common Cause of Mankind. If *Peace* be negotiated, set forth the Advantages of living in *Ease, Indolence,* and an heroick Contempt of the Concerns of the World; magnify the Terms of Pacification, and add to them *Articles* which were never proposed— In other Cases you cannot fail of applying the same Rule.[45]

The Augustan age, then, gave some critical notice to a number of the ways in which their irony revealed itself: the tone of voice, the validity of praise, the likely motives of the speaker, and any internal inconsistencies in what was said: an honest opinion set cheek-by-jowl with an ironic one, the picture of a ridiculous object set in a frame of ironic approval, suspiciously fulsome praises, caricature of the thing being praised.

iv. *The question of clarity*

Recognition of the kinds of clue that could reveal an irony did not mean that ironies were in fact always happily revealed. In actual fact ironies were constantly misunderstood and misinterpreted. Literary people were uncomfortably aware of this fact and their awareness produced some interesting comments on the relation of irony to various audiences. Henry Peacham, in his "Caution" concerning "*Mycterismus,*" "a privie kind of mocke . . . yet not so privie but that it may well be perceived," had admonished his Elizabethan readers that "it is not to be used to simple and ignorant persons, which do want the capacitie & subtlety of wit to perceive it."[46] A hundred years later poor Defoe was wondering that there should be any need to explain the irony of his *Shortest Way,*[47] and in the last chapter of the *Memoirs of Scriblerus* Martin's writings are described as "for the most part Ironical, and the Drift of them often so delicate and refin'd as to be mistaken by the vulgar."[48] But

---

[45] *Humourist* II (1725), pp. 96-105.
[46] Peacham, *Garden of Eloquence* (1593), pp. 38-39.
[47] See p. 73 above.
[48] See Dict. III.B.ii, pp. 147-48 above.

Francis Hutcheson, discussing that incongruous association of great and mean images which produces laughter, including the laughter of burlesque, pointed out that differences between individuals, social groups, time, and place all involve differences of opinion on what is dignified and what is mean, so that there are wide variations in what will cause laughter.[49] The problem is not only the obtuseness of the vulgar. And this the *Craftsman* found to be true in respect of political allegiance. During the years 1727-30 Caleb did some loud complaining about the forced interpretation of his essays into seditious libels. His tongue was in his cheek, and no doubt he hoped to impede prosecution of his own paper by crying out against the prosecution of innocent writers, but the essays illuminate the political mind of the age, which expected to find a second meaning under every period. In his issue of February 7, 1727, Caleb announced the heads of his best argument:

> I design, in a short Time, to consider the Case of *Irony* and *Innuendoes* in a *judicial* Light; and how far a *forced, distant,* or *inverted* Construction of any Sentence is consistent with common *Equity* and the *Liberties* of this Nation, when a *plain, natural* and *obvious* Meaning is ready at Hand.[50]

The *Craftsman*'s complaint was about people who saw ironies where there were none, but the main complaint continued to be about people who couldn't see an irony under their noses. Fielding gave up the irony of his *Jacobite's Journal,* among other reasons, because "there is no kind of Humour so liable to be mistaken"; irony was, consequently, "of all others, the most dangerous to the Writer. An infinite Number of Readers have not the least Taste or Relish for it, I believe I may say do not understand it. . . ."[51] The *World* for Thursday, December 26, 1754,[52] discoursed briefly on this subject:

> In writings of humour, figures are sometimes used of so delicate a nature, that it shall often happen that some people will see things in a direct contrary sense to what the author and the majority of readers understand

[49] Francis Hutcheson, *Reflections upon Laughter* (1750), pp. 5-25.
[50] *Craftsman* (1731), I, 106.
[51] Fielding, *Jacobite's Journal*, No. 17 (March 26, 1748).
[52] *World* (Chalmers), XXVII, pp. 277-79 (No. 104). For additional comments see Charles Jarvis, *Don Quixote* (1742), pp. vi-vii, and *Monthly Review*, IV (April, 1751), 419.

them. To such the most innocent irony may appear irreligion or wickedness. But in the misapprehension of this figure, it is not always that the reader is to blame. A great deal of irony may seem very clear to the writer, which may not be so properly managed as to be safely trusted to the various capacities and apprehensions of all sorts of readers. In such cases the conductor of a paper will be liable to various kinds of censure, though in reality nothing can be proved against him but want of judgment.

The other side of the coin was that some ironists had no wish to be understood. Burton, rambling on about "scoffers," tells the story of Leo Decimus the "scoffing *Pope*" and his co-conspirator Bibiena, who persuaded Baraballius of Caieta that he was as good a poet as Petrarch and so convinced the good man of his genius that when his wiser friends told him of his folly he became very angry with them.[53] Bellegarde warns his English readers against falling into precisely this trap:

The custom of Flattery seems a Trade; or to say better, a Tribute we give, to be repaid in the same Coin. 'Tis difficult to distinguish when Commendation is sincere, and when *Ironical.* Our Prejudice for our personal Merit, makes us think the Praises bestow'd in pure *Complaisance,* to be due to us. To be undeceiv'd, let us fancy our selves the Comedy that is acted. As we make sport with others, on whom we lavish our Incense in pure Flattery, and against our Conscience, we sneer aside the Person we loudly extol and commend with an *Emphasis.* By these counterband Praises, we mean to excite the Compliments made to us in pure Favour, and without Desert. Is not this a pleasant sort of Game? Why are we so greedy after those insipid Flatteries, that only Wheedle and Decoy us?[54]

But it was Shaftesbury, perhaps, who was most sensitive to the abuse, not only in social conversation but in politics and intellectual debate:

the natural free Spirits of ingenious Men, if imprison'd and controul'd, will find out other ways of Motion to relieve themselves in their *Constraint:* and whether it be in Burlesque, Mimickry or Buffoonery, they will be glad at any rate to vent themselves, and be reveng'd on their *Constrainers.*[55]

[53] Burton, *Anatomy of Melancholy* (1621), pp. 196-99.
[54] Bellegarde, *Reflexions upon Ridicule* (1717), II, 149-50.
[55] Shaftesbury, *Characteristics* (Robertson), I, 50-51.

Men in these circumstances resort to speaking their minds "ironically," if necessary involving themselves in "Mysteriousness" and talking "so as hardly to be understood, or at least not plainly interpreted, by those who are dispos'd to do 'em a mischief." Such irony is "the Corruption or wrong Use of Pleasantry and Humour."[56] Elsewhere he objects to people who "go about industriously to confound men, in a mysterious manner, and to make advantage or draw pleasure from that perplexity they are thrown into by such uncertain talk...."[57]

Were there any critical standards in this realm of clarity? How obvious should an irony be? There was first of all the standard inherent in the problem itself and the complaints quoted above. As Peacham said of *mycterismus,* "This figure must not be too obscure and darke, for by that it may loose the vertue and use, if it be not perceived...."[58] At an interval in the performance of their *"ironi-call* confederacie" in *Cynthia's Revells,* Mercury tells Crites to have patience, that he will mimic to the last detail the fantastic affectations of the courtiers, and Crites answers: "I, but you should doe more charitably, to doe it more openly; that they might discover themselves mockt in these monstrous affections."[59] Shaftesbury, as we have seen, objected severely to either political or social raillery which deceived instead of informing its audience. The *Gentleman's Magazine* for 1764,[60] quoting a translation of George Frederick Meier's *Thoughts on Jesting,* offers:

By a jest we imply much more than is expressed; we only give the hearer an opportunity to think; and by starting a jocular conceit, force him to make reflections himself, so as to conceive what was not expressed; but this should be done so as instantly and forcibly to lead the mind to the particular reflection intended....

In addition to the standard that irony should be clear enough to hit its audience, there was a tenuous connection between irony and the doctrine that art should be true to nature. Irony was con-

[56] *Ibid.*
[57] *Ibid.,* I, 45.
[58] Peacham, *Garden of Eloquence* (1593), pp. 38-39.
[59] Jonson, *Works* (Herford-Simpson), IV, 147. See pp. 132-33 above for a full description of the situation.
[60] XXXIV (Supplement, 1764), 614.

sidered one of the four primary tropes,[61] about which Ephraim
Chambers asserted that they "should always be clear; they are vicious, if they be obscure, or too far fetched."[62] Lansdowne's *Essay
upon Unnatural Flights in Poetry* had gone to some poetic length
to say virtually the same thing:

> But Poetry in Fiction takes delight,
> And mounting up in Figures out of Sight,
> Leaves Truth behind in her audacious flight;
> Fables and Metaphors that always lie,
> And rash Hyperboles, that soar so high,
> And every Ornament of Verse, must die.
>
> Mistake me not: No Figures I exclude,
> And but forbid Intemperance, not Food;
>
> . . . .
>
> As Veils transparent cover, but not hide,
> Such metaphors appear, when right apply'd;
> When, thro' the phrase, we plainly see the sense,
> Truth, when the meaning's obvious, will dispense.[63]

Both authors seem to be thinking of metaphor and the other two
tropes more than of irony, although this attitude toward truth had
its effect on judgments of individual ironies. Thus, under the influence of Father Bouhours and this point of view, Lansdowne[64]
and John Oldmixon made a rather curious connection between irony
and hyperbole. Oldmixon writes in that medley of Bouhours and
himself called *The Arts of Logick and Rhetorick:*

> The *Irony* is another Way of passing off an *Hyperbole*. When we
> rally or banter we may say any Thing, but must be more upon our Guard
> when we write seriously; as *Balzac* does when he says, *He could get as
> much Wine out of his Muscadines as would make half* England *drunk;
> that his Vines produce as much as ought to serve a whole Country; that
> there are more Perfumes in his Chamber than in all* Arabia Foelix, *and
> such a Flood of Orange and Jessamine Water, that he and his Servants
> are forced to swim for their Lives.* Had he said this by Way of Banter,
> it had been well enough; but the Misfortune is he says it with a grave
> Tone, and perhaps is the first Man that ever said a Thing so gravely,
> that had so little Truth in it. *Voiture* never offends in this manner.

---

[61] See p. 35 above.
[62] Ephraim Chambers, *Cyclopaedia* (1741, 1743), Vol. II, "Trope."
[63] George Granville, *Unnatural Flights in Poetry* (Spingarn), pp. 292-93.
[64] *Ibid.*, p. 296.

When he introduces the *Hyperbole* 'tis always by Way of Raillery: As in this other Passage of the above-mentioned Letter to Cardinal *de la Valette*, upon the Entertainment at *la Barre*. . . . *The Ball continued very pleas-antly, till a great Noise without Doors drew all the Ladies to the Window, where, at about a hundred Yards distance, so great a Number of arti-ficial Fire-works issu'd out of a Wood, that it seem'd as if all the Branches of the Trees were so many Rockets, that all the Stars were fallen from the Skies, and the Sphere of Fire had taken Place of the middle Region of the Air. These, my Lord, are three Hyperboles, which being rightly appraised and reduced to the just Value of Things, can amount to no more nor no less than three dozen of Rockets.* The Conclusion is Banter and Irony. *Voiture* did not think it seem'd was sufficient to warrant the *Wood* of *Rockets*, the *falling Stars* and the *Sphere of Fire*, he turns it all into Raillery, and brings off all well. . . . Falsehood it self becomes Truth by the Help of an *Irony*, or what we call the *Rule of Contraries*. Thus when we say of a scandalous lewd Woman, she is a very vertuous Per-son, every one understands what is said, or rather what is not said. . . . After all the best Guide we can follow is this admirable Saying of one of the greatest Wits of our Age;

> *Nothing but Truth is lovely, nothing fair,*
> *And nothing pleases us, but Truth is There;*
> *Truth shou'd direct the Poet's fruitful Vein*
> *In all Things, and e'en in the Fable reign.*

'Tis taken from *Boileau*, and is as well exprest by Lord *Lansdown*. . . . These judicious Reflections are a strange Rebuke to those Writers and Readers, who waste their Time about such Stuff as *Robinson Cruso's*, *Gullivers*, &c. Dean *Swift* in all his Tales and Fables, has not shewn that he is at all sensible of the Duty of an Author to have Truth always in View, and to follow that unerring Guide. If he can work his Readers Faces into a *Grin* he reaches the utmost of his Ambition; and if they laugh, he has his noble Reward; tho' like People that are tickled, they would cry if they could, and are, or ought to be, in Pain when he pre-tends to give them Pleasure.[65]

In Oldmixon's censure of Swift we see the truth-to-nature standard rigidly applied to subtle and complicated irony. In the association of irony and hyperbole there is a curious realignment of Aristotle's statement that elaborate, elevated diction is suitable to ironic speech,[66] for Oldmixon and Lansdowne force irony to act as a clarifying agent to the hyperbole. Almost the only conclusion we can draw from

[65] John Oldmixon, *Logick and Rhetorick* (1728), pp. 21-28.
[66] Aristotle *Rhetoric* III. vii. 11.

Oldmixon's various observations is that he approved nothing but rather simple, obvious irony.

A third standard of judgment was concerned primarily with the effectiveness of ridicule and burlesque, but applications of this standard could not but affect the clarity of an irony as well. This standard grew out of consideration of burlesque exaggeration and distortion. Early in the century, speaking of mock-heroic poetry, John Quincy said of his translation of Holdsworth's *Muscipula,*

I have endeavoured the best I am able in this, to keep up to the Humour and Turn of that Way of Writing, which I take principally to consist in raising the Diction, and labouring the Poetry most, where the Matter is lowest, and most proper for Ridicule.[67]

This notion that the more glaring the contrast the better the ridicule was stated succinctly by the *Craftsman:*

The greater the Distance between the *real* and the *affected Qualifications,* the stronger is the Contrast, and the higher the Ridicule. The *Ass in the Lyon's Skin* was much more *ridiculous* than He would have been, if He had contented himself with assuming the kindred Appearance of an *Horse.*[68]

The same approach is pursued by a series of three essays in the *Publick Register* early in 1741. When the mind is in a "State of Ambiguity, upon any Object whatsoever appearing to be thrown out of the Currency of the Species to which it properly belongs, and is as it were passing into the direct contrary, so as not to be wholly either"[69] we laugh. The "Objects of Humour" are the same as those of laughter.[70] The author instances No. 144 of the *Free-holder* as full of humor and quotes several incongruous incidents there described, such as

a drunken Bishop, who reeled from one Side to the other, and was very sweet upon an Indian Queen.

However, this Jarring in the Objects of Humour is not always placed so full in View. It is frequently softned, and the Glare taken off, by being thrown as it were at a Distance, and is rather suggested to the Imagination by a Hint, than mark'd out by strong Lines. Of this Kind is a Passage in the abovemention'd Paper, where our Fox-Hunter (con-

---

[67] Quoted by Richmond P. Bond, *English Burlesque Poetry* (1932), p. 42.
[68] *Craftsman* (1737), XI, 218-19.
[69] *Publick Register*, No. 2, Jan. 10, 1741.
[70] *Ibid.*, No. 3, Jan. 17, 1741.

cluding those whom he saw in Masquerade Habits to be Foreigners) conceives a great Indignation against them, for pretending to laugh at an *English* Country-Gentleman, for he had been the Object of some of their Mirth.

We have here only a Glimpse of the Contrast, and it is upon Imagination bringing to View the Character of a Fox-Hunter, that we see his assuming to himself, as an *English* Country-Gentleman, the Prerogative of not being laugh'd at by Foreigners; it is the Strut of a little Man stretching himself into the Class of Tallness, and is an extending of Magna Charta somewhat beyond its natural Precincts. . . . Where the Mind itself is thus employ'd in compleating the Sentiment, the Humour is both delicate and pleasing, but often escapes a common, or indolent Reader, whose Imagination requires a strong Glare to rouze it.[71]

Speaking of Swift he says, "This Author has a most happy Talent at Banter, or Ridicule, which is a very extensive Kind of Humour, and is rendring an Object ludicrous, by attributing to it Qualities, the Reverse to those it actually possesses." Our critic here is unquestionably discussing irony in the central Augustan sense, although he calls it "banter." He goes on to remark that "a plain Banter" is too easy and insipid; "To render it therefore agreeable, and to give a genuine Edge, it must be either sharpen'd by Wit, or not appearing to be the End in View, must be shaded off, and left to the Imagination to find out." Thus in the "Dedication to Prince Posterity" Swift wisely "makes his Banter indirect."[72]

Although the critic of the *Publick Register* preferred subtle to obvious irony, the scattered opinions collected above suggest the influences at work to produce a rather obvious standard of clarity: the necessity of reaching a possibly obtuse audience, a sometimes narrow-minded application of the truth-to-nature doctrine, the theory that the best ridicule involves a glaring contrast. But these pronouncements were scattered and there was no very positive application of them to irony so named. On the other hand there developed in the early eighteenth century a critical principle which was very much a part of explicit thought about irony. Although this principle grew out of a concern with the effectiveness of an irony rather than its clarity, it inevitably involved clarity in its op-

[71] *Ibid.*
[72] *Ibid.*

eration. It had to do with delivery, and can best be seen in relation to other, different standards of delivery.

v. *The mask of gravity*

The Renaissance tradition that the satirist should inveigh with biting rage has been noticed sufficiently often.[73] Nor was this critical standard limited to formal verse satire; Michael Drayton memorialized Nashe, "though he a Proser were," for being "Sharply *Satirick*":

> ... I surely thinke
> Those words shall hardly be set downe with inke
> Shall scorch and blast so as his could, where he
> Would inflict vengeance. . . .[74]

The "Poets vehemence,"[75] "That Rage, in which his Noble Vigour"[76] lies, issues in "the sharper wit of the bold *satyre*,"[77] "In harsh sarcasmes, dissonant and smart."[78] This point of view required the satirist to charge at full tilt, waving his banner as he came. It remained an available convention for satire in the Augustan age,[79] but in that period a shrewder piece of advice, belonging to the tradition of oratory rather than verse satire, gained prominence. Quintilian had stated the central principle:

The *ethos* which I have in my mind and which I desiderate in an orator is commended to our approval by goodness more than aught else and is not merely calm and mild, but in most cases ingratiating and courteous and such as to excite pleasure and affection in our hearers, while the chief merit in its expression lies in making it seem that all that we say derives directly from the nature of the facts and persons concerned and in the revelation of the character of the orator in such a way that all may recognise it.[80]

... closely dependent on *ethos* are the skilful exercise of feigned emotion or the employment of irony in making apologies or asking questions, irony

---

[73] David Worcester, *Art of Satire* (1940), pp. 3-6,12.
[74] Michael Drayton, *Epistle to Henry Reynolds* (Spingarn), p. 137.
[75] John Stephens, *Essayes and Characters Ironicall* (1615), pp. 29-30.
[76] Dryden, *Prologues and Epilogues* (Gardner), p. 158.
[77] Jonson, *Works* (Herford-Simpson), IV, 323.
[78] Henry Hutton, *Satyres* (Percy Soc.), p. 10.
[79] David Worcester, *Art of Satire* (1940), p. 12.
[80] Quintilian *Institutio* VI. ii. 13.

being the term which is applied to words which mean something other than they seem to express. From the same source springs also that more powerful method of exciting hatred, when by a feigned submission to our opponents we pass silent censure on their violence. For the very fact of our yielding serves to demonstrate their insupportable arrogance, while orators who have a passion for abuse or are given to affect freedom of speech fail to realise that it is a far more effective course to make your antagonist unpopular than to abuse him.[81]

In the mid-seventeenth century John Bulwer was judging from this standard when he criticized excessive use by the orator of an ironical gesture:

Both the *Indexes*, with a countenance averse, directed to one side, doe point out an *ironicall intention*.

This Action although it may with honesty enough be done by an Oratour, yet to doe it often, and to charge them strongly and vehemently against them that are present, as if he would dig out the eyes of his Auditory ... this is rather the garbe of those who rage and rave like madmen, then of those who with understanding and moderation exercise the faculty of the *Hand* in speaking.[82]

The famous droll Andrew Marvell reproved Samuel Parker for his railing; "in my poor opinion," Marvell commented, "I never saw a man thorow all his three Books in so high a Salivation."[83] Marvell's own experience had been:

in my observation, if we meet with an Argument in the Streets, both Men, Women and Boys, that are the Auditory, do usually give it on the modester side, and conclude, that he that rails most has the least reason.[84]

Bayle's *Dictionary*,[85] Shaftesbury,[86] and Blackmore[87] agreed on this point.

During the Restoration and early eighteenth century, laughing satire—ridicule and banter as distinct from raging satire or sweet reason—gave a new tone to all sorts of literary forms. Hugh Mac-

[81] *Ibid.*, VI. ii. 15-16.
[82] John Bulwer, *Chirologia and Chironomia* (1644), pp. 79-80.
[83] Marvell, *Rehearsal Transpros'd* (1672), p. 170.
[84] *Ibid.*, p. 168.
[85] Bayle, *Dictionary* (1734-38), I, 727 col. 1. See also Bayle, *Dictionary* (1734-41), III, 165b, 633b.
[86] Shaftesbury, *Characteristics* (Robertson), II, 222.
[87] Blackmore, *Essays* II (1717), pp. 254-56.

donald observes of the early Restoration period, "the spirit of banter was in the air."[88]   The new tone of verse satire, of prose style,[89] of controversy[90]—in all it is plain enough.   One result of this shift of taste from satire to ridicule was that the theory of jests and laughter became inextricably involved with the critical theory of satire.   Ben Jonson's *Discoveries* had set these two in opposition to each other: "The true Artificer" will be admired for "in inveighing, what sharpenesse; in Jest, what urbanity hee uses."[91]   Now the new fusion had to be rationalized.   The sources of the critical theory that was constructed, and the justifying precedents, were various— French "raillery," Attick "salt," Roman "urbanity"—but for the moment we are concerned only with the one aspect of that theory which came to have an explicit and emphatic application to irony: the manner of delivery.

We have seen above that in the criticism of oratorical and con-troversial satire there was available the precept to dissimulate one's anger; in the theory of jesting there was available a similar sanc-tion for the indifferent manner, and whereas in the criticism of formal verse satire anger had been approved, critics of jesting had never approved of buffoonery.   The buffoonery of farce, the antic grimaces and grotesque costumes of actors, had always been con-sidered a low form of comedy,[92] and in conversational jesting such antics were thought vulgar.   Puttenham spoke for the view with his usual pungency:

when we give a mocke with a scornefull countenance as in some smiling sort looking aside or by drawing the lippe awry, or shrinking up the nose; the Greeks called it *Micterismus*, we may terme it a fleering frumpe, as he that said to one whose wordes he beleved not, no doubt Sir of that. This fleering frumpe is one of the Courtly graces of *hicke the scorner*.[93]

Also speaking of jests, the *Art of Complaisance* warned: "above all, let us beware they be not accompanied with grimaces or disagree-

[88] Hugh Macdonald, "Banter" (1947), pp. 26-27.
[89] *Ibid.*, pp. 21-22.
[90] *Ibid.*, p. 26.
[91] Jonson, *Works* (Herford-Simpson), VIII, 588.
[92] See, for instance, Dryden, *Essays* (Ker), I, 135-37; II, 132-33. John Old-mixon, *Logick and Rhetorick* (1728), pp. 324-25, 355-56.
[93] Puttenham, *Arte of English Poesie* (Willcock-Walker), pp. 186-91.

able gestures, after the manner of Players, Mimicks, and Buffoons."[94] Such advice was current in the Augustan age.

In contrast to buffoonery stood the manner of the gentleman. Cicero had said that "dissimulation" is "extremely pleasing when it is well managed, not in a vehement strain of language, but in a conversational style...,"[95] and in the Restoration and early eighteenth century the conversational style of the gentleman was one of the things the literati thought a great deal of, especially in jesting and raillery. Sprat derives the manner from Horace's "way," which is

the very Original of true Raillery, and differs as much from some of the other Latin *Satyrs,* as the pleasant reproofs of a Gentleman from the severity of a School-master. I know some Men disapprove it, because the Verse seems to be loose, and near to the plainness of common Discourse. . . . the same judgment should be made of Mens styles as of their behaviour and carriage: wherein that is most courtly and hardest to be imitated, which consists of a Natural easiness and unaffected Grace, where nothing seems to be studied, yet everything is extraordinary.[96]

Dryden pointed out that the wit of the writers of the preceding age "was ill-bred and clownish" because they had not associated with gentlemen. But under the influence of Charles II and his court Restoration writers became "easy and pliant to each other in discourse."[97] We see the influence of this ideal in John Hughes' praise of L'Estrange's "Gaiety and seeming Negligence,"[98] and in James Drake's description of Tom Brown's "careless gay Humour, and negligent cheerful Wit."[99] The "purest Source of ... Pleasantry," said Dennis, "what the *French* call *naiveté,* which is a charming Simplicity, dictated by pure Nature, is almost always Original; For there is something in it so easie, so free, so flowing and so natural, as flies the restraint of a Copy."[100] "The simple manner," says Shaftesbury, expresses "the effect of art under the appearance of the greatest ease and negligence. And even when it assumes the

[94] *Art of Complaisance* (1673), pp. 41-42.
[95] Cicero *On Oratory* III. 53.
[96] Sprat, *Cowley* (Spingarn), pp. 136-37.
[97] Dryden, *Essays* (Ker), I, 174-76.
[98] John Hughes, *Of Style* (Durham), p. 84.
[99] Tom Brown, *Works* (1720), I, prefatory materials.
[100] Dennis, *Critical Works* (Hooker), II, 160-61. Cf. II, 282.

censuring or reproving part, it does it in the most concealed and gentle way."[101]   Oldmixon comments on "that *Naivety*...which is the Charm in Voiture."[102]   Easy, negligent, careless, unstudied, unaffected, natural, simple, naive, free, gay, graceful: this was the manner of the gentleman in raillery.

Certain related precepts were offered by critics more interested in results than in *politesse*. The *Art of Complaisance* pointed out that a "facetious *repartie*" is most effective when it appears to be spontaneous,[103] and that

when we would rally, to excite laughter, 'tis best to speak in a cold and serious manner, that the Company may be pleasantly surprised, in seeing us serious in the midst of persons, who rend the air with laughters.[104]

Ferrand Spence commented that Lucian "does things so privately and *underhand*, that very often we cannot tell, whether he be in *Jest* or *Earnest*,"[105] and the *Tatler* for September 10, 1709, suggested that

a certain insensibility in the countenance recommends a sentence of humour and jest.... The jest is to be a thing unexpected; therefore your undesigning manner is a beauty in expressions of mirth....[106]

Charles Rollin[107] and the *Gentleman's* for 1764[108] repeated the idea.

We see, then, that the various sources of critical judgment had supplied somewhat various standards for the delivery of satire and jests, including irony.   On the one hand was the tradition that satire should rage and foam; on the other the rhetorician's practical advice to make satire and argumentative attack appear to be objective, impersonal.   The old notion that irony may well reveal itself in the manner of delivery was circumscribed by the prej-

---

[101] Shaftesbury, *Characteristics* (Robertson), I, 157-70.

[102] Oldmixon, *Logick and Rhetorick* (1728), pp. 197-98.

[103] *Art of Complaisance* (1673), p. 42.

[104] *Ibid.*, p. 59.

[105] Ferrand Spence, *Lucian* (1684-85), I, sig. B7ᵛ-B8ᵛ. Cf. Fielding, *Works* (Stephen), VI, 322-25.

[106] *Tatler* (Aitken), II, 118 (No. 66).   Aitken attributes this essay to Steele; Temple Scott to Swift—see Swift, *Prose Works* (Temple Scott), IX, 18.   See also *Tatler* (Aitken), IV, 234-38 (No. 242, Oct. 26, 1710).

[107] Charles Rollin, *Teaching and Studying the Belles Lettres* (1749), II, 261-62.

[108] *Gentleman's Magazine*, XXXIV (Supplement, 1764), 615.   See also Bellegarde, *Reflexions upon Ridicule* (1717), I, 161; Christopher Smart, *Midwife* (1751-53), III, 49-53.

udice against anything savoring of buffoonery, by idealizations of the gentleman's manner, and by the observation that the most effective raillery is spontaneous and to a considerable extent hidden to a first glance. Out of this confusion the early eighteenth century evolved a single and widely accepted principle by which the delivery of an irony could be judged: mock-heroic and other varieties of irony are most effective when hidden under a mask of seeming gravity.

Gravity of manner in perpetrating an irony had always been, of course, a natural potential of the method. Thinking of Socrates' verbal irony Cicero had said, as Thomas Stanley translated him, "it is a very elegant, sweet and facete kind of speech, acute with gravity, accommodated with Rhetorick words, and pleasant speeches."[109] The 1657 edition of Holland's translation of Plutarch's *Moralia* describes a remark made "in good earnest and great gravity (after the *ironical* manner)."[110] But the grave manner did not crystallize into a critical concept until the first half of the eighteenth century, when people became conscious of it under the dual impact of Cervantes and the popularity of high burlesque,[111] and it was not cemented to irony so called until nearly the middle of the century.

In 1693 a taste for the manner of a gentleman had led Motteux to prefer high burlesque to the low burlesque which had been popular during the Restoration. "Good sence and a Gentleman's manner," he commented, "ought to be preserv'd, or Burlesque dwindles to Buffoonry. . . ." These are more easily preserved by high burlesque, which "is also pleasant to the Reader by the Air of Gravity and ridiculous Affectation, with which Trifles are related as mighty matters."[112] For his skill in this grave fooling John Philips was memorialized by his friend "Rag" Smith:

> Oh, various bard, you all our powers control,
> You now disturb, and now divert the soul:

[109] Thomas Stanley, *History of Philosophy* (1655-62), Part 3, pp. 5-6.

[110] The passage is referred to page 526 of this edition by the files of the *N.E.D.* preserved at the University of Michigan.

[111] High burlesque—mock-heroic and parody—did not come into fashion until the turn of the century. See Richmond P. Bond, *English Burlesque Poetry* (1932), pp. 21-23.

[112] *Gentleman's Journal*, Jan., 1692/93, p. 27.

Milton and Butler in thy Muse combine,
Above the last thy manly beauties shine;
For as I've seen, when rival wits contend,
One gayly charge, one gravely wise defend,
This on quick turns and points in vain relies,
This with a look demure, and steady eyes,
With dry rebukes, or sneering praise, replies:
So thy grave lines extort a juster smile,
Reach Butler's fancy, but surpass his style;
He speaks Scarron's low phrase in humble strains,
In thee the solemn air of great Cervantes reigns.[113]

The "solemn air of great Cervantes" was to be a touchstone for the next half-century, and by the second quarter of the century mock gravity was an aspect of high burlesque which demanded consideration. John Dennis found himself involved in some rather nice distinctions on the subject when he set out to prove the *Rape of the Lock* inferior to the *Lutrin*. The latter, said Dennis, supplies several ridiculous incidents of the kind which are the true source of comic laughter, but "There is not so much as *one,* nor the *Shadow of one,* in the *Rape of the Lock:* Unless the Author's Friends will object here, That his *perpetual Gravity,* after the *Promise* of his Title, makes the whole Poem one continued *Jest.*" In Boileau Dennis found mock-gravity a more positive virtue: "*Boileau* calls his *Lutrin* an *Heroick Poem,* and he is so far from raising an *Expectation* of Laughter, either in the *Title,* or in the *Beginning of the Poem,* that he tells Monsieur *de Lamoignon,* to whom he addresses it, that 'tis a *grave Subject,* and must be read with a *grave Countenance.*"[114]

The Scriblerus circle were of course very much alive to the virtues of mock solemnity. Arbuthnot wrote Swift on March 19, 1728/29, that he was occupied with a work which rose "to a very solemn piece of burlesque,"[115] and we recall two famous characterizations of Swift, Pope's compliment in the *Dunciad*:

---

[113] Edmund Smith, "A Poem to the Memory of Mr. John Philips" (Chalmers), p. 205.

[114] Dennis, *Critical Works* (Hooker), II, 329-31.

[115] Arbuthnot, *Works* (Aitken), p. 126.

> Whether thou chuse Cervantes' serious air,
> Or laugh and shake in Rab'lais' easy Chair,[116]

and Swift's characterization of himself:

> His Vein, ironically grave,
> Expos'd the Fool, and lash'd the Knave:[117]

Not unnaturally the literary output of the group alerted their wide audience to this quality of manner. The *Craftsman*, tongue in cheek as usual, complained about the frequent treatment of serious subjects in a ludicrous manner, a practice introduced by Cervantes and Rabelais:

I could give a Multitude of Instances; but I believe it will be sufficient to mention only two Books lately publish'd; namely, Captain *Gulliver's Voyages*, and *An Enquiry into the Reasons of the Conduct of* Great-Britain, *&c.* the *last* of which seems to be a servile Imitation of the *other*, as that is of the *French* or *Spanish* Author before-mention'd, and might be better entitled *Don Quixote* in *Politicks;* the Reflections of *Pantagruel* on the present State of Affairs; or *Gulliver* turn'd *Statesman.*

It is evident to every Reader of the meanest Capacity, that the Author of this curious Piece proceeds on the Model of those Writers, and that his Design is to ridicule *Statesmen* and *political Matters* in the same Manner that *Cervantes* exposes Books of *Chivalry,* or Captain *Gulliver* the Writings of *Travellers,* by publishing a Collection of the most palpable *Falshoods, Absurdities,* and *Contradictions,* in a grave and serious Manner, with the same solemn Grimace and repeated Professions of *Truth* and *Simplicity.*[118]

After the late Twenties observations of the manner became commonplace. Discussing the techniques of mock-epic, Walter Harte singled out the contribution of language:

> The *Language* next: from hence new pleasure springs;
> For *Styles* are dignify'd, as well as *Things.*
> Tho' Sense subsists, distinct from phrase or sound,
> Yet *Gravity* conveys a surer wound.
> The chymic secret which your pains wou'd find,
> Breaks out, unsought for, in *Cervantes'* mind;
> And *Quixot's* wildness, like that King's of old,
> Turns all he touches, into *Pomp* and *Gold.*

[116] Pope, *Dunciad* (Sutherland), pp. 62-63. See also Pope, *Odyssey* (1725-26), V, 299-300.
[117] Swift, *Poems* (Williams), II, 565.
[118] *Craftsman* (1731), I, 79-81 (No. 14, Jan. 20, 1727).

> Yet in this Pomp discretion must be had;
> Tho' *grave*, not *stiff*; tho' *whimsical*, not *mad*:[119]

William Somervile, undertaking to prove that high burlesque is preferable to low, quoted "Rag" Smith, Dacier, and Boileau's statement that whereas to recount *"une chose grande en stile bas"* is unimpressive, nothing is more ridiculous than to tell a comic story *"en Termes graves & serieux."*[120]   Richard Owen Cambridge arrived at the same conclusion about the proper manner of high burlesque through his rigid notion that good mock-heroic must imitate the true heroic in every particular:

> A Mock-Heroic poem should, in as many respects as possible, imitate the True Heroic. The more particulars it copies from them, the more perfect it will be. By the same rule it should admit as few things as possible, which are not of the cast and color of the ancient Heroic poems. The more of these it admits, the more imperfect will it be. It should, throughout, be serious, because the originals are serious; therefore the author should never be seen to laugh, but constantly wear that grave irony which *Cervantes* only has inviolably preserv'd.[121]

The reviewer for the *Monthly* was willing to go along with this doctrine:

> Our readers probably may not be unanimous in determining, whether throughout a composition of this nature, that is really entertaining, its uninterrupted mock gravity must be an essential and indispensable point. . . : However, if Mr. *Addison*'s pleasant criterion of true humour, *viz.* That it looks grave itself, while it sets all others a laughing, pleases from its justness, we must allow our author the merit of preserving his grave irony with uninterrupted power of face. After the reader has once contracted a settled intimacy with his hero's character, he accompanies him thro' his various adventures with continual emotions of pleasantry, which are now and then heighten'd into irrepressible paroxysms of laughter; while the poet, thro' the tenor of his work, seems, with a well-assumed and persevering gravity, unconscious of the least joke.[122]

The idea seems to have looked like current gospel to William Dodd, author of *A Day in Vacation at College. A Burlesque Poem:*

---

[119] Walter Harte, *Essay on Satire* (1730), pp. 11-13. This poem also appeared in the *Grub-street Journal* for June 18, 1730.

[120] William Somervile, *The Chase* (1749), pp. 109-13.

[121] R. O. Cambridge, *Scribleriad* (1752), pp. iii-iv.

[122] *Monthly Review*, V (July, 1751), 117-19.

The learned Reader will observe how strictly the Writer of this Piece has complied with the Opinions of the ingenious Author of the very grave *Scribleriad*. He, in Imitation thereof, never deigning to let one Smile intrude all the Way through; and in so doing, we hope People of *true* and *nicer Taste* will confess he has hit upon the *true Burlesque*. For in the Preface to that Poem saith the Writer,—'In a *Mock-heroic* Poem, the Author should never be seen to laugh, but constantly wear that grave Irony, which *Cervantes* only has inviolably preserved.'[123]

In the light of this doctrine of gravity Motteux's translation of *Don Quixote* seemed all wrong. Charles Jarvis was severely critical of Motteux's low comic manner:

... nothing can be more foreign to the design of the author, whose principal and distinguishing character is, to preserve the face of gravity, generally consistent throughout his whole work, suited to the solemnity of a *Spaniard*, and wherein without doubt is placed the true spirit of its ridicule.[124]

The *Monthly*, reviewing Smollett's translation, made a like censure:

With regard to those translations from translations, published by *Motteux*, and others, they deserve no farther mention; except to express our wonder, that, under the burlesque veil, and farcical disguise, in which they have envelloped the author, they have not been able totally to divest him of his native dignity. . . .[125]

The extent to which the idea had solidified by mid-century is illustrated in Joseph Warton's praise of *The Splendid Shilling:* "that admirable copy of the solemn irony of Cervantes, who is the father and unrivalled model of the true mock-heroic. . . ."[126]

Although Cervantes was undoubtedly the dominant model of grave irony, by mid-century the grave manner of Swift had achieved nearly equal fame. Pope had suggested Cervantes as Swift's master, but Fielding demurred. It was Lucian, not Cervantes, who had taught the great Dean, says Captain Booth in *Amelia*.[127] Whoever his master may have been, his mock gravity had by mid-century entered the stream of conventional literary observations. The *Monthly*, reviewing *Female Taste*, compared it to Swift:

[123] William Dodd, *A Day in Vacation* (1751), p. 6 of Notes.
[124] Charles Jarvis, *Don Quixote* (1742), pp. iv-v.
[125] *Monthly Review*, XIII (Sept., 1755), 197.
[126] Joseph Warton, *Essay on Pope* (1806), I, 242-43.
[127] Fielding, *Amelia* (Navarre Soc.), II, 181-82.

The principal merit and humour of this satire consists in its being a pursuit of Dean *Swift*'s very droll directions to servants; which, with a seeming gravity, and true comic spirit, constantly enjoins them to commit the very faults, he would, by his peculiar manner, more effectually remind them to reform.[128]

Talking about Swift's *A project for the advancement of religion, and the reformation of manners*, Orrery shows the power of this stereotype of the Dean's manner:

The author appears in earnest throughout the whole treatise, and the dedication, or introduction, is in a strain of serious panegyric. . . . But as the pamphlet is of the satirical kind, I am apt to imagine, that my friend the Dean put a violence upon himself, in chusing to appear candidly serious, rather than to smile under his usual mask of gravity. . . . methinks, upon these occasions, I perceive him writing in shackles.[129]

In the Preface to his unpublished *Charliad* Joseph Spence compares Cervantes, Rabelais, and Swift, and now it is Swift rather than Cervantes who is the exemplar of grave irony:

The Spanish Chief is for Natural Ridicule; the Frenchman puts on a ridiculous Face, in things that are serious; and your countryman [Swift] puts on a serious face, in things that are ridiculous. He is the last to laugh at his own jest; and by that Method perhaps has excell'd both the others.[130]

An interesting application of the concept of grave irony appeared in the theater section of the *London Chronicle* for 1757 or early 1758. The critic is discussing Barry's portrayal of Richard III:

. . . the Humour of Richard, which never should take off the Mask, is with him too free and open. Richard's Pleasantry never rises to Mirth; it always proceeds from what the Poet calls the *mala mentis gaudia*, the wicked Pleasures of the Mind; and it should therefore never become totally jocund, but should ever be a mixed Emotion of Joy and Malice. Where he jokes about his Score or two of Taylors, and finds himself a marvelous proper Man, there should be no free Exultation, because his Mirth is ironical, and he is still sensible of his own Deformity; and therefore he should smile, and smile, and be a villain. This should hold all through, except in the triumphant Self-Congratulations of Ambition.[131]

[128] *Monthly Review*, XII (June, 1755), 510.
[129] Orrery, *Remarks on Swift* (1752), pp. 98-99. See also p. 262.
[130] Quoted by Richmond P. Bond, *English Burlesque Poetry* (1932), p. 166 n.
[131] Quoted by C. H. Gray, *Theatrical Criticism in London to 1795* (1931), pp. 138-39.

Although the notions of irony and the proper ironic manner expressed here are conventional for the time, the subjective orientation which the critic gives them is premonitory of later concepts of irony.

vi. *The virtue of consistency*

With the critical adoption of an appropriate manner for irony came critical recognition that whatever ironic pose is adopted must be consistently maintained. Perhaps the worst aspect of run-of-the-mill controversial irony in the Restoration and first years of the eighteenth century had been its half-heartedness. Even when a combatant found an effective ironic premise or mask he was likely after a few pages to drop it for downright abuse. Shaftesbury noted this failing with considerable acidity:

There cannot be a more preposterous sight than an executioner and a merry-Andrew acting their part upon the same stage. Yet I am persuaded any one will find this to be the real picture of certain modern zealots in their controversial writings. They are no more masters of gravity than they are of good-humour. The first always runs into harsh severity, and the latter into an awkward buffoonery. And thus between anger and pleasure, zeal and drollery, their writing has much such a grace as the play of humorsome children, who, at the same instant, are both peevish and wanton, and can laugh and cry almost in one and the same breath.[132]

It was undoubtedly Swift who first saw the full force of the necessity for sustaining an irony. Craik reports that when Skelton's anonymous *Some Proposals for the Revival of Christianity* (1736), which was an imitation of Swift's ironical style and had been ascribed to him, was brought Swift to examine he remarked, "The author of this has not continued the irony to the end."[133] He made the same criticism of *The Rights of the Christian Church:*

This man hath somewhere heard, that it is a point of wit to advance paradoxes, and the bolder the better. But the wit lies in maintaining them, which he neglecteth, and formeth imaginary conclusions from them, as if they were true and uncontested.[134]

[132] Shaftesbury, *Characteristics* (Robertson), I, 47-48.
[133] Henry Craik, *Life of Swift* (1894), II, 165 n.
[134] Swift, *Prose Works* (Temple Scott), III, 118.

After some of his own relentless ironies had been published the shilly-shallying of weaker ironists was all the more evident. *Fog's Weekly Journal* for Saturday, June 2, 1733 (No. 239), went to work on one. There had recently occurred in the City certain riots which had been made a matter for the Grand Jury. After the Recorder had charged the Jury in rather pointed terms about these riots, the Lord Mayor suggested the Jury distinguish between riots and public rejoicings, which latter the recent congregation had been, in his opinion. The Grand Jury thanked the Lord Mayor, but Walsingham's *Free Briton* for May 17 (No. 182) argued ironically that the Lord Mayor could not possibly have said what he was reported to have said. *Fog's* commented on this essay at some length:

... when he [Walsingham] attempts that Figure called *Irony* he seems to know himself, and the Strength of his own great Genius, for a most excellent Critick has given us the following Definition of it:

Irony (says he) "is not a Work for groveling Pens; but extremely difficult, even to the best. —It is certainly one of the most beautiful Strokes of Rhetorick, and which requires a Master Hand to carry on, and finish with any Success; but when a Bungler attempts it, he finds it beyond his Skill, and his mishapen Work with this awkward polishing becomes intirely deformed, as the false Beauty of Paint upon a Lady's Face is less desirable than no Beauty at all, and the Pertness of a shallow Fop more disagreeable than his Silence."

But Mr. *Walsingham's* Irony has a Delicacy in it peculiar to the Man, and he is known by his Hand, as *Hercules* was by his Foot—he begins his Paper with a Mock-Encomium upon my Lord-Mayor, which I shall not quote, but shall recommend it to be read by all those that may want a Nap this warm Weather....

I shall now produce some of those beautiful Strokes of Rhetorick which my Author says are essential to this Way of Writing; in order to it, I shall quote Word for Word what follows the Sentence before repeated.

"Now to my Apprehension, with humble Submission I speak it, this Intelligence cannot be true, it is either the Dream of mistaken People, or the Forgery of some bad Body, who hath much Malice against his Lordship, the aforesaid Grand Jury, their Friends, and their Cause into the Bargain. Pray let us consider the Fact; here is an Inquest to be taken, and the Lord Mayor, who hardly ever yet gave the Charge to the Grand Jury, since the *Old Bailey* has been a Court of *Oyer* and *Terminer*, his Lordship is made in this unusual Manner to give them a strict Charge, a Charge. —To what Purpose? You shall see, it is to instruct them that they carefully distinguish between Riots and publick Rejoycings, that they may not present as Riots and Misdemeanours, such Acts of Joy and Festivity as may have been celebrated on Account of some great Good which hath lately been done.

"Can it be true then, that his Lordship could give such a Charge? Certainly not, I think; first for that no great Good hath been done; Secondly, that there have been no Rejoycings for great Good, but rather, as wise Men tell us, for great Mischief. Thirdly, because it must shew his Lordship apprehended that such Rejoycings for great Good might be presented by the Grand Jury as riotous Proceedings: And lastly, because it must shew that his Lordship was in some kind of Panick lest this identical Grand Jury actually should, as such Offences against the Peace of the Crown, the Good of the City, and the Laws of the Land."

I only quote this as a Specimen of fine Raillery and most ingenious Satyr—his *Apprehension with his humble Submission*—his *Dream of mistaken People*, and *Forgery of some bad Body*, and so on to the End, do not only convey to you the ingenious Sentiment of an Author who thinks finely, but you see they are convey'd in a most beautiful Stile.

The other Paragraph hath also its Beauties. He is there speaking of the unfeigned Rejoycings made for the Suppression of the Excise-Bill. You see how logically he draws his Consequences; no great Good hath been done; therefore there have been no Rejoycings for great Good, but rather for great Mischief. —Indeed the Irony seems to be dropt here, when he calls it a great Mischief; but it is taken up again the very next Sentence, for there it is a great Good again; but perhaps in Irony a Man may sometimes call a thing black, and sometimes white, and mean the same thing, or mean nothing at all; and who knows but he might have learnt this dodging Way of Reasoning from some Legerdemain Patron, who might be a great Virtuoso at Cups and Balls—*Here you have it, and there you have it not.* . . .

The paper concludes with several passages from Shaftesbury, including the one quoted above. Although *Fog's* criticism here is not to be taken as necessarily valid, it is interesting to note the standards of judgment to which the attack appeals: Walsingham's ironic panegyric is too heavy-handed and obvious; the style is that of neither a gentleman nor an accomplished writer; the ironic pose is not consistently maintained; and the whole thing is dull.

In the realm of mock-heroic, the virtue of consistency was remarked by Pope, Jarvis, and Cambridge, among others. A note to the *Dunciad* points out, in reference to the pissing contest, that

"Our good Poet, (by the whole cast of his work being obliged not to take off the Irony) where he cou'd not show his Indignation, hath shewn. . . ."[135] Charles Jarvis, in his Preface to *Don Quixote*, asserted that of all the kinds of satire, the ironical is

the most difficult to preserve in a work of length. Who is there but observes our author's admirable talent at it? However it must be confessed, he has now and then broke in upon this scheme; which I am persuaded he must have been forced to in compliance with the humour of the age and country he wrote in, and not from any error of judgment.[136]

The sharpness of eye with which Jarvis observed his author's talent is illustrated by his note to a passage in which the dialogue of Sancho and Teresa is called an "impertinent discourse."

So it is in the original (*impertinente:*) but I suspect the irony is here broke by the transcriber or printer, and not by the author himself, and that it should be (*importante*) *important*, which carries on the grave ridicule of the history.[137]

Richard Owen Cambridge's passion for consistency runs through all his theory of the mock-heroic: the author must "never" laugh, he must "constantly" sustain the grave irony which Cervantes had "inviolably" preserved.[138] Commenting on his own *Scribleriad* he says, "To compleat the design of mock-gravity, the Author and Editors are represented full as great enthusiasts as the Hero; therefore, as all things are supposed to appear to them in the same light as they do to him, there are several things which they could not explain without laying aside their assumed character."[139] Thus the "Irony" of the poem is "observed as strictly in the notes as in the text. . . ."[140]

The standard of consistency was finally ensconced in John Lawson's lectures on rhetoric:

The Dangers attending this Figure [irony] are these three; one is ever apt to break in upon it. Your real Sense is ready to burst out, and mingle itself with the ironical, which makes an odd incoherent Mixture.

[135] Pope, *Dunciad* (Sutherland), p. 119.

[136] Charles Jarvis, *Don Quixote* (1742), pp. vi-vii.

[137] *Ibid.*, II, 27 n. Ozell repeats this note—John Ozell, *Don Quixote* (Mod. Lib.), p. 478 n.

[138] R. O. Cambridge, *Scribleriad* (1752), pp. iii-iv.

[139] *Ibid.*, pp. xv-xvi.

[140] *Ibid.*, pp. xiii-xv.

This Fault in long continued Irony seemeth scarcely avoidable, since it is laid to the Charge of *Lucian, Cervantes,* and *Swift,* the three great Masters of this Figure.

Another Danger is, Ironies are often intermixed with serious Truths, which is abrupt and hard: As in the latter of the two following Lines, speaking of Dr. *Swift,*

> Or thy griev'd Country's Copper Chains unbind,
> Or *praise the Court,* or *dignify Mankind.*

All before and after the latter of these Lines are understood in their literal Sense.[141]

Recognition of the virtue was ordinary by mid-century.[142]

vii. *The question of length*

In his seminal discussion Quintilian divided irony into three types according to length: the trope, which extends to a few words set in a non-ironic context; the figure that extends throughout an entire speech; and the figure that extends through an entire life, such as Socrates'.[143] Until the Augustan age, although this division by length was an available idea[144] people usually thought of irony as a brief, whiplash kind of thing—a nipping taunt. But the spate of ironic essays, pamphlets, poems, and even whole books which appeared from the Augustan presses called people's attention to irony as a device capable of sustained manipulation,[145] and Swift pointed the fact out to them in his "Apology" prefixed to the *Tale of a Tub:*

Another Thing to be observed is, that there generally runs an Irony through the Thread of the whole Book, which the Men of Tast will observe and distinguish, and which will render some Objections that have been made, very weak and insignificant.[146]

[141] John Lawson, *Lectures Concerning Oratory* (1760), pp. 257-68.

[142] Additional observations are to be found in Joseph Warton, *Adventurer* Nos. 127, 133 (Augustan Soc.), pp. 195-96 (No. 133, Feb. 12, 1754); Deane Swift, *Essay upon Swift* (1755), pp. 70-72, 135-36.

[143] The passage is quoted above on p. 5.

[144] Thomas Wilson, *Rhetorique* (G. H. Mair), pp. 134-56. Abraham Fraunce, *Arcadian Rhetorike* (1588), Book I, chaps. i, ii, vi. Thomas Stanley, *History of Philosophy* (1655-62), Part 3, pp. 5-6.

[145] See Chapter III above.

[146] Swift, *Tale of a Tub* (Davis), p. 4.

Toward mid-century the utility of irony for the long haul became a question of some critical interest. The *Prompter* for March 23, 1736 (No. 144), brought it up almost accidentally while pursuing his criticism of the *Grub-street Journal* for not sustaining its ironic pose:

I don't know how it happens, that we Writers unwarily permit ourselves to grow *warm*, in our Reasonings, and confound *Things* with *Persons*. No Example ought to have Weight enough to mislead us into so unfruitful a Practice: (I *except* Cases, where *Personal* Qualities are the *Subject* we treat of) But, I judge with the *Partiality* Men are apt to deceive themselves by, or the Gentlemen (whoever they are) at the Head of the *Grub-street Journal*, have been *oftnest to blame*, in this particular Error: tho', if I conceive not a very wrong Notion of the Scheme they *might* pursue with most Honour, and Interest, It is a *Deviation*, of much worse Effect in *Their* Case, than in That of the Authors of any *other* Paper, now publish'd among us.

What I mean, is, that, to allow the full Scope to the *Humour* of their Title, One would expect an *ironical Transversion of Censure;* where (to keep up the *Resemblance* they assume) as They shou'd never bestow *Praise*, but upon the Dull, and Ridiculous, so they should delicately, and pretendedly, level the Seemings of their *Satire*, against Nothing but *Wit*, and *Good Judgment*.

In a Plan, of this Turn, Nothing *gravely* malignant cou'd have Place; and, consequently, *Anger*, and *Invective*, must be excluded. *Satire smiling* her Reproof into Favour even of the *Party corrected*, the Gayety of the *Manner* wou'd serve, as a *Veil*, to the Malice, and afford no Motives to Resentment.

I shall be better understood, if I borrow a Paragraph from our *Great Poet* above-mentioned, as I find it in One of his *Letters* to a Friend, among that beautiful Collection, not long since made publick.

"Dr. SWIFT (says he) much approves what I *proposed*, even to the very *Title;* which I design shall be *The Works of the Unlearned,* published Monthly, in which, whatever Book appears, that *deserves Praise*, shall be *depreciated ironically;* and, in the same manner that modern Critics take, to *undervalue* Works of *Merit*, and to *commend* the *high Productions of Grub-street.*"

If *This*, as seems reasonable to believe, was the *Hint*, that gave Beginning to the *Grub-street Journal*, I am sorry, for the Town's Sake, and the Paper's, that It was not *directly pursued:* The Field it threw open was the most *copious*, and *fruitful*, that cou'd well have been cultivated. —All, that Judgement, and Humour, and Satire, and Fancy, cou'd have *wish'd*, they might have found, in *this Scene....*

The *Grub-street Journal* rose to the bait on April 14:

... we had no occasion to confine our-selves to that *Ironical Transversion of Censure,* which our late unsuccessful Brother *The Prompter,* in No. 144. represented as necessary 'to keep up the Resemblance we had assumed.' Had we, according to his opinion, thought our-selves obliged 'never to bestow *Praise,* but upon the Dull, and Ridiculous, and always to level the Seemings of our *Satire,* against Nothing but *Wit,* and *Good Judgment;*' this, instead of 'allowing the full Scope to the *Humour* of our *Title,*' would have restrained us within narrower limits, and hindered us from pursueing so fully the end and design of it. How could we have published the *Letters* of Correspondents, on so great a variety of subjects written without any manner of *Irony?* Would it have been sufficient to introduce them always with an *Ironical Preface?* Would not the trouble and difficulty of this task have been very great; and the continual repetition of it, tedious and nauseous to the reader, as well as writer? Whereas, consistently with our own Scheme, we might publish the compositions of others, and our own, on all kinds of subjects, and in whatever manner written, whether serious and direct, or ludicrous and ironical. To expose the follies and lesser faults of our Members, the latter way was thought sufficient: but their crimes and greater enormities seemed plainly to require the additional scourge of the former. Self conceited Ignorance and Dullness, when alone, might have been kept perhaps within some bounds by the sneering smiles of Ridicule; whereas nothing but the rugged frowns of Severity would effectually restrain them, when associated with Impudence, Immorality, and Irreligion. Thus, instead of the single *field* of *Irony,* which our Brother surprizingly affirms to be 'the most *copious,* and *fruitful,* that cou'd well have been cultivated;' there was layed open by our Scheme a more spacious plain of double the extent, for the literary exercises of grave, as well as airy authors.[147]

Rather surprisingly, Henry Fielding felt at one point that there was some truth in the *Grub-street* point of view. In the *Jacobite's Journal* for March 26, 1748 (No. 17), he confessed, "I am weary of personating a Character for which I have so solemn a Contempt"; moreover, he continued, discussing irony as a literary method, "An infinite Number of Readers ... are apt to be tired, when it is carried to any Degree of Length." The *Publick Register* for January 17, 1741 (No. 3), had analyzed the problem more carefully, learning from Swift. In managing ironic praise, "a great Delicacy is required to prevent it being trite, and consequently insipid ... as

[147] *Memoirs of Grub-street* (1737), I, viii-x.

nothing is more easy than a plain Banter, the Poignancy is wore off in being handled by every one." The solution is to enliven the irony with wit and indirection.

The Dedication to Prince *Posterity* is throughout a Strain of Banter, which would have been little more than insipid, had the Author only in a sneering Manner attributed Wit, Parts, Politeness, and profound Erudition to his Cotemporaries; but he was too great a Master of his Weapon to handle it in so common a Manner: He gives a Newness to his Subject by Allegory, and makes his Banter indirect, by an Accusation against Time, the Governor of Prince *Posterity,* who with an inveterate Malice, he declares, devours all the Productions of that learned, witty, and polite Age, intent only to keep his Highness in universal Ignorance of their Studies.

Later in the same essay the author points out that

from an Ambiguity in Appearance we are taken into a Laugh, by a kind of Surprize, which Ambiguity upon Reflection soon vanishes; for Judgment steps in, unmasks the Object, and knows it for what it really is. This is the Reason that the same Object of Humour must not dwell long upon the Imagination, but, to preserve the Humour, must be quickly shifted for some other. Thus the solemn and grave Manner of treating trivial Subjects, which is a Species of Humour, requires great Dexterity to render it spirited, otherwise we shall soon separate the Subject from the Manner, and, with the judicious *Cervantes,* quickly dismantle Sancho of his Government Robes.

Peter Motteux had complained fifty years before that the reader "soon grows weary" of mock heroics,[148] but the great model of the form, *Don Quixote,* had patently not been found dull during the intervening period, and Corbyn Morris suggested a reason:

The *Humour* appears, in the Representation of a Person in real Life, fancying himself to be under the most solemn Obligations to attempt *hardy* Achievements; and upon this Whimsy immediately pursuing the most romantic Adventures, with great Gravity, Importance, and Self-sufficiency; To heighten your Mirth, the *hardy* Atchievements to be accomplish'd by this Hero, are wittily contrasted by his own meagre weak Figure, and the *desperate Unfierceness* of his Steed *Rozinante;* —The *Ridicule* appears in the strange Absurdity of the Attempts, upon which the Knight chuses to exercise his Prowess; Its Poignancy is highly quicken'd, and consequently the Pleasure it gives you, by his miserable Disasters, and the doleful Mortifications of all his Importance and Dig-

---

[148] *Gentleman's Journal,* January, 1692/93, p. 27.

nity; —But here, after the Knight, by diverting you in this manner, has brought himself down to the lowest Mark, he rises again and forces your Esteem, by his excellent Sense, Learning and Judgment, upon any Subjects which are not ally'd to his Errantry; These continually act for the Advancement of his Character; And with such Supports and Abilities he always obtains your ready Attention, and never becomes heavy or tedious.[149]

viii. *The new critical importance of irony*

Interesting as some of the critical analyses of irony are, perhaps the most significant development in the Augustan age was the elevation of irony to a place of importance in relation to other ways of literary expression, an importance which entitled it to serious critical consideration.   That criticism should not have taken account of irony, after Swift and Cervantes and the ironic pamphleteers of the age, would surprise us.   Yet the process was slow.   In the Restoration and early eighteenth century people grasped any terms that were handy to describe this new way of writing—*raillery, banter, ridicule, humour, drolling, burlesque, irony*, all were used loosely and interchangeably.   Then, as no doubt usually happens, people began to straighten up the confusion, to analyze the thing and to determine the reference of critical terms.   Here *irony* had the advantage.   In its long life in the rhetorics it had always referred to a limited and identifiable verbal maneuver.   *Raillery, banter, ridicule, humour* had no such strong central references to readily identifiable techniques, they referred to the more general aspects of motive, tone, effect.   It was natural, then, that commentators and critics faced with confusion should prefer *irony* to vaguer words when *irony* was suitable.   And of course it was eminently suitable to a great deal of Augustan writing.   Add to this that Swift had carried irony in its most obtrusive forms to levels of unprecedented effectiveness, and that much of the best writing of the age exhibited irony in a multitude of forms—it would be highly surprising if irony had not become by mid-century a method of more relative critical import than it had had a hundred and fifty years earlier.

[149] Corbyn Morris, *True Standards of Wit* (Augustan Soc.), pp. 38-39.

This is of course not to say that irony was not admired by Renaissance critics. Thomas Wilson, following Cicero, said that by the irony of blame-by-praise we may "even as well set out his noughtinesse this way, as though wee had in very deede uttered al his naughtie conditions plainly,"[150] and of the irony of understatement Hoskins remarked: "It exceedeth speech in silence, and makes our meaning more palpable by a touch than by a direct handling."[151] But the thing was not of first importance, as Abraham Fraunce discloses in an illuminating comparison:

Thus much for Tropes, whereof the most excellent is a *Metaphore;* the next, *Ironia,* then *Metonymia;* lastlie, *Synecdoche:* The most usuall also is a *Metaphore,* then a *Metonymia,* next, *Synecdoche,* lastlie, *Ironia. Metonymia, Metaphora,* and *Synecdoche* oftentimes concurre together.[152]

The trope *irony* was certainly more usual in the Augustan age. Complaints that it was too common, that nothing was safe from bantering wits, are familiar. But more than that, the versatility and brilliance of the method were exhibited in a group of satiric essays, poems, and prose fictions the like of which had not been written before in English. Swift felt, at least so far as prose was concerned, that he had led the way:

> Arbuthnot is no more my Friend,
> Who dares to Irony pretend;
> Which I was born to introduce,
> Refin'd it first, and shew'd its Use.[153]

"I pretend," he wrote to Bathurst, "to have been an improver of irony on the subjects of satire and praise...."[154] And in the context of the sort of controversial irony which was coming off the English presses when Swift began writing, his claim was modest. An estimate of his impact on the age came grudgingly from an antagonistic Whig pamphlet called *An Essay upon the Taste and Writings of the Present Times* (1728):

[150] Thomas Wilson, *Rhetorique* (G. H. Mair), pp. 134-56.
[151] John Hoskins, *Directions for Speech and Style* (Hudson), pp. 25-26. See also Puttenham, *Arte of English Poesie* (Willcock-Walker), p. 184; Anthony Blackwall, *Introduction to the Classics* (1728), pp. 171-72.
[152] Abraham Fraunce, *Arcadian Rhetorike* (1588), Book I, chap. xi.
[153] Swift, *Poems* (Williams), II, 555.
[154] Swift, *Correspondence* (Ball), IV, 166.

But of all those Tyrants that have, in any Age or Nation, made themselves dreadful by any of the various Parts of Ridicule, there was perhaps never one that equall'd in Power our most facetious Countryman
Dr. *Swift*. For by this one single Talent he has reign'd absolute in the
witty World for upwards of 30 Years. —He has open'd a Vein of
Humour, which in the most humorous Nation of the World was never
heard of before.[155]

But Cervantes perhaps equally with Swift though in a different
mode impressed the age with the importance of irony, and Lucian
and Erasmus shone with a brighter light because of this new awareness. The result was a critical respect for irony which began to
show up in occasional writings at about the same time the *Essay
upon ... Taste* memorialized Swift's power, in the late 1720's. Discussing a current pamphlet Anthony Collins remarked:

Must not the fine *Irony* it self, and the Execution of it, with so much
Learning, Sense, and Wit, raise in you the highest Esteem and Admiration of the Author...? ... And can you think of a better *Form* of
Conveyance, or *Vehicle* for Matters of such universal Concern to all in-
telligent People ... than his Method of *Irony?*[156]

Irony, says a gentleman quoted in *Fog's Weekly* for June 2, 1733
(No. 239), "is certainly one of the most beautiful Strokes of Rhetorick...." "The ironical is the most agreeable, and perhaps the
strongest of all kinds of satire," says Jarvis.[157] The *Craftsman* for
April 13, 1745, heads its essay, "Irony the keenest weapon of satire;
an example of ironical panegyric," and begins thus:

Irony, in the hands of a man of fancy and judgment, is one of the
surest and most useful weapons with which satire can be arm'd against
vice and folly.[158]

Even as he abandons the ironical character of his *Jacobite's Journal*
Fielding admits the artistic value of the method: "... Irony is capable of furnishing the most exquisite Ridicule...."[159] The *Tale
of a Tub* and *Don Quixote,* says Allan Ramsay, deal in argumenta-

---

[155] Pp. 5-6.
[156] Anthony Collins, *Discourse concerning Ridicule and Irony* (1729), pp. 45-46.
[157] Charles Jarvis, *Don Quixote* (1742), pp. vi-vii.
[158] *Gentleman's Magazine,* XV (April, 1745), 207-8.
[159] Fielding, *Jacobite's Journal,* No. 17 (March 26, 1748).

tive ridicule, which "is, of all the modes of Ridicule that ever were found out, the fairest as well as the most diverting."[160]   Although Deane Swift writes with more impetuosity than care, one of his comments is indicative of what by mid-century it was possible to say of irony:

> The *Argument against abolishing Christianity* . . . is according to the best of my judgment the most delicate, refined, compleat, unvaried piece of irony, from the beginning to the end, that ever was written since the creation of the world; and without dispute, if in the works of man there can be supposed any such thing as real perfection, we must allow it to consist in those amazing productions of wit and humour, which in all probability can never be excelled by any effort of genius, and beyond which it is impossible to frame any critical or distinct idea of the human faculties.[161]

Joseph Warton praised the "poignant ridicule, and attic elegance" of Erasmus and remarked, "The irony of the Encomium on Folly has never been excelled."[162]   And Dr. Johnson, in his Life of Pope, speaks as admiringly as Deane Swift on the subject of another ironic essay:

> This year was printed in *The Guardian* the ironical comparison between the *Pastorals* of Philips and Pope; a composition of artifice, criticism, and literature, to which nothing equal will easily be found. The superiority of Pope is so ingeniously dissembled, and the feeble lines of Philips so skilfully preferred, that Steele, being deceived, was unwilling to print the paper lest Pope should be offended.[163]

Thus by mid-century the old rhetorical trope irony had become a literary mode capable of the highest achievements and worthy of serious critical attention.   More than that, a small body of theory had been evolved.   It came not fully formed from the forehead of an Aristotle but arose out of the nature of the thing and the trials and errors of the Augustan ironists and their readers.   And it found expression not in a critical scheme but in the casual practical criticism of the time.

[160] Allan Ramsay, *Essay on Ridicule* (1762), pp. 53-54 n.
[161] Deane Swift, *Essay upon Swift* (1755), pp. 135-36.
[162] Joseph Warton, *Essay on Pope* (1806), I, 178-79.
[163] Johnson, *Lives* (Birkbeck Hill), III, 107.

ix. *The meaning of the word again*

In this chapter and the preceding one we have been observing developments in the techniques and criticism of English classical irony so called; did these have any significance for the future of the word *irony*'s meaning? I think they did. We have just now observed that irony so named became a literary mode of critical importance in the second quarter of the eighteenth century. This in itself, by stimulating people to think about irony, would—and did—lead to a deepening analysis of the concept as the century progressed.

But we have also observed several other developments. First, people became increasingly conscious that irony could be the informing principle of a fairly long piece of writing, and in such writing they saw the necessity of sustaining both the ironic point of view and the ironic mask to the end. Second, we have observed that people became increasingly conscious in the second quarter of the eighteenth century that an author could present in an ironic way not only arguments and opinions but also—and most important—characters and action. We have seen that this awareness grew up especially around high burlesque and even, in Fielding's mind,[164] extended to the creation of character in the novel. Let us take for example Richard Owen Cambridge's notions, quoted above, about the irony of his *Scribleriad.* The Author never laughs but always seems to be serious; he wears constantly "that grave irony which *Cervantes* only has inviolably preserv'd." Both "Author and Editors are represented full as great enthusiasts as the Hero; therefore ... all things are supposed to appear to them in the same light as they do to him." If this attitude in presenting the story is successfully sustained, how is the audience to discover the irony? Cambridge gives us a suggestion. Scriblerus is promised the grand elixir he seeks and frequent statements in the poem insinuate that he will succeed in possessing it. But the actual consequence of all his striving is—beggary. Thus we discover the irony, says Cambridge.

Is this not dramatic irony? Here we have the self-effacing author going quietly about his business of depicting blind characters

[164] See pp. 139-40 above.

foolishly pursuing courses which lead to the very reverse of their expectations—and depicting them for all the world as though he saw nothing wrong in their behavior.   Here we have statements which mean one thing to Scriblerus and quite another to Cambridge and to us, the audience.   It is true that Cambridge's motive is that of the satirist rather than of the philosophic observer, but we may suppose an audience would generate a degree of philosophic detachment out of watching the event of Scriblerus' passionate foolishness.

I think it is indeed accurate to say that *Scriblerus* and *Don Quixote* and other fictional narratives which the mid-century Augustans called *irony* do embody dramatic irony, and it is not hard to see how the transferal of the word *irony* from relatively brief ironic praise of an opinion or attitude or argument to the longer burlesque, the fictional character, and the novel was inevitably leading people to use *irony* to name that whole complex of elements in a fictional work which David Worcester has defined as *dramatic irony*. I do not think, however, that the mid-century Augustans had reached the precipice at the end of this path.   They were on the verge, but the uses of *irony* I have collected seem to indicate that at mid-century they still thought of irony in the main simply as the technique of blame-through-praise used by an author in presenting his fiction with mock approval.

FIVE

RAILLERY AND *BANTER*

The word *irony* was not a key word during most of our period, nor was it even widely current until the second quarter of the eighteenth century. But the verbal devices people usually meant when they did use *irony* were current, were omnipresent, throughout the Augustan age. Other words were used to name them, and these words need to be sorted out. Unfortunately the task is far from easy. "Some writers," remarks John W. Draper, "use the comic, the ludicrous, the ridiculous, wit, raillery, humour, and satire in a loosely synonymous fashion...."[1] It was the exceptional writer who used any of these terms with precision. Anthony Collins, for instance, in his *Discourse concerning Ridicule and Irony* often seems to consider all of them available for naming any kind of levity. His usage was representative of run-of-the-mill authors of the age. But distinctions were available and can be ferreted out.

Of *satire,* David Worcester points out that the "soul of the word has shown a progressive change from a specific, narrow meaning to an abstract, broad one."[2] Just as satire itself developed from the crabbedly conventional verse satires of Joseph Hall and Donne through the freer verse satires of Dryden into the variety of prose forms used by Swift and Addison and Mandeville, so the word itself widened its reference from the formal verse satire to any mode of literature which displayed a certain motive and spirit. "More than any other people, the English have associated virulence and malevolence with the idea of satire,"[3] Worcester comments. Dry-

---

[1] John W. Draper, "Theory of the Comic in Eighteenth-Century England" (1938), p. 208.
[2] David Worcester, *Art of Satire* (1940), p. 3.
[3] *Ibid.,* p. 6.

den, trying to define the meaning of *satire* at the end of the seventeenth century, supports this view:

in our modern languages we apply it only to invective poems, where the very name of satire is formidable to those persons, who would appear to the world what they are not in themselves; for in English, to say satire, is to mean reflection, as we use that word in the worst sense....[4]

It was probably this sense of the word which necessitated a stock phrase of the Augustan age, "satire and ridicule." *Ridicule* was felt to indicate something less malevolent and lighter in tone than *satire,* to depend on a real or imagined incongruity that had at least something of the comic in it. As we have seen, the word *irony* had not yet developed either the philosophic or tragic senses which it carries today. It still referred chiefly to certain devices useful for indirect verbal attack. It was, then, most often a tool of satire or ridicule.

A third general term, *humour,* has been interestingly discussed by E. N. Hooker.[5] He distinguishes three senses of the word in the Restoration: (1) "a powerful individual inclination ... a singularity with deep emotional roots";[6] (2) " 'a fainter or weaker passion,' 'without any rule but the present whim'; it is 'a toyish conceit,' or a 'wilfull fansie' ";[7] (3) the "humour of the town," that is, the prevailing taste or fashion. Hooker argues that the early eighteenth century, under various influences, moved away from Restoration disapproval of such aberrations from the norm toward approval of them as admirable, or at least entertaining, individualism. What was the relation of *irony* to *humour?* Presumably either a fictitious character or an author in his own person might display an ironic humour; Congreve asserts that when a humorous character uses wit, "the Manner of *Wit* should be adapted to the *Humour.* As, for Instance, a Character of a Splenetick and Peevish *Humour* should have a Satyrical Wit. A Jolly and Sanguine *Humour* should have a Facetious Wit."[8] When his contemporaries spoke of Swift's "humour" or his "peculiar vein of humour" we assume they were thinking of that irony which was the distinctive characteristic of his writ-

[4] Dryden, *Works* (Scott-Saintsbury), XIII, 67.
[5] E. N. Hooker, "Humour in the Age of Pope" (1947-48).
[6] *Ibid.,* p. 363.
[7] *Ibid.*
[8] Congreve, *Humour in Comedy* (Spingarn), pp. 243-44.

ing and his personal relations with others. But in this meaning of *humour* there is no necessary extension to irony. In the earlier eighteenth century a much looser sense of the word was available, however, roughly encompassing any sort of clever, witty, or light discourse, a sense which Congreve objected to.[9] He seems to have felt that the underlying distinction between *wit* and *humour* was the difference between intellect and character, but in practice this was a difficult line to draw and not many Augustans were interested in drawing it. Consequently *humourous* could often mean "witty." As one of the cleverest and wittiest devices of verbal communication, irony we may suppose was often included under humour thus loosely conceived.

According to Richmond P. Bond's investigation of *burlesque* as it was used to refer to poetry,[10] the word first appeared in English in the second half of the seventeenth century, when it was used in the general sense of "drolish, merry, pleasant,"[11] and in a more precise sense to refer to the travesties and Hudibrastics—the *low* burlesque—popular in the Restoration. After 1700 the word became more elastic. It could refer to (1) the octosyllabic doggerel reminiscent of Butler as an isolated element; (2) poems imitative of Butler's method; (3) "poems aiming at incongruous imitation."[12] In the third sense the word included the old low burlesque and the new high burlesque: mock-heroics and parody. As we have already observed,[13] both high and low burlesque, particularly the former, use the ironic method of blame-by-praise, and so far as poetry is concerned the only sense of *burlesque* which would almost never have a possible relevance for irony as the Augustans conceived it would be that of the verse form.

i. Railing *and* Raillery

In the Augustan age the word *raillery*, which came nearer to *irony* in meaning than any other general term with the possible ex-

[9] *Ibid.*
[10] Richmond P. Bond, *English Burlesque Poetry* (1932).
[11] *Ibid.*, p. 19.
[12] *Ibid.*, p. 20.
[13] See pp. 125 ff. above.

ception of *banter*, achieved wide popular currency. Consequently people found it easier to use the handy *raillery* to name ironic discourse than to reach for the more precise but esoteric *irony*. They often paired *railing* with *raillery*, and there was a degree of confusion and interaction between the two.

Railing, which had been current since the sixteenth century, seems to have had two basic meanings throughout the English classical period. (In the following pages I discuss the various meanings of *railing*, *raillery*, and *banter* under headings numbered (1), (2), and so on.[14] So that my own use of these words will be unambiguous, I have frequently indicated by number which meaning I am invoking, thus: *raillery* #2 or *railing* #1.)

(1) In one sense, the less frequent one, *railing* referred simply to the act of verbal attack or criticism, without limits as to the method employed. In this sense it might involve the irony of Erasmus, the ridicule of Aristophanes, discreet reproof, slanderous gossip, the inspired rumors of politics. Its connotation was unpleasant, even immoral.[15]

(2) In its second and more common meaning *railing* referred specifically to angry invective. Such invective could range from the bluntest of vulgar name-calling to the artful rhetoric of Juvenal or Shakespeare, but always the attack was felt to be a frontal assault, the tone angry, the imputed faults serious and the effect on the object painful. The connotation of the word was highly unfavorable in this sense too, so that *railing* was usually thought of as vulgar name-calling rather than as artfully witty invective. People who liked the witty invective of, say, a particular satirist usually preferred not to call it railing; people who did not used the word as a

---

[14] Several of the footnotes which follow list passages dating from the early sixteenth to the mid-eighteenth century in which *railing*, *raillery*, or *banter* is clearly used in one of the senses defined. There is no attempt to list all the appearances I have noted of the two words.

[15] Philip Sidney, *Apology for Poetry* (G. G. Smith), pp. 181-82. Gabriel Harvey, *Works* (Grosart), I, 164; II, 201. Thomas Nashe, *Works* (McKerrow), I, 283-84. Shakespeare, *Twelfth Night*, I, v, 85 ff. *Raillerie a la Mode* (1673), pp. 40-42. John Oldham, *Works* (1686), pp. 19-20. Tom Brown, *Amusements and Letters* (Hayward), p. 42. Bayle, *Dictionary* (1710), II, 1264L. *Humourist* II (1725), pp. 96-105. *Art of Railing* (1723), *passim.* J. K., *New English Dictionary* (1731), "rail." *Female Spectator* (1755), IV, 110, 121.

device of adverse criticism.[16] Thus Nashe denied Harvey's accusation:

Skolding, thou saiest, is the language of shrewes, railing the stile of rakehels; what concludst thou from thence? Do I scold? do I raile?

Scolding & railing is loud miscalling and reviling one another without wit, speaking every thing a man knows by his neighbor, though it bee never so contrary to all humanitie and good manners, and would make the standers by almost perbrake to heare it. Such is thy invective against *Greene,* where thou talkst of his lowsines, his surfeting, his beggerie, and the mother of *Infortunatus* infirmities. If I scold, if I raile, I do but *cum ratione insanire; Tully, Ovid,* all the olde Poets, *Agrippa, Aretine,* and the rest are all scolds and railers, and by thy conclusion flat shrewes and rakehels: for I doe no more than their examples do warrant mee.[17]

Jonson rebelled against a similar accusation:

> ... all your writing, is meere rayling.
> *Aut.* Ha! If all the salt in the old *comoedy*
> Should be so censur'd, or the sharper wit
> Of the bold *satyre,* termed scolding rage,
> What age could then compare with those, for buffons?
> What should be said of Aristophanes?
> Persius? or Juvenal? whose names we now
> So glorifie in schooles....[18]

This attitude was then and remained representative, but in both the earlier period and the later the word was used at times to recognize invective involving wit of a respectable order. At the end of the seventeenth century, for instance, Dryden could remark: "Juvenal has railed more wittily than Horace has rallied. Horace

---

[16] Thomas More, *Works* (1557), "The deballacion of Salem and Byzance," chap. v, p. 939. Roberte Whytinton, *Tullyes offyces* (1534), sig F7^r. Gabriel Harvey, *Works* (Grosart), II, 129. Thomas Nashe, *Works* (McKerrow), I, 195-96, 324. Shakespeare, *Merchant of Venice,* IV, i, 128-42; *King Lear,* II, ii, 12-24. Jonson, *Works* (Herford-Simpson), V, 24. John Stephens, *Essayes and Characters Ironicall* (1615), sig. A3^r-A4^r. Richard Flecknoe, *Sixty-nine Enigmatical Characters* (Augustan Soc.), pp. 30-31. Dryden, *Works* (Scott-Saintsbury), XIII, 37-38, 97-99, 100; *Prologues and Epilogues* (Gardner), pp. 78, 90. Isaac Barrow, *Works* (1687), I, 227. John Sheffield, "An Essay upon Poetry" (Spingarn), p. 290. Shaftesbury, *Characteristics* (Robertson), I, 11. Myles Davies, *Athenae Britannicae* (1716), II, 163. Nathan Bailey, *Universal Etymological English Dictionary* (1724), "rail." Arbuthnot, *Works* (Aitken), p. 384. Pope, *Works* (Elwin-Courthope), VII, 196, 446; *Prose Works* (Ault), p. 184. *The Bee,* VII, 121 (No. 81, Sept. 7-14, 1734).

[17] Thomas Nashe, *Works* (McKerrow), I, 324.

[18] Jonson, *Works* (Herford-Simpson), IV, 323.

means to make his readers laugh, but he is not sure of his experi-
ment. Juvenal always intends to move your indignation, and he
always brings about his purpose."[19] If in the Augustan age the
onus attached to the word became slighter, it became only imper-
ceptibly slighter.

Although the word *raillery* was used loosely by the Augustans,
there seem to have been three substantial phases of its meaning.

(1) In one sense, perhaps the most frequent, it was more or less
equivalent to *ridicule,* with this difference, that whereas people felt
ridicule could refer to a supposedly objective reality apart from
words (our own *ridiculous* or *ridiculousness*), they always thought
of *raillery* as a verbal act. The motive of raillery ♯1 like that of
ridicule was contempt rather than the genuine or assumed hatred
of railing ♯2, and in contrast to the tone of angry passion characteristic of railing ♯2—this was the most deeply felt difference—raillery
to some extent at least laughed at its object, even if only through
witty indirection or a light manner. On the other hand raillery
♯1 resembled railing ♯2 in aiming at real faults with the intent to
give real pain. Within these limits the contempt of the rallier
might range from hostile to friendly contempt, his technique from
coarse buffoonery to the subtlest and cleverest of invention, his objects might range from serious vices to silly foibles, his effect from
the maximum to the minimum of pain: some raillery bludgeoned,
some cut, some only tickled; some was "low" or "gross," some
"sharp" or "biting," some "fine," "pleasant" or "genteel."[20]

[19] Dryden, *Works* (Scott-Saintsbury), XIII, 100.
[20] Sprat, *Cowley* (Spingarn), pp. 136-37; *Royal Society* (1667), pp. 413-19.
Raillerie a la mode (1673), *passim.* Edward Phillips, *New World of Words*
(1706), "satyrize." *Art of Speaking* (1708), pp. 305-11. Dryden, *Works* (Scott-
Saintsbury), XIII, 59, 97-99, 100; *Essays* (Ker), I, 266; *Lucian* (1710-11), I,
38-48. John Oldham, *Works* (1686), sig. A2^r-v. William Temple, "Of Poetry"
(Spingarn), pp. 101-2. *Plutarch's Morals* (1691), I, sig. A5^v-A6^r. Locke,
Concerning Education (Quick), pp. 121-23. William Wotton, *Reflections upon
Ancient and Modern Learning* (1697), p. 110; *A Defense of the Reflections*
(1705), pp. 47-48. Tom Brown, *Colloquies out of Erasmus* (1699), "Life," sig.
b5^v-b6^v. Dennis, *Critical Works* (Hooker), I, 432 n. Dacier, *Plato* (1701), I,
58-61. Bellegarde, *Reflexions upon Ridicule* (1717), I, "Advertisement," 67-68,
88-89, 99, 126, 179; II, 14, 62, 117, 167. *Tatler* (Aitken), II, 59-61 (No. 57,
Aug. 20, 1709), 70-72 (No. 59, Aug. 25, 1709); IV, 124-26 (No. 219, Sept. 2,
1710), 221 (No. 239, Oct. 19, 1710), 234-38 (No. 242, Oct. 26, 1710). Bayle,
Dictionary (1734-38), II, 148 col. 1; IV, 137 col. b. Shaftesbury, *Characteristics*

Dryden's famous description of "fine raillery," because of its relatively early date, influence, and precision, is worth quoting once more:

Holyday says, "a perpetual grin, like that of Horace, rather angers than amends a man." I cannot give him up the manner of Horace in low satire so easily. Let the chastisement of Juvenal be never so necessary for his new kind of satire; let him declaim as wittily and sharply as he pleases; yet still the nicest and most delicate touches of satire consist in fine raillery.... How easy is it to call rogue and villain, and that wittily! But how hard to make a man appear a fool, a blockhead, or a knave, without using any of those opprobrious terms! To spare the grossness of the names, and to do the thing yet more severely, is to draw a full face, and to make the nose and cheeks stand out, and yet not to employ any depth of shadowing.... Neither is it true, that this fineness of raillery is offensive. A witty man is tickled while he is hurt in this manner, and a fool feels it not. The occasion of an offence may possibly be given, but he cannot take it. If it be granted, that in effect this way does more mischief; that a man is secretly wounded, and though he be not sensible himself, yet the malicious world will find it out for him; yet there is still a vast difference betwixt the slovenly butchering of a man, and the fineness of a stroke that separates the head from the body, and leaves it standing in its place.... I wish I could apply it to myself, if the reader would be kind enough to think it belongs to me. The character of Zimri in my "Absalom," is, in my opinion, worth the whole poem: it is not bloody, but it is ridiculous enough; and he, for whom it was intended, was too witty to resent it as an injury. If I had railed, I might have

---

(Robertson), I, 21-22, 43-44, 47-48, 50-51, 85-86; II, 337-38, 354. Shaftesbury, *Life, Letters, Regimen* (Rand), pp. 504-5. *Spectator* (G. G. Smith), No. 266 (Jan. 4, 1712). Myles Davies, *Athenae Britannicae* (1716), I, 322-23. Pope, *Works* (Elwin-Courthope), VI, 164-65; VII, 134. Pope, *Miscellanies* (1728), III, vii-x. Pope, *Iliad* (1756), II, 56-58 n.; IV, 36-38 n., 164-72 n., 232 n., 239-40 n. Swift, *Tale of a Tub* (Davis), pp. 2, 10; *Poems* (Williams), I, 86-88, 214-19, 631, 634-38; *Prose Works* (Temple Scott), XI, 71; *Correspondence* (Ball), IV, 328-31. "An Essay on Gibing" (1727), pp. 5-10, 16-22. *Essay upon the Taste and Writings of the Present Times* (1728), p. 39. Anthony Collins, *Discourse concerning Ridicule and Irony* (1729), pp. 5-7, 38. J. K., *New English Dictionary* (1731), "satyrize." *Gentleman's Magazine*, III (July, 1733), 348; XII (Sept., 1742), 479-81. *London Magazine*, VII (Oct., 1738), 500-501. *Fog's Weekly Journal*, No. 239 (June 2, 1733). *The Bee*, IV, 393 (No. 49, Jan. 26-Feb. 2, 1734). Fielding, *Works* (Stephen), VI, 322-25. Corbyn Morris, *True Standards of Wit* (Augustan Soc.), pp. 6-7, 36-37. *Female Spectator* (1755), III, 319-20; IV, 136-49. John G. Cooper, *Socrates* (1750), pp. 57-59 n., 87-88. *Monthly Review*, IV (Jan., 1751), 223; V (June, 1751), 78-79; X (March, 1754), 193-96. John Ozell, *Don Quixote* (Mod. Lib.), pp. 24, 138. John Brown, *Essays on Characteristics* (1751), pp. 41-43, 49-50, 53-54, 100-102. *World* (Chalmers), XXVI, 67 (No. 14, April 5, 1753).

suffered for it justly; but I managed my own work more happily, perhaps more dexterously. I avoided the mention of great crimes, and applied myself to the representing of blindsides, and little extravagances; to which, the wittier a man is, he is generally the more obnoxious. It succeeded as I wished; the jest went round, and he was laughed at in his turn who began the frolic.[21]

For Dryden fine raillery involves the laughter arising from ridicule, indirection, artistic finesse, and a concern with minor rather than major failings. He does not deny that the object of fine raillery is actually hurt—"severely" rebuked—but thinks a "witty" man is sufficiently amused not to be offended. An even more sensitive conscience in this regard was demonstrated by the *Tatler*:

This is the true art of raillery, when a man turns another into ridicule, and shows at the same time he is in good humour, and not urged by malice against the person he rallies. Obadiah Greenhat has hit this very well: for to make an apology to Isaac Bickerstaff, an unknown student and horary [*sic*] historian, as well as astrologer, and with a grave face to say, he speaks of him by the same rules with which he would treat Homer or Plato, is to place him in company where he cannot expect to make a figure; and makes him flatter himself, that it is only being named with them which renders him most ridiculous.[22]

All of Dryden's specifications were met by Pope's *Rape of the Lock*: as Warton commented, "I hope it will not be thought an exaggerated panegyric to say that the Rape of the Lock is the best satire extant; ... in point of delicacy, elegance, and fine-turned raillery, on which they [the French] have so much valued themselves, they have produced nothing equal to the Rape of the Lock."[23]

A letter of Swift's takes us into the realm of "sharp raillery," raillery meant to hurt and, often, to hurt as much as possible. It could deal with serious failings and its author's contempt was not necessarily friendly nor his ridicule delicate.

As I am conjectured to have generally dealt in raillery and satire, both in prose and verse, if that conjecture be right, although such an opinion has been an absolute bar to my rising in the world, yet that very world must suppose that I followed what I thought to be my talent, and

[21] From the "Discourse concerning . . . Satire" in Dryden, *Works* (Scott-Saintsbury), XIII, 97-99.
[22] *Tatler* (Aitken), II, 70-72 (No. 59, Aug. 25, 1709).
[23] Pope, *Works* (Elwin-Courthope), II, 116.

charitable people will suppose I had a design to laugh the follies of mankind out of countenance, and as often to lash the vices out of practice.
And then it will be natural to conclude, that I have some partiality for
such kind of writing, and favour it in others. I think you acknowledge,
that in some time of your life, you turned to the rallying part, but I
find at present your genius runs wholly into the grave and sublime, and
therefore I find you less indulgent to my way by your dislike of the
Beggar's Opera, in the persons particularly of Polly Peachum and
Macheath, whereas we think it a very severe satire upon the most pernicious villainies of mankind. And so you are in danger of quarrelling
with the sentiments of Mr. Pope, Mr. Gay the author, Dr. Arbuthnot,
myself, Dr. Young, and all the brethren whom we own. Dr. Young
is the gravest among us, and yet his satires have many mixtures of
sharp raillery. At the same time you judge very truly, that the taste of
England is infamously corrupted by shoals of wretches who write for
their bread; and therefore I had reason to put Mr. Pope on writing
the poem, called the Dunciad. . . .[24]

Earlier in the game *Raillerie a la mode* (1673), antagonistic toward the common professors of raillery, had remarked:

. . . they have their Figures, Graces, and Ornaments peculiar to their kind
of Speech, though they do not distinguish or use them Grammatically,
by the Names of *Sarcasmus, Asteismus, Micterismus, Antiphrasis, Charientismus,* or *Ironia,* yet have they their Dry *Bobs,* their Broud *Flouts,*
Bitter *Taunts,* their Fleering *Frumps,* and Privy *Nips.* Besides the use
of their admirable Art of Canting, they have a cunning way of Jeering,
accusing others by justifying themselves, and saying, I never did—or
by asking the Question general, Who did so and so? Why who did you
Whore cries 'tother? did I? and so the Game begins; but by this
evasive way of Abuse they will be sure to keep wide off the Law's Tenter-
hooks.[25]

Only a thin veneer of jocosity, crude indirection, or heavy wit apparently distinguished such stuff from railing #2, and most people
of taste would have called it gross raillery. It differed only in degree from the works Dryden and Swift admired, however, and in
trying to canvass the range of things called raillery in sense #1 we
are well advised by John Brown: "What is high Humour at *Wapping,* is rejected as nauseous in the *City:* What is delicate Raillery
in *the City,* grows *coarse* and *intolerable* as you approach *St.*

---

[24] Swift, *Correspondence* (Ball), IV, 329-31.
[25] Pp. 40-42.

James's...."[26]   Thus Shaftesbury, who resided at the St. James end, carried delicacy to the point of finding burlesque itself a type of gross raillery.[27]

But in all raillery (♯1) as ridicule, fine, sharp, or gross, contemptuous laughter was an essential ingredient, as John Brown succinctly stated:

> Pure *Wit*, when not applied to the Characters of Men, is properly a Species of Poetry. It amuses and delights the Imagination by those sudden Assemblages and pleasing Pictures of Things which it creates: and from every common Occasion can raise such striking Appearances, as throw the most phlegmatic Tempers into a Convulsion of good-humoured Mirth, and *undesigning Laughter*.
>
> But *Ridicule* or *Raillery*, which is the Subject of our Inquiry, hath a further Scope and Intention. It solely regards the Opinions, Passions, Actions, and Characters of Men: and may properly be denominated "that Species of Writing which excites Contempt with Laughter."[28]

Pope, in a letter to Caryll of November 19, 1712, had expressed the same idea with more grace:

> You may conclude from what I here say that it was never in my thoughts to offer you my poor pen in any direct reply to such a scoundrel, who, like Hudibras, need fear no blows but such as bruise, but only in some little raillery in the most contemptuous manner thrown upon him, not as in your defence expressly, but as in scorn of him *en gaiete de coeur*.[29]

We must remember, however, that the content of laughter and gaiety might be only a glint in the eye, a clever allusion, the use of some device for projecting an apparent impersonality.

(2) In a second sense *raillery* referred to a kind of verbal attack which sounded exactly like that ridicule to which *raillery* in sense ♯1 referred. But this raillery (♯2) was not motivated by contempt, it did not attack real failings, and it did not hurt. One type of such raillery (♯2) was praise-by-blame irony: under the clever hand of the rallier mock faults turned into real virtues and mock ridicule turned into real praise.[30]   (Here Voiture was considered

---

[26] John Brown, *Essays on Characteristics* (1751), pp. 53-54.
[27] Shaftesbury, *Characteristics* (Robertson), I, 50-51.
[28] John Brown, *Essays on Characteristics* (1751), pp. 41-43.
[29] Pope, *Works* (Elwin-Courthope), VI, 164-65.
[30] Richard Flecknoe, *Enigmaticall Characters* (1658), pp. 30-31. Locke, *Concerning Education* (Quick), pp. 121-23. Swift, *Poems* (Williams), I, 214-19;

the master.) The second type attacked either imaginary failings or real peccadilloes and aberrations so minor in nature no one could mind having them noticed. The motive of the rallier was friendly affection or simply the desire to furnish a little entertainment, and the effect was like that of being tickled, as the Augustans were fond of saying.[31]

In his "Of Raillerie," Richard Flecknoe described the raillery of praise-by-blame, and we notice that *raillery* in this sense connoted elegance, as it continued to do.

There is as much difference betwixt *Raillerie* and *Satyrs, Jesting* and *Jeering, &c.* as betwixt *gallantry* and *clownishnesse;* or betwixt a *gentle Accost* and *rude Assault.* And if I would habit them in their several properties, I would cloath *Satyr* in haircloth, *jeering* in home spun-stuff, *jesting* in motley, and *Raillery* in silk. It being a gentle exercise of wit and witty harmlesse *calumny,* speaks ill of you by contraries; and the *reverse* or tother side of complement, as far beneath as that above reality. There's nothing in it of abusive, and only as much in it of handsome invective and reproach as may well be owned without a blush: publishing those praises of you without shame, which flattery would make you ashamed to hear. It differs from *Gybing* as gentle smiles from scornfull laughter, and from rayling as Gentlemens playing at foyls, from Butchers and Clowns playing at Cudgels. Tis nothing bitter, but a poignant sauce of wit, for curious pallats, not for your vulgar Tasts.[32]

The full range of raillery #2 was defined by Henry Fielding a century later. He is unusually clear and concrete:

True raillery indeed consists either in playing on peccadillos, which, however they may be censured by some, are not esteemed as really blemishes in a character in the company where they are made the subject

Prose Works (Temple Scott), XI, 71, 88; *Correspondence* (Ball), I, 62-63, 65. Fielding, *Works* (Stephen), VI, 322-25. *Female Spectator* (1755), IV, 136-49. *Monthly Review,* IV (April, 1751), 419.

[31] Richard Bulstrode, *Essays* (1715), p. 56. William Wotton, *Reflections upon Ancient and Modern Learning* (1697), p. 149. Bruyère, *Manners of the Age* (1699), pp. 6, 113-14. Tom Brown, *Works* (1720), III, 146. Bellegarde, *Reflexions upon Ridicule* (1717), I, 21, 22, 52-53, 153-54; II, 9. *Tatler* (Aitken), II, 85 (No. 61, Aug. 30, 1709). Pope, *Works* (Elwin-Courthope), VI, 96-97, 118-19, 226-28, 295-97; VII, 232-34, 236, 249. Swift, *Journal to Stella* (Williams), I, 267; II, 436. Swift, *Poems* (Williams), II, 747, 751-52. Swift, *Prose Works* (Temple Scott), XI, 72, 88. Swift, *Correspondence* (Ball), I, 153, 341-43. Fielding, *Works* (Stephen), VI, 322-25. *Female Spectator* (1755), IV, 122-23, 136-49. Letitia Pilkington, *Memoirs* I & II (1749), II, 21-22, 49. Christopher Smart, *Midwife* (1751-53), III, 49-53.

[32] Richard Flecknoe, *Enigmaticall Characters* (1658), pp. 30-31.

of mirth; as too much freedom with the bottle, or too much indulgence with women, &c.

Or, secondly, in pleasantly representing real good qualities in a false light of shame, and bantering them as ill ones. So generosity may be treated as prodigality; economy as avarice, true courage as fool-hardiness: and so of the rest.

Lastly, in ridiculing men for vices and faults which they are known to be free from. Thus the cowardice of A--le, the dulness of Ch--d, the unpoliteness of D--ton, may be attacked without danger of offence; and thus Lyt--n may be censured for whatever vice or folly you please to impute to him.

And however limited these bounds may appear to some, yet, in skilful and witty hands, I have known raillery, thus confined, afford a very diverting, as well as inoffensive entertainment to the whole company.[33]

But raillery #2 could do more than entertain, as Pope pointed out:

As the fooling and toying with a mistress is a proof of fondness, not disrespect, so is raillery with a friend. I know there are prudes in friendship, who expect distance, awe, and adoration; but I know you are not of them: and I, for my part, am no idol-worshipper, though a papist.... I know some philosophers define laughter, *a recommending ourselves to our own favour by comparison with the weakness of another:* but I am sure I very rarely laugh with that view....[34]

This "delicate" raillery, as it was often called, this raillery which could be flattering, entertaining, and affectionate, was not work for every hand. "There are," said La Bruyère, "abundance of obscene, a great many more railing and satyrical Wits, but very few delicate. A Man must have manners and politeness to trifle with a good grace, and a copious fancy to play handsomely on little things, to create matter of raillery, and make something out of nothing."[35] Swift seems to have been thinking of delicate raillery debased and turned gross when he made the following observation:

There is a sort of rude familiarity, which some people, by practising among their intimates, have introduced into their general conversation, and would have it pass for innocent freedom or humour.... This, among the Romans, was the raillery of slaves, of which we have many instances in Plautus. It seemeth to have been introduced among us by

---

[33] Fielding, *Works* (Stephen), VI, 322-25.
[34] Pope, *Works* (Elwin-Courthope), VI, 118-19.
[35] Bruyère, *Manners of the Age* (1699), p. 6.

Cromwell, who, by preferring the scum of the people, made it a court entertainment. . . .[36]

An even lower type Fielding notes in "that kind of raillery ... which is concerned in tossing men out of their chairs, tumbling them into water, or any of those handicraft jokes which are exercised on those notable persons, commonly known by the name of buffoons. . . ."[37] Perhaps it will be useful to illustrate what the great wits of the age thought of as "delicate" raillery. In his *Journal to Stella* Swift wrote on December 11, 1711, a day when it looked as though Oxford's ministry would fall:

Lord treasurer came in to see her [Mrs. Masham], and seeing me in the outer room fell a rallying me; says he, You had better keep company with me, than with such a fellow as Lewis, who has not the soul of a chicken, nor the heart of a mite. . . . He asked, whether I was not afraid to be seen with him?[38]

Erasmus Lewis, of course, was a good friend of both men and Swift's loyalty was not being seriously questioned. A much wittier and more graceful sample of delicate raillery comes from the pen of John Gay, in a joint letter with Pope to Caryll, Senior, during April of 1715:

Sir, —Mr. Pope is going to Mr. Jervas's, where Mr. Addison is sitting for his picture. In the meantime, amidst clouds of tobacco at William's Coffee-house, I write this letter. We have agreed to spend this day in visits. He is to introduce me to a lord and two ladies, and on my part, which I think will balance his visits, I am to present him to a duchess. . . . Mr. Rowe's Jane Grey is to be played in Easter week, when Mrs. Oldfield is to personate a character directly opposite to female nature—for what woman ever despised sovereignty? Chaucer has a tale where a knight saves his head by discovering that it was the thing which all women most coveted. Col. Frowde puns upon his play, and declares that most of the ladies of Drury Lane will not accept of a crown when it is offered them, unless you give them a supper into the bargain, and wonders how people can admire the uncommonness of the character. Mr. Pope's Homer is retarded by the great rains that have fallen of late, which cause the sheets to be long a-drying. This gives Mr. Lintot great uneasiness, who is now endeavouring to corrupt the curate of his parish to pray for fair weather, that his work may go on the faster. There is

[36] Swift, *Prose Works* (Temple Scott), XI, 72.
[37] Fielding, *Works* (Stephen), VI, 322-25.
[38] Swift, *Journal to Stella* (Williams), II, 436.

a sixpenny criticism lately published upon the tragedy of the What d'ye Call it, wherein he with much judgment and learning calls me a blockhead, and Mr. Pope a knave. . . . Mr. Pope will make his conditions before he will venture into your company, that you shall not allow him any of your conversation in the morning. He is obliged to pay this self-denial in complaisance to his subscribers. For my part, who do not deal in heroes or ravished ladies, I may perhaps celebrate a milk-maid, describe the amours of your parson's daughter, or write an elegy upon the death of a hare; but my articles are quite the reverse of his, that you will interrupt me every morning, or ten to one I shall be first troublesome and interrupt you. . . .

Thus far Mr. Gay, [Pope has taken over the pen] who in his letter has forestalled all the subjects of raillery and diversion. . . .[39]

Such delightful raillery as this occasionally shows its head even today, but in the much more favorable Augustan atmosphere it was the rage.

(3) It is not surprising that a word as comprehensive in reference as we have seen *raillery* to be should also have been used to name jesting of any sort at all, regardless of whether the jest attacked anything.[40] In the extremes of *railing* (#1) as any sort of attack and *raillery* (#3) as any sort of jest we see the possible range of the words. Perhaps the clearest indication of sense #3 is that the Augustans sometimes used *raillery* to name that entire branch of rhetoric which is concerned with jesting. In translating Cicero's *De officiis* I, 29, the sixteenth-century translation of Roberte Whytinton had given "two maners of jestynge gentyll boorde and ray-lynge,"[41] and later translators had also used "jesting" in this place, but Roger L'Estrange gives: "There are two sorts of *Raillery*, or *Mirth*; the one is *Course, Petulant, Criminal*, and *Foul*; the other,

[39] Pope, *Works* (Elwin-Courthope), VI, 226-28.
[40] (Cotgrave, *Dictionarie* [1611], "Raillerie.") Thomas Blount, *Glossographia* (1656), "Raillery." Edward Phillips, *New World of Words* (1662), "Raillery." *Art of Complaisance* (1673), pp. 38-44, 58-62. Elisha Coles, *English Dictionary* (1676), "Raillery." Roger L'Estrange, *Tully's Offices* (1681), p. 51. Ferrand Spence, *Lucian* (1684-85), I, sig. C4ᵛ-C5ᵛ. Isaac Barrow, *Works* (1687), I, 193-94, 199. Tom Brown, *Remains* (1720), pp. 233-34. Dennis, *Critical Works* (Hooker), I, 16-17. Edward Cocker, *English Dictionary* (1704), "Raillery." Bayle, *Dictionary* (1734-38), II, 85 col. 2. J. K., *New English Dictionary* (1731), "Rallery." Charles Rollin, *Teaching and Studying the Belles Lettres* (1749), II, 261-63. John Brown, *Essays on Characteristics* (1751), pp. 70-71.
[41] Roberte Whytinton, *Tullyes offyces* (1534), sig. F7ʳ.

Cleanly, Gracious, Ingenious, and *Facetious....*"[42] Isaac Barrow speaks of "St. *Paul's* meaning...concerning *Eutrapelia,* (that is, facetious speech, or raillery, by our Translatours rendred *Jesting,*)"[43] and when in his *Teaching and Studying the Belles Lettres* (1749) Charles Rollins translates from Quintilian and *De oratore* on prudence and moderation in the use of jests, he uses *raillery* as a synonym for *jesting.*[44] It should be noted here that Shaftesbury makes a point of calling a particular type of jest *raillery,* a type which falls between *raillery* (♯3) as harmless jesting and *raillery* (♯1) as ridicule. It is the playful elaboration of a fiction simply for the fun of mystifying all or part of the audience (see that sense of *irony* discussed under Dict. VII above). The fiction itself has no satiric content, but the act of mystification is the sort of "playing upon a person" which could be thought of as mocking attack.

'Tis real humanity and kindness to hide strong truths from tender eyes. And to do this by a pleasant amusement is easier and civiller than by a harsh denial or remarkable reserve. But to go about industriously to confound men, in a mysterious manner, and to make advantage or draw pleasure from that perplexity they are thrown into by such uncertain talk, is as unhandsome in a way of raillery as when done with the greatest seriousness, or in the most solemn way of deceit. It may be necessary, as well now as heretofore, for wise men to speak in parables, and with a double meaning, that the enemy may be amused, and they only who have ears to hear may hear. But 'tis certainly a mean, impotent, and dull sort of wit which amuses all alike, and leaves the most sensible man, and even a friend, equally in doubt, and at a loss to understand what one's real mind is, upon any subject.

This is that gross sort of raillery which is so offensive in good company. And indeed there is as much difference between one sort and another as between fair-dealing and hypocrisy, or between the genteelist wit and the most scurrilous buffoonery.[45]

Although the important distinctions between *railing* (♯2) as angry invective, *raillery* (♯1) as ridicule, and *raillery* (♯2) as a harmless verbal gambit are not difficult to draw, it is obvious that even abstractly considered the one type of thing modulates into the

---

[42] Roger L'Estrange, *Tully's Offices* (1681), p. 51.
[43] Isaac Barrow, *Works* (1687), I, 193-94.
[44] II, 261-63.
[45] Shaftesbury, *Characteristics* (Robertson), I, 45. See also *ibid.,* I, 65; II, 240, 295.

next without any pause. Equally important, the bases of the distinctions are the meaning of a tone, the touchiness of an audience, the seriousness of a failing—all of them qualities susceptible of various judgment in Wapping, the City, and St. James'. The connotations of *raillery* added a third spur to confusion. In friendly relationships delicate raillery (♯2) was felt to be an elegant grace, but sharp raillery (♯1) was thought cruel or rude; in controversy, satire, and instruction sharp raillery (♯1) was felt to be the most effective and graceful method of attack available, but railing (♯2) was thought vulgar. Whether from a failure of taste or disingenuousness, people utilized the most favorable connotation they could manage for their verbal offspring, and the lack of either clear-cut or objective demarcations between the various types of raillery and railing made it all the easier for them to succeed. Thus the range of discourse to which the words in their different senses were actually applied was considerable. This unhappy state of affairs did not go unnoticed.

The most frequent complaint was that what passed as delicate raillery (♯2) with some people was really too sharp not to hurt or too blunt to be called raillery. Probably more than any other great wit of his time Swift loved the social uses of raillery (♯2) and objected to its misuse. In a vivid little poem "To Betty the Grizette" (1730) he describes the sort of vulgar raillery which to his own discriminating taste seemed so blunt and direct it could only be called railing (♯2):

> Sets of Phrases, cut and dry,
> Evermore thy Tongue supply.
> And, thy Memory is loaded
> With old Scraps from Plays exploded.
> Stock't with Repartees and Jokes,
> Suited to all Christian Fokes:
> Shreds of Wit, and senseless Rhimes,
> Blunder'd out a Thousand Times.
> Nor, wilt thou of Gifts be sparing,
> Which can ne'er be worse for wearing.
> Picking Wit among Collegions,
> In the Play-House upper Regions;

> Where, in Eighteen-penny Gall'ry,
> *Irish* Nymphs learn *Irish* Raillery:
> But, thy Merit is thy Failing,
> And, thy Raillery is Railing.
>   Thus, with Talents well endu'd
> To be scurrilous, and rude;
> When you pertly raise your Snout,
> Fleer, and gibe, and laugh, and flout;
> This, among *Hibernian* Asses,
> For sheer Wit, and Humour passes!
> Thus, indulgent Chloe bit,
> Swears you have a World of Wit.[46]

Betty, however, because her manner was jocose flattered herself she was employing delicate raillery (#2). In another place Swift castigated that raillery (#2) which is too sharp for friendly conversation, though not too blunt.

Raillery is the finest part of conversation; but, as it is our usual custom to counterfeit and adulterate whatever is too dear for us, so we have done with this, and turned it all into what is generally called repartee, or being smart; just as when an expensive fashion cometh up, those who are not able to reach it, content themselves with some paltry imitation. It now passeth for raillery to run a man down in discourse, to put him out of countenance, and make him ridiculous, sometimes to expose the defects of his person or understanding; on all which occasions he is obliged not to be angry, to avoid the imputation of not being able to take a jest. It is admirable to observe one who is dexterous at this art, singling out a weak adversary, getting the laugh on his side, and then carrying all before him. The French, from whence we borrow the word, have a quite different idea of the thing, and so had we in the politer age of our fathers. Raillery was to say something that at first appeared a reproach or reflection; but, by some turn of wit unexpected and surprising, ended always in a compliment, and to the advantage of the person it was addressed to. And surely one of the best rules in conversation is, never to say a thing which any of the company can reasonably wish we had rather left unsaid; nor can there anything be well more contrary to the ends for which people meet together, than to part unsatisfied with each other or themselves.[47]

Swift was wrong in his notion that *raillery* had formerly been limited to praise-by-blame irony, but his objection to sharp ralliers

[46] Swift, *Poems* (Williams), II, 523.
[47] Swift, *Prose Works* (Temple Scott), XI, 71.

(#1) in polite conversation had been a common complaint from the beginning, and continued to be. Eliza Haywood does not limit polite raillery (#2) to praise-by-blame, but her objection parallels Swift's:

The difference between *ridicule* and *raillery* is so very small, that the one is often mistaken for the other. —The latter, therefore, ought never to be attempted but by people of fine taste, nor played off but on those equally qualified to return it; and as it has also some distant affinity to *satire*, should never have for its subject matters of too serious a nature. —What exposes any thing we wish to have concealed, though it may be done with an air of pleasantry, leaves a sting behind it which is not easily forgiven, and will be taken for *ridicule*, whether meant as such or not.

I know nothing in effect that sticks longer on the mind than a bitter sarcasm, especially when conscious of its having some foundation in truth. —But you will say this is not *raillery*. I grant it is *ridicule*,—it is invective; yet it is that which, with people of narrow understandings, passes for *raillery*, and as such is excused, if not applauded.

As your sentiments are gay, to railly well, your expressions must be so too, yet accompanied with a certain softness, which will render what you say tickling, not wounding, to the heart.[48]

The difficulties of the situation and the popular standards of the age are manifest in a passage from Bellegarde:

There are certain Circumstances wherein *Politeness* makes it requisite to understand Raillery; as a good means to avoid Differences, and preserve a Man's Repose. ... When the Raillery is innocent, and turns upon indifferent Subjects, it must be brutish to take fire, and to complain of it. If it be too cutting, 'tis enough to signify that we feel it. If the Drolling Person after this pursues his Jest, it manifests he is a Wretch that is defective in Brain and Breeding. I have seen *Clarinda* put herself in a Passion, because she was told she made an aukward Curtsey, and enter'd a Room with an ill Grace. Those that rallied her upon that Score, did it without the least design of affronting her; and instead of making a Quarrel of it, as she did, she ought to have thank'd 'em for the Advice they gave her.[49]

An occasional complaint was that what passed as witty ridicule with some people was really such crass, blunt stuff that it should be called not raillery (#1) but railing (#2). True raillery (#1), said Sprat, differs from railing (#2) "as the pleasant reproofs of a

[48] *Female Spectator* (1755), IV, 136-49.
[49] Bellegarde, *Reflexions upon Ridicule* (1717), II, 9.

Gentleman from the severity of a School-master,"[50] but *Raillerie a la mode* could find little of this difference in the popular practice of the time:

> It is a Vitious sort of *Buffoonry*, that this mistaken Age is ready to cry up for a high acquir'd *Ornament* and Piece of Refin'd *Education*, while a *sober* Judgment, or *modest* Innocence, is as much mistook, and exploded for meer *Dulness* and *Ignorance*. He that can *abuse* another *handsomely*, is presently applauded for a *shrewd* Wit, a *notable* Man, which indeed imports no better than an abusive K--- as a good *harmless honest* Man is but the better word for a *Fool*.[51]

> ... to Buy or Read these *Cudgel-playing* Books, is but to make *Billings-gate* your Diversion; or to know the best way how to give *bad* Language: 'tis no better than downright *Railing*, Frenchifi'd into *Raillerie a la mode*.[52]

Finally, John Brown pointed out Shaftesbury's vital confusion of *raillery* #1 and *raillery* #3:

> ... the noble Writer often ... confounds *Mirth*, *Urbanity*, or *Good-humour*, with *Raillery* or *Ridicule:* Than which, no two Things in Nature are more diametrically opposite. The first, as it ariseth solely from *sudden* and *pleasing Resemblances* impressed on the Imagination, is justly regarded by all, as the best *Mediator* in every Debate. The last, as it ariseth solely from *Contempt*, is therefore no less justly regarded by most, as an *Embroiler* and *Incendiary*.[53]

In the sixteenth and early seventeenth century the words *rail*, *railing*, *railer* were in common use. Shortly after the middle of the seventeenth century the word *raillery* was imported from France. At first the French *raillerie* was also likely to be used and Sprat was obliged to call practitioners of the art "*Railleurs*,"[54] but from the beginning of its use in England *raillery* seems to have comprehended all three of the meanings defined above.[55] The definition

[50] Sprat, *Cowley* (Spingarn), pp. 136-37.
[51] *Raillerie a la mode* (1673), pp. 1-3.
[52] *Ibid.*, pp. 6-10.
[53] John Brown, *Essays on Characteristics* (1751), pp. 70-71.
[54] Sprat, *Royal Society* (1667), pp. 413-19.
[55] Hugh Macdonald asserts that when it first came into use *raillery* was "more or less equivalent to what we now mean by 'banter'" and had much the same meaning as *drollery*, "although it had acquired other meanings by 1672." If I know what Mr. Macdonald means I am obliged to argue that the word had a wider range of meaning even this early. See Hugh Macdonald, "Banter" (1947), pp. 23, 27.

which had appeared in Cotgrave's French dictionary of 1611 was repeated for English *raillery* by Blount and Phillips: "Raillerie: f. Jeasting, boording, sport, merriment; also, a flowt, or scoffe; a flowting, or scoffing."[56] Richard Flecknoe described the raillery of praise-by-blame in his *Enigmaticall Characters* (1658). In his life of Cowley and the history of the Royal Society Sprat used the word to mean ridicule. If any sense was slow in coming to clear conception it was that of the delicate raillery (♯2) which plays upon imaginary or negligible failings.

There was bound to be confusion between the old *railing* and the new *raillery*. Steele's remark in the *Tatler* may not indicate that Steele was confused but it probably misled some of his readers: "... they [would-be satirists] may as well pretend to flatter, as rail agreeably without being good-natured."[57] What have agreeableness and good nature to do with angry invective? But of course there was precedent for the use of *railing* (♯1) as any sort of attack, including good-natured raillery (♯1). The opposite of the foregoing instance is supplied us by the *Censor*, who seriously referred to the following passage as "raillery":

... the World is grown so Vicious and Degenerate, that I am perfectly sick of being one of its Inhabitants. Interest, and Prejudice are the Two great Bias's that turn every Inclination. The whole Universe is but one large Family of Knaves and Fools, that, like Flint and Steel, are perpetually striking Fire out of each other. The Friend, you think, you may confide in, betrays his Trust: The Tradesman from whom you promised your self fair Dealing, puts the Tricks of his Vocation upon you: The Lawyer, that should do you Justice in his way, lets the Adversary into the Weakness of your Cause, and sells your Interest for a Cross Fee: In short, we are hem'd in, and besieg'd with Villany. . . .[58]

He prefaced his "raillery" with the observation that he was not "able to bring my self into a Form of Gaiety. . . ."[59] Some people refused to bother their heads over distinctions; others manipulated the connotations of the words without scruple as to the denotations. Three essays will further illuminate the situation. All of them are

[56] Cotgrave, *Dictionarie* (1611), "Raillerie."
[57] *Tatler* (Aitken), IV, 236 (No. 242, Oct. 26, 1710).
[58] *Censor* (1717), I, 11-12 (No. 2, April 13, 1715).
[59] *Ibid.*, I, 10.

complaints about the spate of detraction and defamation which op-
pressed the Augustan age, and all of them deal with the same
wide variety of Augustan methods of attack. Their titles are *Raillerie a la mode* (1673), "Of Libels,"[60] and *The Art of Railing*
(1723). But a remedy was at hand. As *raillery* had become more
popular after the Restoration other forms of the word were required.
Rally, rallies, rallied, rallying[61] became the most popular verb
forms, and apparently out of these grew a new spelling of the
noun: *rallery*.[62] Bailey's dictionaries set out to use this difference
in spelling as a means of clearing up the confusion. The *Universal
Etymological English Dictionary* II (1727) gives these entries:

RAILERY ... scolding, harsh, opprobrious Language.
RALLERY ... merry Drolling or Playing on a Person in Words,
Jeering, Jesting, a close Jibe.

This largely artificial distinction was continued in other Bailey dictionaries,[63] and B. N. Defoe's dictionary copied it,[64] but it does not
seem to have caught on. *Raillery* and *rallery* were still used interchangeably in contrast to *railing*.

The association of *railing* and *irony* was not especially close.
Railing (#1) as any kind of verbal attack of course included all the
ironies of attack and sometimes obviously referred to one. As angry
invective *railing* (#2) of an especially rhetorical nature could conceiv-
ably refer to the more virulent ironies, but since the essence of irony
was indirection and railing was usually thought of as blunt and direct,
irony was not likely to be considered a normal tool of railing (#2).
Raillery and *irony*, however, were very closely related. *Raillery*
(#2) as praise-by-blame was identical in reference with one of the
central meanings of *irony* (see Dict. III.B.i above), though *raillery*
in this sense probably suggested to most people a primarily conversational gambit, and *irony* did not. *Raillery* (#2) as the friendly playing upon imaginary failings or negligible peccadilloes—again
felt to be especially a conversational thing—used the same verbal

[60] *Humourist* II (1725), pp. 96-105.
[61] *Art of Complaisance* (1673), p. 59.
[62] *Art of Speaking* (1708; first published 1676?), pp. 305-11.
[63] *Dictionarium Britannicum* (1730); *Universal Etymological English Dictionary* (1766).
[64] B. N. Defoe, *Compleat English Dictionary* (1735).

techniques that *raillery* (‡1) as ridicule did, and in that sense *raillery* was both wider and narrower in reference than *irony* was. *Raillery* ‡1 comprehended a wide range of techniques in which the specific ironic methods useful for attack were certainly included; on the other hand *raillery* ‡1 implied a certain motive and effect, whereas *irony* could include motives and effects other than those of ridicule. The irony of understatement, for instance, did not necessarily function as ridicule. Nevertheless, ironies were used more frequently by the Augustans for the purpose of ridicule than for any other. More important, they had such a taste for ironic methods in their raillery (‡1)—chiefly blame-by-praise—that they often found themselves alternating *raillery* and *irony* as though the two words were not far from synonymous.[65] Thus Bailey could define *ironically* to mean "by way of Irony or Raillery," and Sprat could admonish the wits of his age:

...the Family of the *Railleurs* is deriv'd from the same Original with the *Philosophers*. The Founder of Philosophy is confess'd by all to be *Socrates*; and he also was the famous Author of all *Irony*.

Of course, *irony* (Dict. IX) as any kind of derisive attack was in fact synonymous with *raillery* (‡1) as ridicule. Similarly *raillery* in Shaftesbury's sense of aimless mystification was coextensive with *irony* used in the same sense (Dict. VII), and *raillery* (‡3) as any kind of jesting could include nearly all the ironies.

ii. *Banter*

Apparently the word *banter* began to appear in more or less polite company toward the end of Charles II's reign. Although it was not included in Edward Phillips' *New World of Words* for 1662, 1671, or 1678, nor in Elisha Coles' *English Dictionary* of 1676, Tom D'Urfey picked it up for his *Madam Fickle*, given at

---

[65] Sprat, *Royal Society* (1667), pp. 413-19. Dryden, *Lucian* (1710-11), I, 38-48. Shaftesbury, *Characteristics* (Robertson), I, 50-51; *Life, Letters, Regimen* (Rand), pp. 504-5. Bailey, *Universal Etymological English Dictionary* II (1727), "Ironically." "An Essay on Gibing" (1727), pp. 5-10. Anthony Collins, *Discourse concerning Ridicule and Irony* (1729), p. 38. *Female Spectator* (1755), III, 319-20.

the Dorset Garden Theatre in November, 1676,[66] and Anthony Wood used it in an almanac entry dated September 6, 1678.[67] In another entry Wood settled on 1676 as the year that bantering as a social gambit had become popular at Oxford.

1676: this yeare (I speak as neare as I can) came up at Oxon the way of bantering among certaine bachelors and masters, used by them in public places and coffey houses. The cheif <were> Thomas Birton. . . . Uttering fluently romantic nonsense, unintelligible gibberish, florishing lyes and nonsense.[68]

For the 1680's the *New English Dictionary* quotes three passages (from Buckingham, Tom Brown, and Shadwell) in which the word appears, each time referring to some sort of verbal deception, as it had in D'Urfey and Wood, and in 1690 *banter* was included in *A New Dictionary of the Canting Crew*.[69]

Of unknown etymology, the word apparently had been picked up from the vulgar cant of the period by the men about town. It was some time, however, before more discriminating wits would admit its respectability. In 1710 Swift was still complaining:

The Author cannot conclude this Apology, without making this one Reflection; that, as Wit is the noblest and most useful Gift of humane Nature, so Humor is the most agreeable, and where these two enter far into the Composition of any Work, they will render it always acceptable to the World. Now, the great Part of those who have no Share or Tast of either, but by their Pride, Pedantry and Ill Manners, lay themselves bare to the Lashes of Both, think the Blow is weak, because they are insensible, and where Wit hath any mixture of Raillery; 'Tis but calling it *Banter*, and the work is done. This Polite Word of theirs was first borrowed from the Bullies in *White-Fryars*, then fell among the Footmen, and at last retired to the Pedants, by whom it is applied as properly to the Productions of Wit, as if I should apply it to Sir *Isaac Newton's* Mathematicks, but, if this *Bantring* as they call it, be so despisable a Thing, whence comes it to pass they have such a perpetual Itch towards it themselves? To instance only in the Answerer already mentioned; it is grievous to see him in some of his Writings at every turn going out of his way to be waggish, to tell us of a *Cow that prickt up*

---

[66] *New English Dictionary*, "*banter.*" The play was published in 1677.
[67] *Ibid.*
[68] Anthony Wood, *Life and Times* (Clark), II, 334.
[69] Hugh Macdonald, "Banter" (1947), p. 27.

her Tail, and in his answer to this Discourse, he says *it is all a Farce and a Ladle;* With other Passages equally shining.[70]

Again, in the *Tatler* for September 26-28, 1710, Swift remarked that "banter" was the invention of "some *pretty fellows*" and that he had been struggling against its increasing use for some years past.[71]   His struggle was a failure, however; the word had been used widely and in polite company ever since the turn of the century.   Edward Cocker's *English Dictionary* of 1704 had included it, giving a rather limited definition: "*Bantering,* a thwarting jocularly with half witted people," and it was added to the 1706 edition of Phillips' dictionary: "To *Banter,* to Jest or Jeer; to Amuse or Play upon."[72]

We notice in both Swift's comment and Phillips' definition that *banter* could now be used to indicate ridicule in general, often with a pejorative connotation.   Although verbal deception of various sorts seems to have been the original referent of the word, this sense was gradually extended to include ridicule of any kind.   The extension may have been in process in the following passage from Tom Brown, 1691: "One while he rails at the Priests, another at the French, laughs at the *Irish;* and in the whole, banters all, and the work's done."[73]   Defoe, in that passage of his *Explanation of the Shortest Way,* 1703, which we have quoted before for different reasons, remarks:

> If any man takes the pains seriously to reflect upon the contents, the nature of the thing, and the manner of the style, it seems impossible to imagine it should pass for anything but a banter upon the high-flying churchmen.[74]

William Wotton's *A Defense of the Reflections,* 1705, uses *banter* repeatedly and easily to mean, roughly, ridicule.[75]   Although the reference of the word may occasionally have been extended even further, to include jesting of any sort regardless of its content of

---

[70] Swift, *Tale of a Tub* (Davis), p. 10.
[71] Swift, *Prose Works* (Temple Scott), IX, 35.
[72] Edward Phillips, *New World of Words* (1706), "Banter."
[73] Tom Brown, *Wit for Money* (1691), p. 5.
[74] (Trevelyan), p. 55.
[75] Pp. 56, 60, 62-63, 68.

ridicule,[76] ordinarily its meaning fell within the range from deception-without-ridicule to ridicule-without-deception, and the sense of ridicule came to overshadow the original sense of verbal deception.

(1) *Banter* as deception was most often used to denote a verbal fiction of some sort offered with enough ostensible conviction to bamboozle an audience, temporarily at least. The motive behind this game was the desire for fun, playfulness; no ridicule was involved except insofar as the object was deceived he looked foolish and obtuse.[77] Such a banter might run to considerable length, as did the one Tom Brown commented on: " ... the Town has been banter'd near two Months with a sham Account of the Weather, pretended to be taken from Barometers, Thermometers...."[78] On the other hand it might be quite brief. In a letter to the Reverend William Tisdall of December 16, 1703, Swift described a popular amusement:

I will teach you a way to outwit Mrs. Johnson: it is a new-fashioned way of being witty.... You must ask a bantering question, or tell some damned lie in a serious manner, and then she will answer or speak as if you were in earnest; and then cry you, "Madam, there's a *bite*." I would not have you undervalue this, for it is the constant amusement in Court, and everywhere else among the great people; and I let you know it, in order to have it obtain among you, and teach a new refinement.[79]

The extremes to which such bamboozling went are illustrated by a note in *The Bee*, No. 61. After reprinting from the *Grub-street Journal* an advertisement that Eustace Budgell had been set up as candidate for Parliament, *The Bee* commented: "We believe we need not inform our Readers that this *Advertisement* is designed

---

[76] Bellegarde, *Reflexions upon Ridicule* (1717), I, 21-22, 100-101. Blackmore, *Satyr against Wit* (Spingarn), pp. 326, 327. Bailey, *Dictionarium Britannicum* (1730), "Banter."

[77] *New English Dictionary*, "banter" in its various forms. Anthony Wood, *Life and Times* (Clark), II, 334. Tom Brown, *Works* (1720), I, 163. Dennis, *Critical Works* (Hooker), II, 348. Edward Cocker, *English Dictionary* (1704), (1724), "Banter." Swift, *Correspondence* (Ball), I, 40; V, 245-46. John Oldmixon, *Logick and Rhetorick* (1728), pp. 21-28. Anthony Collins, *Discourse concerning Ridicule and Irony* (1729), pp. 57-58. *Grub-street Journal*, July 9, 1730. *The Bee*, V, 387 (No. 61). *Publick Register*, XII (March 21, 1741), 179.

[78] Tom Brown, *Works* (1720), I, 163.

[79] Swift, *Correspondence* (Ball), I, 40.

for a *Banter;* that there never was any such Meeting as is mentioned in it, and that Mr. *Budgell* never presumed to offer himself as a Candidate for Member of Parliament for the City of *London....*" Here, of course, the banter itself—the fictitious structure—may be taken not as harmless but as high burlesque of Budgell's pretensions.   As such it becomes ridicule in sense ♯2 of *banter.*   John Dennis applies our word interestingly to a common device of burlesque, in his *Remarks on the Rape of the Lock*, 1728:

Of the same Nature are those numerous Banters in Rhyme, which are to be found throughout this Poem, which are so uniform, and so much of a piece, that one would swear the Author were giving a Receipt for dry Joking: For by placing something important in the Beginning of a Period, and making something very trifling follow it, he seems to take pains to bring *something* into a Conjunction Copulative with *nothing*, in order to beget *nothing*.   Of this there are divers Instances in *Ariel*'s Speech in the *2d Canto;*

> This Day black Omens threat the brightest Fair
> That e'er deserv'd the watchfull'st Spirit's Care;
> Some dire Disaster, or by Force or Sleight,
>
> . . . .
>
> Whether the Nymph shall break Diana's Law,
> Or some frail China Jar receive a Flaw,[80]
>
> . . . .

In deceiving the audience and then disappointing its expectations Pope is bantering it—and using a basic device of irony and burlesque.

Banter as deception was also used, though not quite so frequently, to denote a verbal fiction perpetrated not out of playfulness but out of a desire to gain some practical end.[81]   The context of this use is usually argument or controversy, in which the imputed banterer attempts to convince his audience of the truth of something which his opponent thinks is arrant nonsense.   Thus Charles Leslie accuses Hoadly of consciously manipulating words in a deceitful way:

[80] Dennis, *Critical Works* (Hooker), II, 348.
[81] *New English Dictionary*, "banter" in its various forms.   Dennis, *Critical Works* (Hooker), I, 316.   Anthony Collins, *Grounds and Reasons of the Christian Religion* (1724), p. 43; *Discourse concerning Ridicule and Irony* (1729), pp. 8-9, 29.   Charles Leslie, *Best Answer Ever was Made* (1709), p. 8.   John Ozell, *Don Quixote* (Mod. Lib.), p. 664.

... If Mr. *Hoadly* knows that the Word *Power* is sometimes us'd to mean only *Force* or *Strength,* and sometimes to mean a Just and Lawful *Authority;* then he studiously and on Purpose sets himself to *Banter* Mankind, by the *Sound* only of this *Word.*[82]

Anthony Collins accuses his Popish adversaries of perpetrating real fictions:

But what are these *clearest Miracles God ever wrought?* Why, the most extravagant, whimsical, absurd, and ridiculous Legends and Stories imaginable; such as that of *St. Dominick,* who when the Devil came to him in the Shape of a *Monkey,* made him hold a Candle to him while he wrote, and keep it so long between his *Toes,* till it burnt them; and his keeping the Devil, who sometimes came to him in the shape of a *Flea,* and by skipping on the Leaves of his Book disturb'd his Reading, in that Shape, and using him for a Mark to know where he left off reading: Such as St. *Patrick*'s heating an Oven with Snow, and turning a Pound of Honey into a Pound of Butter: Such as *Christ*'s marrying Nuns, and playing at Cards with them. . . .

Are these, or such as these the *clearest Miracles God ever wrought?* Do such Miracles deserve a serious Regard? And shall the *Gravity* with which Mankind is thus banter'd out of their common Sense, excuse these Matters from *Ridicule?*[83]

Calling such tactics "banters" was of course a means of discrediting them. The truth of the charge was a matter of opinion and loyalty. But *banter* #1 could also be used to denote an outright lie provable by an appeal to facts. In the second part of *Don Quixote,* for instance, the Duchess made inquiries of Sancho about the first part:

I find that the good *Sancho* had never seen *Dulcinea* . . . nor carried her his Master's Letter, as having left the Table-Book behind him in *Sierra Morena;* how then durst he feign an Answer, and pretend he found her winnowing Wheat? A Fiction and Banter so injurious to the Reputation of the peerless *Dulcinea*. . . ![84]

It is a mildly interesting fact that although the Augustans never, so far as I know, used *irony* to mean the irony of Fate, they did on at least two occasions use *banter* in this way. On the third of August, 1714, Bolingbroke wrote to Swift: "The Earl of Oxford was removed on Tuesday; the Queen died on Sunday. What a

---

[82] Charles Leslie, *Best Answer Ever was Made* (1709), p. 8.
[83] Anthony Collins, *Discourse concerning Ridicule and Irony* (1729), pp. 8-9.
[84] John Ozell, *Don Quixote* (Mod. Lib.), p. 664.

world is this, and how does fortune banter us!"[85]   And in Ozell's
revision of *Don Quixote* appear these verses to the Don:

> May Fortune's Curse
> From bad to worse,
> Turn all thy best Adventures;
> Thy Joys to Dumps,
> Thy Brags to Thumps,
> And thy best Hopes to Banters.[86]

(2) *Banter* as ridicule.   *Banter* (‡1) as deception did not necessarily involve any other ridicule than the making a dupe of its
audience.   However, a satirist who can dupe his object at the same
time he is ridiculing him in other ways has managed to add insult
to injury, an accomplishment that warms his heart.   No great portion of Augustan satire did really deceive its objects, but a great
deal of it used fictitious structures and apparently innocuous indirection of a sort intended to mislead an audience momentarily,
until the light dawned, or to confuse an audience by its ambiguity
and complexity.   We have only to think of the *Tale of a Tub*,
Gulliver's Travels, the *History of John Bull*, Pope's essay on pas-
toral, Defoe's *Shortest Way*, and hosts of periodical essays and pamphlets to realize how in love with indirect attack the Augustans
were, and when we compare their attacks with the satires and pamphlets of the Restoration, to see that this love was a development
in artistic skill out of rather crude and obvious beginnings.   Since
so much eighteenth-century ridicule utilized at least to a degree the
device of banter (‡1) as deception, it need not surprise us that the
word *banter* was in turn extended to almost any sort of ridicule.   It is
clear, in fact, that the word came to be used in this sense (‡2)
more often than in the first.

Within the range indicated *banter* was occasionally used to denote a piece of ridicule that actually did deceive its object.   In this
use *banter* really fused the two senses of deception (‡1) and ridicule (‡2).   Bellegarde offers an instance:

'Tis a surprizing thing, that Conceitedness of Authors: They reduce all the Discourse, and most commonly very impertinently, to their

[85] Arbuthnot, *Works* (Aitken), p. 77.
[86] John Ozell, *Don Quixote* (Mod. Lib.), p. 825.

Works. Nothing but Flattery will content them; they praise themselves without Reserve, and drink, like *Nectar*, the ironical Encomiums that are made them: The Prejudice in Favour of their Merit, hinders them from perceiving how they are banter'd.[87]

Here "bantered" very evidently refers to the deception practiced— possibly only to that; but the deception is also the vehicle of a satiric attack, so that one feels the word *banter* was chosen be- cause it could refer to ridicule and deception at the same time. The *Tatler* gives us another instance of the same sort:

... when he has a mind thoroughly to correct a man, he never takes from him anything, but he allows him something for it; or else, he blames him for things wherein he is not defective, as well as for matters where- in he is. This makes a weak man believe he is in jest in the whole. The other day he told Beau Prim, who is thought impotent, that his mistress had declared she would not have him, because he was a sloven, and had committed a rape. The beau bit at the banter, and said very gravely, he thought to be clean was as much as was necessary; and that as to the rape, he wondered by what witchcraft that should come to her ears; but it had indeed cost him a hundred pounds to hush the affair.[88]

Such bantering was discussed briefly by the *Humourist:*

The Wit of this Set of Men consists either in the Scandal of the Ab- sent, . . . or else in a sly Artificial *Banter* of the Person present: This is an Abuse but of late Growth. It was born within a Court, and is generally confined to it. A Man must live there to become a Master in it. It consists in a certain low Sort of Craft, a Cant unworthy of an Honest Man, tho' it be every Day practis'd in the very Presence-Cham- ber itself. To excel in this worthy Mystery, you are to invent Expres- sions, which the Person to be abused may well enough construe in his own Favour, and which every one else may be able to expound in his Derision and Contempt. I would fain have Men of Honour be ashamed of this mean sort of Cousenage, which the most ordinary Tradesman is as capable of as themselves, and which an honest Foot-Soldier would heartily despise.[89]

Anthony Collins, discussing Charles II, illustrates his argument with an anecdote in which the bantering (#1) ridicule is clearly of a bur- lesque nature, yet the audience is meant actually to be deceived:

[87] Bellegarde, *Reflexions upon Ridicule* (1717), I, 170.
[88] *Tatler* (Aitken), II, 70-72 (No. 59, Aug. 25, 1709).
[89] *Humourist* II (1725), pp. 184-86.

It is well known how he banter'd the Presbyterian Ministers, who out of Interest came over to him at *Breda;* where they were placed in a Room next to his Majesty, and order'd to attend till his Majesty had done his Devotions; who, it seems, pray'd so artfully, and poured out so many of their Phrases, which he had learned when he was in *Scotland,* where he was forced to be present at religious Exercises of six or seven Hours a-day; and had practis'd among the *Huguenot* Ministers in *France,* who reported him to have a *sanctify'd Heart,* and to *speak the very Language of* Canaan. This *Ridicule* he *cover'd* with *Seriousness;* having at that time Occasion for those Ministers, who were then his great Instruments in reconciling the Nation to his *Restoration.* When he had no farther Occasion for them, he was open in his *Ridicule,* and would say, that *Presbyterianism was not a Religion for a Gentleman.*[90]

Again, in Pope's *Shakespeare*[91] the following interesting entries occur in the "Index of fictitious Persons":

Hamlet ... banters the Messengers the K. and Q. sent to him. Act. 3 Scene. 8
Hamlet ... examin'd by the King, banters him, and is order'd to go to *England.* Act. 4 Scene. 3
Hamlet ... banters a Fop who brought a Challenge from *Laertes,* and accepts it. Act. 5 Scene. 4

The first scene named is that (III.ii.303-405) in which, after the play has been acted, first Rosencrantz and Guildenstern and then Polonius come to fetch Hamlet to the Queen. Hamlet plays upon them unmercifully. His banter sounds superficially like the "fluently romantic nonsense, unintelligible gibberish" which Wood complained of in the Oxford scholars. But of course it is more than that. In such a speech as "We shall obey, were she ten times our mother" the seeming nonsense is the vehicle of bitter satire, and the episode with the recorder moves from satire concealed in banter (♯1) to outright attack. The same analysis can be made of Hamlet's scene with the King (IV.iii.17-55) and with Osric (V.ii.81-189), in which there is much obvious burlesque. As applied to these scenes *banter* seems to denote not deception exactly but mystification acting as the vehicle of satire and ridicule.

[90] Anthony Collins, *Discourse concerning Ridicule and Irony* (1729), pp. 44-45.
[91] Pope, *Shakespeare* (1728), VIII, Indexes.

Banter was used most often, however, simply to denote ridicule and laughing satire of any sort.[92] Thus Bellegarde's defense of fools against ridicule could be translated:

Concur not with those Banterers that droll upon their [the fools'] Stupidity, nor applaud their [the Banterers'] foolish Jests.

'Tis somewhat inhuman, by insulting Railleries to aggravate his Confusion, who has said a foolish Thing; and yet 'tis the Custom for some to laugh at the Cost of others, who are the ridiculous Subjects.

Such people, Bellegarde goes on, use all their attention "to observe the Incongruities that escape you, which she [the Character-example being used] catches up with a sneering Laughter...."[93] In December of 1733 the *Gentleman's Magazine*[94] quoted from the *Daily Courant:*

Banter is not capable of being answered by Reason; not, because it has any Strength in it; but because it runs out of all the Bounds of Reason and good Sense, by extravagantly joining together such Images, as have not in themselves any Manner of Similitude or Connection; by which Means all things are alike easy to be render'd ridicule, *by being represented only in an* absur'd [*sic*] *Dress.*—Christianity has suffer'd from no one thing so much as from *Ridicule* and *Buffoonery.* So far is it

[92] Edward Phillips, *New World of Words* (1706), "banter." William Wotton, *A Defense of the Reflections* (1705), pp. 48-49, 56, 60, 62-63, 68. Dennis, *Critical Works* (Hooker), II, 397. Defoe, *Explanation of the Shortest Way* (Trevelyan), p. 55. Bellegarde, *Reflexions upon Ridicule* (1717), I, 126. Bayle, *Dictionary* (1734-38), II, 117 col. 2. Shaftesbury, *Characteristics* (Robertson), II, 325. Bailey, *Dictionarium Britannicum* (1730), "banter." Swift, *Tale of a Tub* (Davis), p. 10. *A Complete Key to the Tale of a Tub* (1710), p. 7. Swift, *Poems* (Williams), III, 870-71. Swift, *Correspondence* (Ball), IV, 163-64, 166, 167-69, 213. Walter Moyle, *Works* (1726), p. 306. "An Essay on Gibing" (1727), pp. 5-7, 20. *Craftsman* (1731), I, 79-81, 102-4. *Gulliveriana* (1728), pp. 3, 316. John Oldmixon, *Logick and Rhetorick* (1728), pp. 27-28. Anthony Collins, *Discourse concerning Ridicule and Irony* (1729), pp. 25, 50, 63-64; pp. 59-60 and Charles Leslie, *Best Answer Ever was Made* (1709); p. 5 and Edward Stillingfleet, *Works* (1709), V, 27; p. 66 and Robert South, *Animadversions upon Sherlock* (1693), pp. 329-55. *Gentleman's Magazine*, III (July, 1733), 348; III (Dec., 1733), 641; IV (Dec., 1734), 700; V (Jan., 1735), 42. *The Bee*, IV, 234 (No. 45, Dec. 29-Jan. 5, 1733); VI, 195 (No. 70, June 22-29, 1734). John Constable, *Accuracy of Style* (1734), pp. 65-66. William Somervile, *The Chace* (1749), p. 113. Fielding, *Works* (Stephen), VI, 322-25. *Female Spectator* (1755), III, 319-20. John Ozell, *Don Quixote* (Mod. Lib.), p. 112. Letitia Pilkington, *Memoirs* I and II (1749), II, 21-22. John Brown, *Essays on Characteristics* (1751), pp. 49-50, 100-102. *Connoisseur* (1755), I, 161-62 (No. 27).

[93] Bellegarde, *Reflexions upon Ridicule* (1717), I, 126.

[94] III, 641.

from being true that *Ridicule is the surest Test of Truth and real Worth* &c. that it is evidently false both as to Religion and Politicks.

Here "Banter" occupies exactly the place usually reserved for "Ridicule" and obviously means neither more nor less. Some of the things called *banter* in this wide sense were pretty blunt and open. Here, for instance, is a *"Banter on* Pope, *as Translator of* Homer":

> *Homer* describing the divine Abodes,
> Mingled a crippl'd *Vulcan* with his Gods;
> And the same Bard, when he his Heroes sings,
> Crouds a *Thersites* in among his Kings;
> A crooked, petulant, malicious Wight,
> Unfit for Converse, Friendship, Love, or Fight;
> The Scum and Shame of *Greece,* whose Mother Nature
> Impress'd the Scoundrel strong on every Feature.
>   Should *Homer* now revive, and sing agen,
> Of Gods Immortal, or of God-like Men;
> As a strong Foil, he'd make his Murd'rer *P--e*
> The *Vulcan,* and *Thersites* of the Group.[95]

Letitia Pilkington's anecdote about an elderly admirer uses *banter* to denote blunt teasing:

> He used to hire me to write Love Letters to him, which, as a Proof of his being a young Man, he shewed at *White's.* . . . . They [two noblemen who frequented White's] bantered me on my Taste, in writing so many fine Things to an old Fellow, when so many young ones, themselves in particular, would be proud of them—I assured their Lordships, I would oblige them on the same Terms I did the Colonel, who always paid me handsomely for my Compliments.
> This turned all their Raillery on the Colonel. . . .[96]

Nevertheless, about many appearances of *banter* in which the primary referent is simply the spirit of ridicule we feel the overtone of deception adhering to the word. Since much ridicule and raillery did involve a degree of bamboozling, a general term for ridicule was bound to be associated with it. Consequently it is difficult to prove that *banter* any more than *raillery* or *drollery* emphasized the deceptive aspect of a piece of ridicule. Yet such a carryover would have been quite natural, and in some instances the contexts seem to justify saying that an author has chosen to use *banter*

[95] *Gulliveriana* (1728), p. 316.
[96] Letitia Pilkington, *Memoirs* I and II (1749), II, 21-22.

instead of *ridicule* or *raillery* or *satire* because *banter* emphasizes the fictitious structure or ambiguous complexity or misleading tack of the ridicule he is discussing. We may say this of Wotton's remark about an episode in the *Tale of a Tub*:

The ridiculous multiplying of the *Virgin Mary's Milk* among the Papists, he banters under the Allegory of a *Cow* which gave as much Milk at a Meal, as would fill Three thousand Churches. . . .[97]

Defoe's explanation of his *Shortest Way*, already quoted,[98] seems to be similarly indicative, and in the *Craftsman*'s critique on a contemporary pamphlet *banter* unquestionably refers not only to the spirit of ridicule but also to the semi-bantering (♯1) vehicle of that ridicule:

. . . his Design is to ridicule *Statesmen* and *political Matters* in the same Manner that *Cervantes* exposes Books of *Chivalry*, or Captain *Gulliver* the Writings of *Travellers*, by publishing a Collection of the most palpable *Falshoods*, *Absurdities*, and *Contradictions*, in a grave and serious Manner, with the same solemn Grimace and repeated Professions of *Truth* and *Simplicity*.

But I must observe, that this *Mock-Enquirer* is not only guilty of very unseasonable and indecent Mirth, by turning to Jest things of the highest Concern, but is also somewhat unhappy in his Imitation of those great Masters; for tho' the Account which he gives of publick Affairs is full as *romantick* and *incredible* as the *Adventures*, which they relate; yet he falls infinitely below them in Diction and manner of Writing; which in them is elegant and majestick; whereas in this Author the Stile is manifestly as *indigested* and *ungrammatical*, as the Tenour of his Book is *fabulous* and *improbable*; but perhaps this may be done on purpose, in order to make the *Banter* the stronger.[99]

The Bee No. 70 quotes the *Daily-Courant*'s complaint about the *Craftsman*'s veiling its criticism of those in power under parables and fictions.

As this Manner of *Writing* on *Topicks* the most important, is extremely *unjust* in its Nature, and eviden[t]ly *unfair* as to those against whom it is *pointed*, so as I have, already hinted, it is a *glaring Insult* on such as it is intended to move. It is neither better nor worse than telling them, "Gentlemen, you are a Pack of silly laughing Knaves, on whom Reason will do no Good, but who may be led by the Nose

[97] William Wotton, *A Defense of the Reflections* (1705), p. 56.
[98] See p. 210 above.
[99] *Craftsman* (1731), I, 79-81 (No. 14, Jan. 20, 1727).

with Banter. Therefore instead of saying, that the M--- robs the Treasury, for which you might be dull enough to expect Proof, we need but tell you, *Robin Goodfellow* skims the *Bowls*, and you swallow the Thing without chewing, as if *Innuendo's* were better than *Evidence*.[100]

Here again *banter* clearly refers not only to the verbal attack but to the techniques of indirection used in the attack.

Given this fusion in *banter* (♯2) of ridicule and various degrees of deception, we are not surprised that *irony* should be closely linked with *banter* in people's minds. Although the two words were often coupled with each other as though synonyms,[101] the use of such terms was so casual that this fact should not be given undue importance. It is more important that people actually used *banter* with considerable frequency to refer to blame-through-praise, the dominant referent of *irony*. Out of thirty-six passages chosen at random from the first half of the eighteenth century, passages in which *banter* as ridicule is applied to a perfectly clear verbal situation, slightly over half of the references are to instances of blame-by-praise. That is to say, the sort of ridicule for which people tended to use *banter* was blame-by-praise irony, although they also used *banter* for other types of ridicule—as indeed they did *irony* at times.

In relating *banter* to the other terms we have discussed it is possible to see why *banter* became an important word in the Augustan age. For the Augustans *wit* and *humour* circumscribed the necessary capacities of the creator, *raillery* and *ridicule* emphasized his purpose. They had a number of words to describe his techniques: *irony, burlesque, invective, sarcasm,* and so on. But many of these techniques put the author in a somewhat new relationship to his audience, a playful, disingenuous, deceptive relationship, and there was no suitable word to emphasize it. We have seen that both *irony* and *raillery*, especially in Shaftesbury, moved toward adopting a

---

[100] *The Bee,* VI, 195 (No. 70, June 22-29, 1734).
[101] Bayle, *Dictionary* (1734-38), III, 631. Shaftesbury, *Characteristics* (1714), Index under "Irony." Shaftesbury, *Characteristics* (Robertson), I, 44-45, 50-51. "An Essay on Gibing" (1727), pp. 5-10. Anthony Collins, *Discourse concerning Ridicule and Irony* (1729), pp. 55, 59, and *passim. Craftsman* (1731), I, 102-4 (No. 18, Feb. 7, 1727). John Oldmixon, *Logick and Rhetorick* (1728), pp. 21-28. William Guthrie, *Quinctilianus His Institutes* (1756), II, 29-30. *Female Spectator* (1755), III, 319-20.

sense of this deceptiveness, but it was *banter* that came to be widely used for it.

No doubt this scheme is too neat. The Augustans used this group of terms in a highly casual way. Yet the satiric spirit of the age demanded terms for discussing it, and as usual such a need was met, haphazardly at first, but it was met. The meaning of *humour* underwent basic modifications; *wit* underwent somewhat futile analysis; *ridicule* became a philosophy. *Burlesque* and *raillery* were imported from the Continent; *banter* was picked up from the streetcorners; *irony* came out of the classroom into the market place.

BIBLIOGRAPHY

[In the following Bibliography are listed the titles referred to in the text and other sources upon which this work is based. Not listed are bibliographies and general surveys which contributed nothing directly, sources examined which contain no relevant material, and books and articles on irony published since about 1760 not referred to in the text.]

Abercromby, David. *A Discourse of Wit*. London, 1686.

Addison, Joseph. *The Free-Holder*, No. 45, Friday, May 25, 1716. (Augustan Reprint Society, Ser. 1, Essays on Wit No. 1, 1946.)

Ainsworth, Robert. *Thesaurus Linguae Latinae compendiarius ... Improvements By Samual [sic] Patrick*. Third edition; London, 1751.

Aldridge, Alfred Owen. "Shaftesbury and the Test of Truth," *PMLA*, XL (1945), 129-60.

[Apsley, Allen.] *Order and Disorder: or, the World Made and Undone. Being Meditations upon the Creation and the Fall. . . .* London, 1679.

Arbuthnot, John. *Life and Works*. Edited by George A. Aitken. Oxford, 1892.

Aristophanes. *The Birds*. Translated by Benjamin Bickley Rogers. Loeb Classical Library.

—— *The Clouds*. Translated by Benjamin Bickley Rogers. Loeb Classical Library.

—— *The Wasps*. Translated by Benjamin Bickley Rogers. Loeb Classical Library.

Aristotle. *The "Art" of Rhetoric*. Translated by John Henry Freese. Loeb Classical Library.

—— *The Nicomachean Ethics*. Translated by H. Rackham. Loeb Classical Library.

Aristotle's Rhetoric; Or the True Grounds and Principles of Oratory; Shewing, The Right Art of Pleading and Speaking in full Assemblies and Courts of Judicature. Made English By the Translators of the Art of Thinking. In Four Books. London, 1686.

The Art of Complaisance or the Means to oblige in Conversation. London, 1673.

The Art of Railing at Great Men: being a Discourse upon Political Railers Ancient and Modern. London, 1723.

The Art of Speaking: Written in French by Messieurs Du Port Royal: In persuance of a former Treatise, Intituled, The Art of Thinking. Rendred into English. Second edition; London, 1708 (first published in 1676?).

Atkins, J. W. H. *English Literary Criticism: The Renascence.* London, 1947.

Bacon, Francis. "An Advertisement touching the Controversies of the Church of England." In *Collotype Facsimile & Type Transcript of an Elizabethan Manuscript Preserved at Alnwick Castle, Northumberland.* Edited by Frank J. Burgoyne. London, 1904.

———— *Certain Considerations For the better Establishment of the Church of England....* London, 1689 (first published in 1603).

———— Selections from *The Twoo Bookes of the Proficience and Advancement of Learning, Divine and Humane.* In J. E. Spingarn, *Critical Essays of the Seventeenth Century,* Vol. I. Oxford, 1908.

———— *Works.* Edited by James Spedding, R. L. Ellis, and D. D. Heath. London, 1857—.

Bailey, Nathan. *Dictionarium Britannicum: Or a more Compleat Universal Etymological English Dictionary Than any Extant.* London, 1730.

———— ————. London, 1736.

———— *An Universal Etymological English Dictionary.* Second edition; London, 1724.

———— ————. Sixth edition; London, 1733.

———— ————. Eleventh edition; London, 1745.

———— ————. Seventeenth edition; London, 1757.

———— ————. Twenty-first edition; London, 1766.

———— ————. Twenty-fifth edition; London, 1790.

———— *The Universal Etymological English Dictionary.* Vol. II. London, 1727.

———— *The New Universal Etymological English Dictionary.* Vol. II. Fifth edition; London, 1760.

Baldensperger, F. "Les Définitions de l'Humour." *Annales De L'Est,* pp. 177-200. 1900.

Barclay, Alexander, trans. *The Ship of Fools.* Edinburgh, 1874. Two volumes.

Baret, John. *An Alvearie or Quadruple Dictionarie, containing foure sundrie tongues: namelie, English, Latine, Greeke, and French. Newlie enriched....* [Second edition; 1580.]

Barker, Henry, trans. *The Polite Gentleman; or, Reflections Upon the several Kinds of Wit, viz. In Conversation, Books, and Affairs of the World. Done out of French.* London, 1700.

Barrow, Isaac. *Works.* Published by the Reverend Dr. Tillotson, Dean of Canterbury. Second edition; London, 1687. Three volumes.

Baxter, Richard. *A Paraphrase on the New Testament, with Notes, Doctrinal and Practical.* Third edition; London, 1701.

Bayle, Peter. *The Dictionary Historical and Critical.* Second edition; London, 1734-38. Five volumes.

—— *A General Dictionary, Historical and Critical: in which A New and Accurate Translation of that of the Celebrated Mr. Bayle is included.... By ... John Peter Bernard ... Thomas Birch ... John Lockman; and other Hands.* London, 1734-41. Ten volumes.

—— *An Historical and Critical Dictionary.* Translated into English.... London, 1710. Four volumes.

The Bee: or, Universal Weekly Pamphlet. February, 1733—June, 1735.

Bellegarde, L'Abbé de. *Models of Conversation For Persons of Polite Education.* London, 1765.

[——] *Reflexions upon Ridicule; or, What it is that makes a Man ridiculous, and the Means to avoid it.* Third edition; London, 1717 (first published in 1706).

Birney, Earle. "English Irony before Chaucer," *University of Toronto Quarterly,* VI (1936-37), 538-57.

Blackmore, Richard. *Essays upon Several Subjects.* Vol. I; London, 1716. Vol. II; London, 1717.

—— Preface to *Prince Arthur, an Heroick Poem.* 1695. In J. E. Spingarn, *Critical Essays of the Seventeenth Century,* Vol. III. Oxford, 1909.

—— *Satyr against Wit.* 1700. In J. E. Spingarn, *Critical Essays of the Seventeenth Century,* Vol. III. Oxford, 1909.

Blackwall, Anthony. *An Introduction to the Classics: containing a Short Discourse on their Excellencies; and Directions how to Study them to Advantage. With an Essay on the Nature and Use of those Emphatical and Beautiful Figures which give Strength and Ornament to Writing.* Fourth edition; London, 1728.

—— *The Sacred Classics Defended and Illustrated: or, An Essay Humbly offer'd towards proving the Purity, Propriety, and True Eloquence Of the Writers of the New Testament.* Second edition; London, 1727.

—— *The Sacred Classics Defended... The Second and Last Volume.* London, 1731.

Blount, Thomas. *The Academie of Eloquence. Containing a Compleat English Rhetorique....* London, 1654.

———— *Glossographia, or a Dictionary interpreting all such hard words ... as are now used in our refined English Tongue.* London, 1656.

———— ————. Fourth edition; London, 1674.

Boileau's Lutrin: A Mock-Heroic Poem. In Six Canto's. Render'd into English Verse. To which is prefix'd some Account of Boileau's Writings, and this Translation. By N. Rowe Esq. London, 1708.

Bolton, Edmund. *Hypercritica, or a Rule of Judgement, for writing or reading our History's.* 1722. In J. E. Spingarn, *Critical Essays of the Seventeenth Century,* Vol. I. Oxford, 1908.

Bond, Richmond P. *English Burlesque Poetry 1700-1750.* Cambridge, Mass., 1932.

A briefe examination for the tyme, of a certaine declaration, lately put in print in the name and defence of certaine Ministers in London, refusyng to weare the apparell prescribed by the lawes and orders of the Realme. [1566.]

Brinsley, John. *The first Booke of Tullies Offices Translated Grammatically....* London, 1631.

Brown, John. "Essay on Satire." In *A Collection of Poems,* Vol. III. London, 1770.

———— *Essays on the Characteristics.* London, 1751.

Brown, Tom. *Amusements Serious and Comical. Letters on Several Occasions.* Edited by Arthur L. Hayward. London, 1927.

———— *The Remains of Mr. Tho. Brown, Serious and Comical, in Prose and Verse. In One Volume. Collected from scarce Papers and Original Mss. Which makes his Works Compleat....* London, 1720.

———— *Twenty Select Colloquies out of Erasmus Roterodamus. By Sir Roger L'Estrange. To which are added, Seven New Colloquies, As Also The Life of Erasmus. By Mr. Brown.* London, 1699.

[————] *Wit for Money: or, Poet Stutter....* London, 1691.

———— *The Works of Mr. Thomas Brown, Serious and Comical, In Prose and Verse.* Fifth edition; London, 1720. Four volumes.

Browne, Thomas. *Christian Morals ... Published from the Original and Correct Manuscript of the Author; by John Jeffery, D.D. Arch-Deacon of Norwich.* Cambridge, 1716.

———— *Pseudodoxia Epidemica or Enquiries into Very Many Received Tenents and Commonly Presumed Truths.* In *Works.* Edited by Charles Sayle. London, 1904.

Bruyère, Jean de la. *The Character, or the Manners of the Age ... Made English by several hands. With the Characters of Theophrastus, Translated from the Greek. And a Prefatory Discourse to them, by Monsieur de la Bruyere.* London, 1699 (a separate title page for the *Characters of Theophrastus* dated 1698).

Budgell, Eustace, trans. *The Moral Characters of Theophrastus.* Second edition; London, 1714 (first published in 1713).

Bullitt, John M. *Jonathan Swift and the Anatomy of Satire.* Cambridge, Mass., 1953.

Bullokar, John. *An English Expositor: Teaching the Interpretation of the hardest words used in our Language.* . . . London, 1621.

—— *The English Expositor Improv'd . . . And now carefully Revised.* . . . *By R. Browne.* . . . Twelfth edition; London, 1719.

Bulstrode, Richard. *Miscellaneous Essays.* London, 1715.

B[ulwer], J[ohn]. *Chirologia: or the Naturall Language of the Hand. Composed of the Speaking Motions, and Discoursing Gestures thereof. Whereunto is added Chironomia: Or, the Art of Manuall Rhetoricke.* London, 1644.

—— *Pathomyotomia or a Dissection Of the significative Muscles of the Affections of the Minde.* London, 1649.

Burton, Robert. *The Anatomy of Melancholy, What It Is.* Oxford, 1621.

—— *The Anatomy of Melancholy.* Edited by Floyd Dell and Paul Jordan-Smith. New York [1927?].

Butler, Samuel. *Characters and Passages from Note-Books.* Edited by A. R. Waller. Cambridge, 1908.

Cambridge, Richard Owen. *The Scribleriad: An Heroic Poem In Six Books.* London, 1752.

—— *Works.* London, 1803.

Casa, Giovanni della. *Galateo, of Manners and Behaviours in Familiar Conversation.* Translated by Robert Peterson. 1576. Edited by Herbert J. Reid. 1892.

Catherall, Samuel. Εἰϰων Σωϰρατιϰη *or, A Portraiture of Socrates, Extracted out of Plato. In Blank Verse.* Oxford, 1717.

Cawdry, Robert. *A Table Alphabeticall, conteyning and teaching the true writing, and understanding of hard usuall English wordes, borrowed from the Hebrew, Greeke, Latine, or French. etc. With the interpretation thereof by plaine English words.* . . . London, 1604. (Modern Language Association of America, photographic facsimile.)

Censor, The. [Lewis Theobald.] London, 1717. Three volumes.

Chaloner, Thomas, trans. *The praise of Folie.* London, 1549.

Chambers, Ephraim. *Cyclopaedia: or, an Universal Dictionary of Arts and Sciences.* London, 1728. Two volumes.

—— ——. Fifth edition; London, 1741, 1743. Two volumes.

—— *Cyclopaedia: or, an Universal Dictionary of Arts and Sciences*

... *revised by Abraham Rees, D.D.* London, 1778-88. Four volumes.

Chandler, Samuel. *The History of Persecution, In Four Parts.* London, 1736.

———— *Reflections on the Conduct of the Modern Deists, In their late Writings against Christianity.* ... London, 1727.

Chesterfield, Philip Dormer Stanhope, Fourth Earl of. *Letters.* Edited by Bonamy Dobrée. London, 1932. Six volumes.

———— *Letters ... to His Son.* Edited by Charles Strachey with Notes by Annette Calthrop. New York, 1901. Two volumes.

Chevalier, Haakon M. *The Ironic Temper: Anatole France and His Time.* New York, 1932.

Cibber, Colley. *Dramatic Works.* Vol. III. London, 1760.

Cicero. *Academica.* Translated by H. Rackham. Loeb Classical Library.

———— *Brutus.* Translated by G. L. Hendrickson. *Orator.* Translated by H. M. Hubbell. Loeb Classical Library.

———— *De officiis.* Translated by Walter Miller. Loeb Classical Library.

———— *On Oratory and Orators with his Letters to Quintus and Brutus.* Translated by J. S. Watson. London, 1862. (Bohn Library.)

Clark, Donald Lemen. *Rhetoric and Poetry in the Renaissance.* New York, 1922.

Clarke, John. *An Essay upon Study.* London, 1731.

Clarke, M. L. *Greek Studies in England 1700-1830.* Cambridge, 1945.

Cobb, Samuel. "A Discourse on Criticism" and "Of Poetry" from *Poems on Several Occasions.* 1707. (Augustan Reprint Society, Ser. 2, Essays on Poetry and Language No. 1, 1946.)

Cocker, Edward. *Cocker's English Dictionary.* ... London, 1704.

———— ————. Third edition; London, 1724.

Cockeram, Henry. *The English Dictionarie: or, An Interpreter of hard English Words.* ... Second edition; London, 1626.

———— ————. Sixth edition; London, 1639.

———— ————. London, 1623. Reprinted with a prefatory note by C. B. Tinker. New York, 1930.

Cockman, Thomas. *Tully's Offices, In English.* Third edition; London, 1714 (first published in 1699).

Coles, Elisha. *A Dictionary English-Latin, and Latin-English.* Second edition; London, 1679.

———— *An English Dictionary.* London, 1676.

———— *An English Dictionary. Newly Corrected, and much Improved.* London, 1732.

[Collins, Anthony.] *A Discourse concerning Ridicule and Irony in Writing, in a Letter To the Reverend Dr. Nathanael Marshall.* London, 1729.

[————] *A Discourse of the Grounds and Reasons of the Christian Religion.* London, 1724.

[————] *A Letter To the Reverend Dr. Rogers, on Occasion of his Eight Sermons, concerning the Necessity of Divine Revelation, and the Preface prefix'd to them.* London, 1727.

[————] *Priestcraft in Perfection: or, a Detection of the Fraud of Inserting and Continuing this Clause (The Church hath Power to Decree Rites and Ceremonys, and Authority in Controversys of Faith) In the Twentieth Article of the Articles of the Church of England.* London, 1710.

[————] *The Scheme of Literal Prophecy Considered; in a View of the Controversy, Occasioned by a late Book, intitled, A Discourse of the Grounds and Reasons.* . . . London, 1727.

A Complete Key to the Tale of a Tub. London, 1710.

Congreve, William. *Concerning Humour in Comedy.* 1695. In J. E. Spingarn, *Critical Essays of the Seventeenth Century,* Vol. III. Oxford, 1909.

Connoisseur, The. London, 1755. Two volumes.

Constable, John. *Reflections upon Accuracy of Style.* London, 1734.

Cooper, John Gilbert. *The Life of Socrates.* . . . Second edition; London, 1750.

Cooper, Lane. *An Aristotelian Theory of Comedy with an Adaptation of the Poetics and a Translation of the 'Tractatus Coislinianus.'* New York, 1922.

Cooper, Thomas. *Thesaurus Linguae Romanae & Britannicae.* . . . London, 1578.

Cornford, Francis Macdonald. *The Origin of Attic Comedy.* Cambridge, 1934.

Cotgrave, Randle. *A Dictionarie of the French and English Tongues.* London, 1611.

———— *A Dictionarie of the French and English Tongues. Whereunto is also annexed a most copious Dictionarie, of the English set before the French. By R.* [*obert*] *S.* [*herwood*] *L.* [*ondoner*]. London, 1632.

[Cotton, Charles.] *Burlesque upon Burlesque: or, The Scoffer Scoft. Being some of Lucians Dialogues Newly put into English Fustian.* . . . London, 1675.

Coverdale, Miles. *A confutacion of that treatise which one John Standish made agaynst the protestacion of D. Barnes in the yeare M.D. XL.* In *Remains of Myles Coverdale.* Edited by the Rev. George Pearson. Cambridge, 1846. (Parker Society.)

Cowley, Abraham. Preface to *Poems*. 1656. In J. E. Spingarn, *Critical Essays of the Seventeenth Century*, Vol. II. Oxford, 1908.

Craftsman, The. 1726—.

Craftsman, The. Vols. I-VII. London, 1731.

Craftsman, The. Vols. VIII-XIII. London, 1737.

Craik, Henry. *The Life of Jonathan Swift.* Second edition; London, 1894. Two volumes.

Cranmer, Thomas. *An Answer unto A crafty and sophisticall cavillation devised by M. Steven Gardiner....* London, 1551.

Croll, Morris W. " 'Attic Prose' in the Seventeenth Century," *Studies in Philology*, XVIII (1921), 79-128.

Cross, Wilbur L. *The History of Henry Fielding.* New Haven, 1918. Three volumes.

Dacier, André. *The Works of Plato, With an Account of his Life, Philosophy, Morals, and Politicks. Together with a Translation of his choicest Dialogues.... Illustrated with Notes. By M. Dacier. Translated from the French.* London, 1701. Two volumes.

Danett, Thomas, trans. *The History of Comines Englished by Thomas Danett anno 1596.* With an Introduction by Charles Whibley. Vol. II. London, 1897.

Daniel, George. *The Poems of George Daniel.* Edited by Alexander B. Grosart. 1878. Four volumes.

Davies, Myles. *Athenae Britannicae: or, A Critical History of the Oxford and Cambridge Writers and Writings....* London, 1716. Two volumes.

Davis, Herbert. *The Satire of Jonathan Swift.* New York, 1947.

Day, Angel. *The English Secretorie: Or, plaine and direct Method, for the enditing of all manner of Epistles or Letters.... Studiously, now corrected, refined & amended ... Together (also) with the second part....* London, 1595 (the first part first published in 1586).

The D--n of W---r still the same: Or, His New Defence of the Lord Bishop of Bangor's Sermon, &c. consider'd As the Performance of a Great Critick, a Man of Sense, and a Man of Probity. London, 1720. (On authorship see Richard Steele, *Correspondence* [Blanchard], p. 118.)

[De Britaine, William.] *Humane Prudence, or the Art By which a Man may Raise Himself and his Fortune to Grandeur.* Eighth edition; London, 1700.

Dedekind, Friedrich. *Grobianus; or, the Compleat Booby. An Ironical Poem ... Done into English, from the Original Latin of Friderick Dedekindus, By Roger Bull, Esq.* London, 1739.

Defoe, B. N. *A Compleat English Dictionary.* Westminster, 1735.

Defoe, Daniel. *The Compleat English Gentleman.* Edited by Karl D. Bülbring. London, 1890.

────── *Explanation of the Shortest Way with the Dissenters.* In *Select Documents for Queen Anne's Reign.* . . . Edited by G. M. Trevelyan. Cambridge, 1929.

[──────] *The Pacificator. A Poem.* London, 1700.

────── *The True-Born Englishman.* London, 1910.

Delaney, Patrick. *Observations upon Lord Orrery's Remarks on the Life and Writings of Dr. Jonathan Swift.* London, 1754.

Demosthenes. *Philippics.* Translated by J. H. Vince. Loeb Classical Library.

────── *Several Orations of Demosthenes, To encourage the Athenians To Oppose the Exorbitant Power of Philip of Macedon. English'd from the Greek by several Hands.* London, 1702.

Dennis, John. *Critical Works.* Edited by Edward Niles Hooker. Baltimore, 1939, 1943. Two volumes.

[Dodd, William.] *A Day in Vacation at College. A Burlesque Poem.* London, 1751.

Douay, English College of. *The Second Tome of the Holie Bible Faithfully Translated into English.* . . . Rouen, 1635.

Dove, John. *Atheism Defined and confuted by undeniable Arguments; Drawne from Scripture & Reason.* London, 1656. [Second title page:] *A Confutation of Atheisme.* London, 1640 (first published in 1605).

Draper, John W. "The Theory of the Comic in Eighteenth-Century England," *JEGP,* XXXVII (1938), 207-23.

Drayton, Michael. *Epistle to Henry Reynolds, of Poets and Poesie.* 1627. In J. E. Spingarn, *Critical Essays of the Seventeenth Century,* Vol. I. Oxford, 1908.

Dryden, John. *The Best of Dryden.* Edited by Louis I. Bredvold. New York, 1939.

────── *Essays.* Edited by W. P. Ker. Oxford, 1900.

────── "The Life of Lucian, A Discourse on his Writings" in *The Works of Lucian, Translated from the Greek, by several Eminent Hands.* London, 1710-11. Four volumes.

────── Life of Plutarch in *Plutarch's Lives. Translated From the Greek by Several Hands.* London, 1683-86. Five volumes.

────── *The Prologues and Epilogues.* Edited by William Bradford Gardner. New York, 1951.

────── *Works.* Edited by Sir Walter Scott and George Saintsbury. London, 1882-93. Eighteen volumes.

Dyche, Thomas. *A New General English Dictionary . . . Originally begun by the late Reverend Mr. Thomas Dyche . . . and now finished by William Pardon.* . . . Twelfth edition; London, 1765.

Eachard, John. *The Grounds & Occasions of the Contempt of the Clergy and Religion Enquired into. In a Letter written to R. L.* London, 1670.

────── *Some Opinions of Mr Hobbs Considered in a Second Dialogue between Philautus and Timothy.* London, 1673.

Earbery, Matthias. *A Serious Admonition to Doctor Kennet, in order to Perswade him to forbear the Character of an Impartial Historian.* London [n.d].

Edwards, John. *A Discourse Concerning the Authority, Stile, and Perfection of the Books of the Old and New Testament.* Vol. III. London, 1695.

────── *Some New Discoveries of the Uncertainty, Deficiency, and Corruptions of Human Knowledge and Learning ... To which is added, A Defence of Sharp Reflections and Censures on Writers and Their Opinions....* London, 1714.

Eliot, John. *Ortho-epia Gallica. Eliots Fruits for the French: Enterlaced with a double new Invention, which teacheth to speake truely, speedily and volubly the French-tongue.* London, 1593.

Elyot, Thomas. *Bibliotheca Eliotae ... the second tyme enriched ...* by Thomas Cooper.... London, 1552.

────── *Bibliotheca Eliotae ... by Thomas Cooper the third tyme corrected....* London, 1559.

────── *The Boke Named the Governour.* Edited by H. H. S. Croft. London, 1880. Two volumes.

Erasmus. *The Praise of Folly.* Translated by John Wilson. 1668. Edited by Mrs. P. S. Allen. Oxford, 1925.

"An Essay on Gibing." In *Miscellanea*, Vol. II, pp. 1-22. London, 1727.

An Essay on the New Species of Writing founded by Mr. Fielding: With a Word or Two upon the Modern State of Criticism. London, 1751.

An Essay on Wit: To which is annexed, A Dissertation on Antient and Modern History. London, 1748. (Augustan Reprint Society, Ser. 1, Essays on Wit No. 2, 1946.)

An Essay upon Sublime. Translated from the Greek of ... Longinus ... Compar'd with the French of ... Boileau. Oxford, 1698.

An Essay upon the Taste and Writings of the Present Times ... Occasion'd by a late Volume of Miscellanies by A. Pope, Esq.; and Dr. Swift. Inscrib'd to the Right Honourable Sir Robert Walpole. London, 1728.

Essays Divine, Moral, and Political ... By the Author of the Tale of a Tub, sometime the Writer of the Examiner, and the Original Inventor of the Band-Box-Plot. London, 1714.

Farquhar, George. *A Discourse upon Comedy, in Reference to the English Stage.* 1702. In W. H. Durham, *Critical Essays of the Eighteenth Century 1700-1725.* New Haven, 1915.

Felltham, Owen. *Resolves: Divine, Moral, Political. The Eighth Impression.* London, 1661.

[Felton, Henry.] *A Dissertation On Reading the Classics, And Forming a Just Style. Written in the Year 1709.* London, 1713.

The Female Spectator. [Eliza Haywood.] Fifth edition; London, 1775 (first issued in 1744-46). Four volumes.

Fenelon, Salignac de la M. *Dialogues concerning Eloquence ... Translated from the French ... By William Stevenson.* Glasgow, 1750.

Ferguson, Robert. *The Interest of Reason in Religion; with the Import & Use of Scripture-Metaphors....* London, 1675.

Fielding, Henry. *Amelia.* London [n.d.] (Navarre Society, Ltd., three volumes.)

[———] *Common Sense: or, the Englishman's Journal.* London, 1738.

——— *The Covent-Garden Journal.* Edited by G. E. Jensen. New Haven, 1915. Two volumes.

[———] *The Jacobite's Journal.* December 5, 1747———.

——— *Jonathan Wild.* London [n.d.]. (Navarre Society, Ltd.)

——— *Joseph Andrews.* New York, 1939. (Modern Library.)

[———] *A Proper Answer To A Late Scurrilous Libel, entitled, An Apology for the Conduct of a late celebrated Second-rate Minister.* Second edition; London, 1748.

——— *Tom Jones.* Modern Library.

——— *Works.* Edited by Leslie Stephen. London, 1822. Ten volumes.

——— and Edward Young. *Plutus, the God of Riches. A Comedy. Translated from the Original Greek of Aristophanes....* London, 1742.

[Fielding, Sarah.] *The Cry: A New Dramatic Fable.* Vol. III. London, 1754.

Fiske, George Converse. "The Plain Style in the Scipionic Circle," *University of Wisconsin Studies in Language and Literature,* No. 3 (1919), pp. 62-106.

Flecknoe, Richard. *Enigmaticall Characters, All Taken to the Life, from severall Persons, Humours, & Dispositions.* 1658.

F.[lecknoe], R.[ichard]. *Sixtynine Enigmatical Characters, All Very exactly drawn to the Life....* Second edition; London, 1665. (Augustan Reprint Society, Ser. 1, Essays on Wit No. 2, 1946.)

Florio, John. *A Worlde of Wordes, Or Most copious, and exact Dictionarie in Italian and English....* London, 1598.

Fog's Weekly Journal, No. 239, Saturday, June 2, 1733.

The Fox with his Fire-brand Unkennell'd and Insnar'd: Or, a Short Answer to Mr. Daniel Foe's Shortest Way with the Dissenters. As also to his Brief Explanation of the same. London, 1703.

Foxe, John. *Actes and Monuments.* 1596.

Fraunce, Abraham. *The Arcadian Rhetorike.* London [1588].

The Free-Holder, or Political Essays. [Joseph Addison.] London, 1716.

Fuller, Thomas. *The Holy State. The Profane State.* Cambridge, 1642.

———— *Two Sermons: The first, Comfort in Calamitie. . . . The other, The Grand Assizes. . . .* London, 1654.

Gally, Henry. *The Moral Characters of Theophrastus. Translated from The Greek, with Notes. To which is prefix'd A Critical Essay on Characteristic-Writings.* London, 1725.

Gascoigne, George. *Certayne Notes of Instruction.* London, 1575. In G. Gregory Smith, *Elizabethan Critical Essays*, Vol. I. Oxford, 1904.

Gay, John. *The Present State of Wit, in a Letter to a Friend in the Country.* London, 1711. (Augustan Reprint Society, Ser. 1, Essays on Wit No. 3, 1947.)

Gayton, Edmund. *Festivous Notes on the History and Adventures Of the Renowned Don Quixote. Revised, with Corrections, Alterations, and Additions . . . By the Editor.* London, 1768.

———— *Pleasant Notes upon Don Quixot.* London, 1654.

Geddes, James. *An Essay on the Composition and Manner of Writing of the Antients, particularly Plato.* Glasgow, 1748.

The Gentleman's Journal: or the Monthly Miscellany. January, 1692 —November, 1694.

The Gentleman's Magazine. 1731————.

Gildon, Charles. "To my Honoured and Ingenious Friend Mr. Harrington, for the Modern Poets against the Ancients." 1694. In W. H. Durham, *Critical Essays of the Eighteenth Century 1700-1725.* New Haven, 1915.

[Glanvill, Joseph.] *A Blow at Modern Sadducism In some Philosophical Considerations about Witchcraft . . . With some Reflections on Drollery, and Atheisme.* London, 1668.

———— *A Seasonable Defence of Preaching: and the Plain Way of it.* London, 1678.

[Gother, John.] *Good Advice to the Pulpits, Deliver'd in a few Cautions For the keeping up the Reputation of those Chairs, And Preserving the Nation in Peace.* London, 1687.

Goulston, Theodore. *Aristotelis de Rhetorica. . . .* London, 1619.

Granger, Thomas. *Syntagma Logicum, or, The Divine Logike. Serving especially for the use of Divines in the practise of preaching, and for the further helpe of judicious Hearers, and generally for all.* London, 1620.

Grant, Mary A. *The Ancient Rhetorical Theories of the Laughable.* Madison, Wisc., 1924. (University of Wisconsin Studies in Language and Literature, No. 21.)

Granville, George, Lord Lansdowne. *An Essay upon Unnatural Flights in Poetry.* 1701. In J. E. Spingarn, *Critical Essays of the Seventeenth Century,* Vol. III. Oxford, 1909.

Gray, Charles Harold. *Theatrical Criticism in London to 1795.* New York, 1931.

Greville, Fulke. *The Life of the Renowned Sr Philip Sidney.* London, 1652.

Grey, Zachary. *Critical, Historical, and Explanatory Notes upon Hudibras . . . with A Dissertation upon Burlesque Poetry. By Montagu Bacon. . . .* London, 1752.

Grimalde, Nicolas, trans. *Marcus Tullius Ciceroes thre bookes of duties, to Marcus his sonne.* [London] 1558 (first published in 1553).

The Grub-street Journal. 1730———.

The Guardian. In *The British Essayists,* Vols. XIII-XV. Edited by Alexander Chalmers. Boston, 1856.

Guazzo, Steeven. *The Civile Conversation of M. Steeven Guazzo. . . .* With an Introduction by Sir Edward Sullivan. London & New York, 1925. Two volumes. (Tudor Translations, Second series, VII.)

Guilletiere [Georges Guillet de St. Georges]. *An Account of a Late Voyage to Athens, containing the Estate both Ancient and Modern of that Famous City. . . . Now Englished.* London, 1676.

Gulliver Decypher'd: or Remarks On a late Book, intitled, Travels into several Remote Nations of the World. By Capt. Lemuel Gulliver. Vindicating The Reverend Dean on whom it is maliciously Father'd. Second edition; London [1726?].

Gulliveriana: or, a Fourth Volume of Miscellanies. Being a Sequel of the Three Volumes, published by Pope and Swift. To which is added, Alexanderiana; or, A Comparison between the Ecclesiastical and Poetical Pope. And many Things, in Verse and Prose, relating to the latter. [Jonathan Smedley.] London, 1728.

Guthrie, William, trans. *M. Fabius Quinctilianus His Institutes of Eloquence. . . .* London, 1756. Two volumes.

——— *The Morals of Cicero.* London, 1744.

——— *M. T. Cicero De Oratore. . . .* Boston, 1882 (first published in 1742?).

—— *M. T. Cicero His Offices....* London, 1755.

Guyse, John. *The Scripture-notion of preaching Christ further clear'd and vindicated....* London, 1730.

H[all], J[ohn]. Περὶ ὕψους, *Or Dionysius Longinus of the Height of Eloquence. Rendred out of the Originall.* London, 1652.

[Hall, Joseph.] *Virgidemiarum, Sixe Bookes....* London, 1597.

—— *Works.* Oxford (D. A. Talboys), 1837. Twelve volumes.

Hall, Thomas. *Vindiciae Literarum, The Schools Guarded: or, the Excellency and Usefulnesse of Humane Learning in Subordination to Divinity, and preparation to the Ministry; As Also, Rules for the expounding of the Holy Scriptures: With a Synopsis of the most materiall Tropes and Figures contained in the Sacred Scriptures.* London, 1655.

[Hanmer, Thomas?] *Some Remarks on the Tragedy of Hamlet....* 1736. (Augustan Reprint Society, Ser. 3, Essays on the Stage No. 3, 1947.)

[Hare, Francis.] *The Difficulties and Discouragements Which attend the Study of the Scriptures In the Way of Private Judgment; Represented in a Letter to a Young Clergyman ... To which is annexed, The Censure of the Lower House of Convocation upon This Book.* Seventh edition; London, 1716 (first published in 1714).

—— *A New Defence of the Lord Bishop of Bangor's Sermon on John xviii.30.* London, 1720.

Harington, Sir John. *A Preface, or rather a Briefe Apologie of Poetrie, and of the Author and Translator,* prefixed to Harington's translation of *Orlando Furioso.* 1591. In G. Gregory Smith, *Elizabethan Critical Essays,* Vol. II. Oxford, 1904.

Harris, John. *Lexicon Technicum: or, an Universal English Dictionary of Arts and Sciences....* London, 1704.

—— ——. Vol. I. Third edition; London, 1726.

Harte, Walter. *An Essay on Satire, Particularly on the Dunciad. To which is added, A Discourse on Satires, Arraigning Persons by Name. By Monsieur Boileau.* London, 1730.

Hartley, David. *Observations on Man, His Frame, His Duty, and His Expectations.* London, 1749.

Harvey, Gabriel. *Letter-Book.* Edited by E. J. L. Scott. 1884. (Camden Society, New ser., Vol. 33.)

—— *Marginalia.* Edited by G. C. Moore Smith. Stratford-upon-Avon, 1913.

—— *Works.* Edited by Alexander B. Grosart. 1884. Three volumes. (Huth Library.)

Healey, John. *Epictetus Manuall. Cebes Table. Theophrastus Characters.* London, 1616.

Heltzel, Virgil Barney. "Chesterfield and the Tradition of the Ideal Gentleman." Unpublished Ph.D. thesis, University of Chicago, 1925.

Henley, John. *An Oration on Grave Conundrums, and Serious Buffoons; Justifying Burlesque Teaching ... Being No. VI of Oratory-Transactions.* London, 1729.

Herbert, Thomas. *Some Years Travels into Divers Parts of Africa and Asia the Great.* Fourth impression; London, 1677.

Heywood, Thomas. *Pleasant Dialogues and Dramma's, Selected out of Lucian, Erasmus, Textor, Ovid, &c.* ... London, 1637.

Hickes, Francis. *Certaine Select Dialogues of Lucian: Together with His True Historie, Translated from the Greeke.* ... *Whereunto is added the life of Lucian ... by T.*[homas] *H.*[ickes]. ... Oxford, 1634.

Hobbes, Thomas. *The Answer ... to Sr. Will. D'Avenant's Preface Before Gondibert.* 1650. In J. E. Spingarn, *Critical Essays of the Seventeenth Century,* Vol. II. Oxford, 1908.

———— *The Art of Rhetoric Plainly Set Forth.* London, 1681. In *English Works,* Vol. VI. Edited by Sir William Molesworth. London, 1840.

[————] *A Briefe of the Arte of Rhetorique. Containing in substance all that Aristotle hath written in his Three Bookes of that subject, Except onely what is not applicable to the English Tongue.* London [1637?].

———— *Hobbes's Leviathan. Reprinted from the Edition of 1651.* With an Essay by W. G. Pogson Smith. Oxford, 1909.

Hoby, Thomas, trans. *The Book of the Courtier by Count Baldassare Castiglione Done into English ... 1561.* Everyman's Library.

Holland, Philemon, trans. *The Philosophie, commonlie called, The Morals Written by the learned Philosopher Plutarch of Chaeronea.* London, 1603.

Holyoke, Francis. *Dictionarium Etymologicum Latinum ... Lastly* [John] *Riders Dictionarie.* ... Oxford, 1627.

Hooker, Edward N. "Humour in the Age of Pope," *Huntington Library Quarterly,* XI (1947-48), 361-85.

Hooper, John. *A Declaration of the Ten Holy Commandments of Almighty God.* 1548. In *Early Writings of John Hooper, D.D. Lord Bishop of Gloucester and Worcester, Martyr, 1555.* Cambridge, 1843. (Parker Society.)

Hoskins, John. *Directions for Speech and Style.* Edited by Hoyt H. Hudson. Princeton, 1935. (Princeton Studies in English, No. 12.)

An Hue and Cry after Dr. S---t; Occasion'd by a True and Exact Copy of Part of his own Diary, found in his Pocket-Book, wherein he has set down a faithful Account of himself, and of all that happen'd to him for the last Week of his Life. Second edition; London, 1714.

Hughes, John. *Of Style.* 1735 (first published in 1698). In W. H. Durham, *Critical Essays of the Eighteenth Century 1700-1725.* New Haven, 1915.

Huloet, Richard. *Huloets Dictionarie, newelye corrected, amended, set in order and enlarged. . . . And in eche place fit Phrases, gathered out of the best Latin Authors. Also the Frenche thereunto annexed. . . . By John Higgins late student in Oxeforde.* London, 1572.

Hultzén, Lee Sisson. "Aristotle's Rhetoric in England to 1600." Unpublished Ph.D. thesis, Cornell University, 1932.

The Humourist. [Thomas Gordon.] Vol. I; London, 1720. Vol. II; London, 1725.

Hutcheson, Francis. *Reflections upon Laughter, and Remarks upon The Fable of the Bees. Carefully corrected.* Glasgow, 1750 (first published in 1726).

Hutton, Henry. *Follie's Anatomie: or Satyres & Satyricall Epigrams . . . From the original tract printed in 1619.* Edited by E. F. Rimbault. London, 1842. (Percy Society.)

Jarvis, Charles, trans. *The Life and Exploits Of the ingenious gentleman Don Quixote De La Mancha.* London, 1742. Two volumes.

[Jeffery, Thomas.] *A Review of the Controversy Between the Author of a Discourse of the Grounds and Reasons of the Christian Religion, And his Adversaries.* London, 1726.

Johnson, Samuel. *A Dictionary of the English Language.* Second edition; London, 1755-56. Two volumes.

———— *Lives of the English Poets.* Edited by George Birkbeck Hill. Oxford, 1905. Three volumes.

Jones, Richard F. "The Attack on Pulpit Eloquence in the Restoration: An Episode in the Development of the Neo-Classical Standard for Prose," *JEGP*, XXX (1931), 188-217.

Jonson, Ben. Dedicatory epistle before *Volpone.* 1607. In J. E. Spingarn, *Critical Essays of the Seventeenth Century*, Vol. I. Oxford, 1908.

———— *Works.* Edited by C. H. Herford and Percy Simpson. Oxford, 1925————. Ten volumes.

K., J. [John Kersey?]. *A New English Dictionary.* Third edition; London, 1731.

[Kennett, White, trans.] *Moriae Encomium: or, a Panegyrick upon Folly. Written in Latin by Desiderius Erasmus. Done into English.* . . . London, 1709 (first published in 1683).

[King, William.] *Some Remarks on the Tale of a Tub* . . . *By the Author of the Journey to London.* London, 1704.

Knowles, Edwin B., Jr. "Allusions to *Don Quixote* before 1660," *Philological Quarterly,* XX (1941), 573-86.

———— *Four Articles on Don Quixote in England.* New York, 1941.

Lawson, John. *Lectures Concerning Oratory. Delivered in Trinity College, Dublin.* Third edition; Dublin, 1760.

[Leigh, Richard.] *The Transproser Rehears'd: or the Fifth Act of Mr. Bayes's Play.* . . . Oxford, 1673.

Le Roux, Philibert Joseph. *Dictionaire Comique, Satyrique, Critique, Burlesque, Libre & Proverbial.* . . . Alion, 1735.

———— *Dictionaire Comique, Satyrique, Critique, Burlesque, Libre & Proverbial.* Amsterdam, 1750.

[Leslie, Charles.] *The Best Answer Ever was Made. And to which no Answer Ever will be Made.* London, 1709.

[————] *The Bishop of Salisbury's Proper Defence, from a Speech Cry'd about the Streets in his Name, and Said to have been Spoken by him in the House of Lords, upon the Bill Against Occasional Conformity.* London, 1704.

L'Estrange, Roger. *Tully's Offices* . . . *Turned out of Latin into English.* Second edition; London, 1681 (first published in 1680).

Lloyd, David. *Memoires of the Lives, Actions, Sufferings & Deaths of those Noble, Reverend, and Excellent Personages, That Suffered* . . . *for the Protestant Religion, And the great Principle thereof, Allegiance To their Soveraigne, In our late Intestine Wars.* . . . London, 1668.

[————] *The Worthies of the World: or, The Lives Of the most Heroick Greeks and Romans Compared, By* . . . *Plutarch* . . . *Englished and Abridged* . . . *To which are added More Lives* . . . *By several Hands.* London, 1665.

Locke, John. *Some Thoughts Concerning Education.* Edited by R. H. Quick. Cambridge, 1902.

The London Journal, No. 938, Saturday, July 9, 1737.

The London Magazine: or, Gentleman's Monthly Intelligencer. 1732————.

Longinus. *On Literary Excellence.* In Allan H. Gilbert, *Literary Criticism: Plato to Dryden.* New York [1940].

Lucian. *The Works of Lucian of Samosata.* Translated by H. W. Fowler and F. G. Fowler. Oxford, 1905. Four volumes.

Lucretius. *De Rerum Natura.* Translated by W. H. D. Rouse. Loeb Classical Library.

McCutcheon, Roger Philip. "The Beginnings of Book-Reviewing in English Periodicals," *PMLA*, XXXVII (1922), 691-706.

Macdonald, Hugh. "Banter in English Controversial Prose after the Restoration," *Essays and Studies by Members of the English Association*, Vol. XXXII, 1946.

———— *John Dryden: A Bibliography of Early Editions and of Drydeniana.* Oxford, 1939.

McGrew, J. Fred. "A Bibliography of the Works on Speech Composition in England during the Sixteenth and Seventeenth Centuries," *Quarterly Journal of Speech*, XV (1929), 381-412.

Manningham, John. *Diary of John Manningham...1602-1603.* Edited by John Bruce. Westminster, 1868. (Camden Society, No. 99.)

Marbeck, John. *A Booke of Notes and Common places, with their expositions, collected and gathered out of the workes of divers singular Writers....* London, 1581.

Marshall, Stephen. *Emanuel; a thanksgiving sermon before the house of commons, upon the victory of the parliamentary forces in South Wales.* London, 1648.

Martin, Benjamin. *Bibliotheca Technologica: or, a Philological Library of Literary Arts and Sciences.* London, 1737.

———— *Lingua Britannica Reformata. A New Universal English Dictionary.* London, 1749.

[Marvell, Andrew.] *Mr. Smirke: or, the Divine in Mode: being Certain Annotations, upon the Animadversions on the Naked Truth. By Andreas Rivetus, Junior.* 1676.

[————] *The Rehearsal Transpros'd: or, Animadversions Upon a late Book, entituled, A Preface, Shewing What Grounds there are of Fears and Jealousies of Popery.* London, 1672.

Mason, John E. *Gentlefolk in the Making: Studies in the History of English Courtesy Literature and Related Topics from 1531 to 1774.* Philadelphia, 1935.

Mayne, Jasper. *Part of Lucian Made English from the Originall. In the Yeare 1638.* Oxford, 1663.

Memoirs of the Society of Grub-street. London, 1737. Two volumes.

Meres, Francis. *Palladis Tamia, Wits Treasury.* 1598. In G. Gregory Smith, *Elizabethan Critical Essays*, Vol. II. Oxford, 1904.

Middleton, Thomas, and William Rowley. *A Courtly Masque: The Device called, The World tost at Tennis.* [1620.]

Milton, John. *Works.* New York, 1931-40. Twenty volumes.

Mitchell, W. Fraser. *English Pulpit Oratory from Andrewes to Tillotson.* London, 1932.

The Monthly Review. 1749——.

More, Henry. *A Modest Enquiry into the Mystery of Iniquity, The First Part, Containing A Careful and Impartial Delineation of the True Idea of Antichristianism.* London, 1664.

More, Thomas. *The Apologye of Syr Thomas More, Knyght.* Edited by Arthur Irving Taft. London, 1930. (Early English Text Society, Orig. Ser. No. 180.)

—— Epistle Dedicatory to his translations of Lucian, translated by C. R. Thompson, *The Translations of Lucian by Erasmus and St. Thomas More.* Ithaca, 1940.

—— *Works.* London, 1557.

[Morris, Corbyn.] *An Essay Towards Fixing the True Standards of Wit, Humour, Raillery, Satire, and Ridicule.* London, 1744. (Augustan Reprint Society, Ser. 1, Essays on Wit No. 4, 1947.)

Moryson, Fynes. *An Itinerary Written By Fynes Moryson Gent.* London, 1617.

Moyle, Walter. "A Dissertation Upon the Age of the Philopatris, A Dialogue, Commonly Attributed to Lucian: In several Letters to Mr. K---." In *The Works of Walter Moyle, Esq.*, Vol. I. London, 1726.

Muses Library; Or a Series of English Poetry..., *The.* [Mrs. Elizabeth Cooper.] Vol. I. London, 1737.

Nashe, Thomas. "To the Gentleman Students of Both Universities." In G. Gregory Smith, *Elizabethan Critical Essays*, Vol. I. Oxford, 1904.

—— *Works.* Edited by Ronald B. McKerrow. London, 1904-10. Five volumes.

Ness, Christopher. *A Compleat History and Mystery of the Old and New Testament, Logically Discust and Theologically Improved.* London, 1696. Four volumes.

Nicholls, William. *An Answer to an Heretical Book Called the Naked Gospel....* London, 1691.

North, Roger. *Examen: or, an Enquiry into the Credit and Veracity of a Pretended Complete History....* London, 1740.

North, Thomas, trans. *The Lives of the Noble Grecians and Romanes, compared together by that Grave Learned Philosopher and Historiographer, Plutarke....* London, 1595 (first published in 1579).

Oldham, John. *The Works ... Together with his Remains.* London, 1686.

Oldmixon, John. *The Arts of Logick and Rhetorick ... Interpreted and Explain'd By that Learned and Judicious Critick, Father Bouhours. To which are added, Parallel Quotations Out of the Most Eminent English Authors....* London, 1728.

Orrery, John Boyle, Earl of. *Remarks on the Life and Writings of Dr. Jonathan Swift ... In a Series of Letters....* London, 1752.

Otway, Thomas. *Complete Works.* Edited by Montague Summers. Vol. I. Bloomsbury (Nonesuch Press), 1926.

Overbury, Thomas. *The Overburian Characters.* Edited by W. J. Paylor. Oxford, 1936. (The Percy Reprints XIII.)

Ozell, John, trans. *Don Quixote.* New York [n.d]. (Modern Library.)

Patrick, Simon. *A Commentary upon the Historical Books of the Old Testament.* Third edition; London, 1727. Two volumes.

———— *A Friendly Debate between a Conformist and a Non-Conformist.* Third edition; London, 1669.

P[eacham], H[enry]. *The Garden of Eloquence, conteining the most excellent Ornaments, Exornations, Lightes, flowers, and formes of speech, commonly called the Figures of Rhetorike. Corrected and augmented by the first Author.* London, 1593.

———— "Of Poetrie" from *The Compleat Gentleman.* 1622. In J. E. Spingarn, *Critical Essays of the Seventeenth Century*, Vol. I. Oxford, 1908.

Pell, Daniel. *Nec inter Vivos, nec inter Mortuos, Neither Amongst the living, nor amongst the Dead. Or, An Improvement of the Sea, Upon the Nine Nautical Verses in the 107. Psalm. . . .* London, 1659.

Pepys, Samuel. *Diary.* Edited by Henry B. Wheatley. London, 1899. Nine volumes.

Perceval, Richard. *A Dictionarie in Spanish and English ... Now enlarged and amplified ... All done by John Minsheu....* London, 1599.

———— ————. London, 1623.

Phillips, Edward. *The New World of English Words....* London, 1662.

———— ————. Third edition; London, 1671.

———— ————. Fourth edition; London, 1678.

———— *The New World of Words ... Revised ... By J.*[ohn] *K.*[ersey]. Sixth edition; London, 1706.

———— Preface to *Theatrum Poetarum, or a Compleat Collection of the Poets.* 1675. In J. E. Spingarn, *Critical Essays of the Seventeenth Century,* Vol. II. Oxford, 1908.

Philostratus. *The Life of Appollonius of Tyana.* Translated by F. C. Conybeare. Loeb Classical Library. Two volumes.

Philpott, John. *A \Defence of the true and old authority of Christ's Church. An Oration of Coelius, the second Curio, for the true and ancient authority of Christ his Church, against Antony Florebell of Mutiny. . . . Translated out of Latin into English.* In *The Examinations and Writings of John Philpot, B. C. L. Archdeacon of Winchester: Martyr, 1555.* Edited by the Rev. Robert Eden. Cambridge, 1842. (Parker Society.)

Pilkington, Letitia. *Memoirs . . . Written by Herself. . . .* Vols. I & II; Dublin, 1749. Vol. III; Dublin, 1754.

Plato. *Apology.* Translated by H. N. Fowler. Loeb Classical Library.

———— *Cratylus.* Translated by H. N. Fowler. Loeb Classical Library.

———— *Euthydemus.* Translated by W. R. M. Lamb. Loeb Classical Library.

———— *Gorgias.* Translated by W. R. M. Lamb. Loeb Classical Library.

———— *Laws.* Translated by R. G. Bury. Loeb Classical Library.

———— *The Lovers.* Translated by W. R. M. Lamb. Loeb Classical Library.

———— *The Republic.* Translated by Paul Shorey. Loeb Classical Library.

———— *The Sophist.* Translated by H. N. Fowler. Loeb Classical Library.

———— *Symposium.* Translated by W. R. M. Lamb. Loeb Classical Library.

Plato his Apology of Socrates, and Phaedo or Dialogue concerning the Immortality of Mans Soul, and Manner of Socrates his Death: Carefully translated from the Greek. London, 1675.

Plutarch. *Plutarch's Lives.* Translated by Bernadotte Perrin. Loeb Classical Library. Eleven volumes.

———— *Plutarch's Moralia.* Translated by Frank Cole Babbitt. Loeb Classical Library. Fourteen volumes.

Plutarch's Morals: Translated from the Greek by Several Hands. London, 1691 (first published in 1683-84?). Five volumes.

A Pocket Dictionary or Complete English Expositor. . . . London, 1753.

Poole, Joshua. *The English Parnassus: or, A Helpe to English Poesie. . . .* London, 1657.

Pope, Alexander. *Complete Poetical Works*. Edited by Henry W. Boynton. Boston and New York, 1903.

───── *The Dunciad*. Edited by James Sutherland. London, 1943.

───── *The Iliad of Homer*. London, 1756. Six volumes.

───── *Martinus Scriblerus, Peri Bathous: or, Of the Art of Sinking in Poetry. Written in the Year 1727*. In *The Works of Alexander Pope*, Vol. VI. London, 1751.

───── *Memoirs Of the Extraordinary Life, Works, and Discoveries of Martinus Scriblerus*. In *The Works of Alexander Pope*, Vol. VI. London, 1751.

───── *Miscellanies in Prose and Verse*. London, 1728. Three volumes.

───── *The Odyssey of Homer*. London, 1725-26. Five volumes.

───── *Prose Works*. Edited by Norman Ault. Vol. I. Oxford, 1936.

───── *Works*. Edited by Whitwell Elwin and William John Courthope. London, 1871-89. Ten volumes.

───── *The Works of Shakespeare*. Second edition; London, 1728. Eight volumes.

Potter, John. *Archaeologia Graeca, or the Antiquities of Greece ... A New Edition. To which is added, An Appendix, containing A Concise History of the Grecian States, And a Short Account of the Lives and Writings of the Most Celebrated Greek Authors. By G. Dunbar. ...* Edinburgh, 1818. Two volumes.

Prideaux, John. *Sacred Eloquence: Or, the Art of Rhetorick, As it is layd down in Scripture*. London, 1659.

The Prompter. November 12, 1734—July 2, 1736.

The Publick Register: or, the Weekly Magazine. January 3, 1741—June 13, 1741.

P.[ulteney], J. *A Treatise of the Loftiness or Elegancy of Speech. Written Originally in Greek by Longin; and now Translated out of French. ...* London, 1680.

Purchas, Samuel. *Purchas his Pilgrimage. ...* Second edition; London, 1614.

Puttenham, George. *The Arte of English Poesie*. Edited by Gladys Doidge Willcock and Alice Walker. Cambridge, 1936.

Quintilian. *Institutio oratoria*. Translated by H. E. Butler. Loeb Classical Library. Four volumes.

Raillerie a la Mode Consider'd: or the Supercilious Detractor. A Jocoserious Discourse; shewing the open Impertinence and Degenerosity of Publishing Private Pecques and Controversies to the World. London, 1673.

Ramsay, Allan. Preface to the *Ever Green*. 1724. In W. H. Durham, *Critical Essays of the Eighteenth Century 1700-1725*. New Haven, 1915.

Ramsay, Allan (the younger). *An Essay on Ridicule*. London, 1753. In *The Investigator*. London, 1762.

[Rapin, René.] *The Comparison of Plato and Aristotle . . . Translated from the French*. London, 1673.

——— *Reflections upon the Eloquence of these times; Particularly of the Barr and Pulpit*. London, 1672.

Remarks upon Remarques: or, A Vindication of the Conversations of the Town, In another Letter directed to the same Sir T. L. London, 1673.

Remarques on the Humours and Conversations of the Town. Written in a Letter to Sr. T. L. London, 1673.

Reyner, Edward. *Rules for the Government of the Tongue*. . . . Third edition; London, 1658 (first published in 1656).

Reynolds, Henry. *Mythomystes*. [1633?] In J. E. Spingarn, *Critical Essays of the Seventeenth Century*, Vol. I. Oxford, 1908.

Robertson, Jean. *The Art of Letter Writing. An Essay on the Handbooks Published in England during the Sixteenth and Seventeenth Centuries*. Liverpool, 1942.

Rogers, John. *A Discourse of the Visible and Invisible Church of Christ*. London, 1719.

——— *The Necessity of Divine Revelation, and the Truth of the Christian Revelation Asserted; in Eight Sermons*. Second edition; London, 1729.

——— *Twelve Sermons, Preached upon Several Occasions*. London, 1730.

——— *A Vindication of the Civil Establishment of Religion . . . With an Appendix containing a Letter from the Reverend Dr. Marshal*. . . . London, 1728.

Rollin, Charles. *The Method of Teaching and Studying the Belles Lettres . . . Translated from the French*. Fourth edition; London, 1749. Four volumes.

Rollins, Hyder E. *An Analytical Index to the Ballad-Entries (1557-1709) in the registers of the Company of Stationers of London*. Chapel Hill, N. C., 1924.

The Roman Antiquities of Dionysius of Halicarnassus. Translated by Earnest Cary. Loeb Classical Library. Seven volumes.

Samuel, Irene. *Plato and Milton*. Ithaca, 1947.

Sandford, William Phillips. *English Theories of Public Address, 1530-1828*. Columbus, Ohio, 1931.

[Sandys, George.] *A Relation of a Journey begun An. Dom: 1610.* Fifth edition; London, 1615.

Sedgewick, G. G. "Dramatic Irony: Studies in its History, its Definition, and its Use Especially in Shakespere and Sophocles." Unpublished Ph.D. thesis, Harvard University, 1913.

―――― *Of Irony Especially in Drama.* Toronto, 1948.

Select Letters taken from Fog's Weekly Journal. Vol. I. London, 1732.

S.[ergeant], J.[ohn]. *Raillery Defeated by Calm Reason: or, the New Cartesian Method of Arguing and Answering Expos'd. In a Letter to all Lovers of Science, Candour and Civility.* London, 1699.

―――― *Reason against Raillery: or, A Full Answer to Dr. Tillotson's Preface Against J. S.* 1682.

Shadwell, Thomas. Preface to *The Humorists, A Comedy.* 1671. In J. E. Spingarn, *Critical Essays of the Seventeenth Century,* Vol. II. Oxford, 1908.

―――― Preface to *The Sullen Lovers, or The Impertinents, A Comedy.* 1668. In J. E. Spingarn, *Critical Essays of the Seventeenth Century,* Vol. II. Oxford, 1908.

Shaftesbury, Anthony Ashley Cooper, Third Earl of. *Characteristics of Men, Manners, Opinions, Times.* Second edition; 1714. Three volumes.

―――― *Characteristics of Men, Manners, Opinions, Times, etc.* Edited by John M. Robertson. New York, 1900. Two volumes.

―――― *The Life, Unpublished Letters, and Philosophical Regimen.* Edited by Benjamin Rand. London and New York, 1900.

―――― *Second Characters or The Language of Forms.* Edited by Benjamin Rand. Cambridge, 1914.

Shakespeare, William. *Works.* Edited by W. A. Wright. London, 1891. Nine volumes.

Sheffield, John, Earl of Mulgrave and Duke of Buckingham. "An Essay upon Poetry." 1682. In J. E. Spingarn, *Critical Essays of the Seventeenth Century,* Vol. II. Oxford, 1908.

―――― "An Essay upon Satyr." In *Poems on Affairs of State: from the time of Oliver Cromwell, to the Abdication of K. James the Second,* pp. 187-97. 1697.

Sherry, Richard. *A Treatise of the Figures of Grammer and Rhetorike....* [1555.]

Shortest-Way with the Dissenters ... With its Author's Brief Explication Consider'd; His Name Expos'd, His Practices Detected, and his Hellish Designs set in a true Light.... Second edition; London, 1703.

Sidney, Philip. *An Apology for Poetry.* 1595. In G. Gregory Smith, *Elizabethan Critical Essays,* Vol. I. Oxford, 1904.

Skeat, Walter W. *A Concise Etymological Dictionary of the English Language.* New York, 1882.

Smart, Christopher. *The Hilliad.* 1752. In *The Works of the English Poets,* Vol. XVI. Edited by Alexander Chalmers. London, 1810.

[————] *The Midwife, or the Old Woman's Magazine.* London, 1751-53. Three volumes.

Smectymnuus. *A Vindication of the Answer to the Humble Remonstrance, from the Unjust Imputations of Frivolousnesse and Falsehood....* London, 1641.

Smith, David Nichol, editor. *Characters from the Histories & Memoirs of the Seventeenth Century.* Oxford, 1918.

Smith, Edmund. "A Poem to the Memory of Mr. John Philips." In *The Works of the English Poets,* Vol. IX, pp. 204-6. Edited by Alexander Chalmers. London, 1810.

Smith, John. *The Mysterie of Rhetorique Unvail'd, Wherein above 130 The Tropes and Figures are severally derived from the Greek into English....* London, 1657.

Smith, William. *Dionysius Longinus on the Sublime: Translated from the Greek....* Second edition; London, 1743 (first published in 1739).

Smollett, Tobias, trans. *Don Quixote.* London, 1755. Two volumes.
———— *Peregrine Pickle.* Oxford, 1925. Four volumes.

Somers Tracts. *A Collection of Scarce and Valuable Tracts, on the most Interesting and Entertaining Subjects....* Vol. I. London, 1748.

Somervile, William. *The Chace. To which is added, Hobbinol....* Fourth edition; London, 1749.

[South, Robert.] *Animadversions upon Dr. Sherlock's Book, Entituled A Vindication of the Holy and Ever-Blessed Trinity, &c....* Second edition; London, 1693.

The Spectator. Edited by G. Gregory Smith. Everyman's Library. Four volumes.

Spence, Ferrand. *Lucian's Works, Translated From the Greek. To Which is Prefixt, The Life of Lucian.* London, 1684-85. Five volumes.

Spenser, Edmund. *Minor Poems.* Edited by Ernest de Selincourt. Oxford, 1910.

Sprat, Thomas. *An Account of the Life and Writings of Mr. Abraham Cowley: Written to Mr. M. Clifford.* 1668. In J. E. Spingarn, *Critical Essays of the Seventeenth Century,* Vol. II. Oxford, 1908.

———— *The History of the Royal-Society of London, For the Improving of Natural Knowledge.* London, 1667.

Spurgeon, C. H. *The Treasury of David: containing an original exposition of the book of Psalms; a collection of illustrative extracts from the whole range of literature....* Vol. II. New York, 1885.

Stanley, Thomas. *The History of Philosophy.* London, 1655-62.

Stanyhurst, Richard. Dedication of *Thee First Foure Bookes of Virgil his Aeneis translated in too English Heroical Verse.* 1582. In G. Gregory Smith, *Elizabethan Critical Essays,* Vol. I. Oxford, 1904.

Steele, Richard. *Correspondence.* Edited by Rae Blanchard. Oxford, 1941.

Stephens, John. *Essayes and Characters Ironicall, and Instructive. The second impression. With a new Satyre in defence of Common Law and Lawyers: Mixt with reproofe against their common Enemy. With many new Characters, & divers other things added; & every thing amended....* London, 1615.

———— *Satyrical Essayes Characters and Others. Or Accurate and quick Descriptions, fitted to the life of their Subjects.* London, 1615.

Stevens, George Alexander. *Distress upon Distress: or, Tragedy in True Taste. A Heroi-Comi-Parodi-Tragedi-Farcical Burlesque. In Two Acts.* London, 1752.

———— *Songs, Comic and Satyrical. A New Edition, Corrected. With the New Edition of the Lecture upon Heads.* London, 1788.

Stillingfleet, Benjamin. *An Essay on Conversation.* Second edition; London, 1738.

Stillingfleet, Edward. *Works.* London, 1709. Six volumes.

———— *Works.* Vol. I. London, 1710.

Stocker, Thomas, trans. *A Righte noble and pleasant History of the Successors of Alexander surnamed the Great, taken out of Diodorus Siculus: and some of their lives written by the wise Plutarch. Translated out of French into Englysh.* London, 1569.

Sweeting, Elizabeth J. *Early Tudor Criticism Linguistic & Literary.* Oxford, 1940.

Swift, Deane. *An Essay upon the Life, Writings, and Character, of Dr. Jonathan Swift.* London, 1755.

Swift, Jonathan. *Correspondence.* Edited by F. Elrington Ball. London, 1910-14. Six volumes.

———— *The Examiner and Other Pieces Written in 1710-11.* Edited by Herbert Davis. Oxford, 1940.

———— *Journal to Stella.* Edited by Harold Williams. Oxford, 1948. Two volumes.

———— *Letters to Charles Ford.* Edited by David Nichol Smith. Oxford, 1935.

———— *Poems*. Edited by Harold Williams. Oxford, 1937. Three volumes.

———— *Prose Works*. Edited by Temple Scott. London, 1897-1908. Twelve volumes.

———— *A Tale of A Tub with Other Early Works 1696-1707*. Edited by Herbert Davis. Oxford, 1939.

The Tatler. Edited by George A. Aitken. London, 1898. Four volumes.

Taylor, Warren. *Tudor Figures of Rhetoric*. Chicago, 1937.

Temple, William. *An Essay upon the Ancient and Modern Learning*. 1690. In J. E. Spingarn, *Critical Essays of the Seventeenth Century*, Vol. III. Oxford, 1909.

———— "Of Poetry." 1690. In J. E. Spingarn, *Critical Essays of the Seventeenth Century*, Vol. III. Oxford, 1909.

Theobald, Lewis, trans. *The Clouds. A Comedy. Translated from the Greek of Aristophanes*. London, 1715.

Theophrastus. *The Characters of Theophrastus*. Translated by J. M. Edmonds. Loeb Classical Library.

Thompson, Alan Reynolds. *The Dry Mock: A Study of Irony in Drama*. Berkeley & Los Angeles, 1948.

Thompson, C. R. "Lucian and Lucianism in the English Renaissance." Unpublished Ph.D. thesis, Princeton University, 1937.

———— *The Translations of Lucian by Erasmus and St. Thomas More*. Ithaca, 1940.

Thompson, Elbert N. S. *The Controversy between the Puritans and the Stage*. New York, 1903.

———— *Literary Bypaths of the Renaissance*. New Haven, 1924.

Thomson, J. A. K. "Erasmus in England." In *Vorträge der Bibliothek Warburg*. London (London University, Warburg Institute), 1930-31.

———— *Irony: An Historical Introduction*. Cambridge, Mass., 1927.

Thordynary of Crysten men. (Wynken de Worde), 1506.

Thornton, Bonnell. *Have At You All: or, the Drury-Lane Journal. By Madam Roxana Termagant*. London, 1752.

Topsell, Edward. *The Historie of Foure-Footed Beastes . . . Collected out of all the Volumes of Conradus Gesner, and all other Writers to this present day*. London, 1607.

Trissino, Giangiorgio. *Poetica*. Selections in Allan H. Gilbert, *Literary Criticism Plato to Dryden*. New York [1940].

A True History, Translated from the Greek. London, 1744.

Turner, F. McD. C. *The Element of Irony in English Literature*. Cambridge, 1926.

Tuve, Rosemond. *Elizabethan and Metaphysical Imagery: Renaissance Poetic and Twentieth-century Critics.* Chicago, 1947.

Ustick, W. Lee. "Changing Ideals of Aristocratic Character and Conduct in Seventeenth-Century England," *Modern Philology,* XXX (1932-33), 147-66.

Vanbrugh, John. *A Short Vindication of the Relapse and the Provok'd Wife, from Immorality and Prophaneness.* In *The Complete Works of Sir John Vanbrugh,* Vol. I. Edited by Bonamy Dobrée. London, 1927.
The Vanity of Scoffing: or a Letter to a Witty Gentleman, Evidently Shewing the Great Weakness and Unreasonableness of Scoffing at the Christian's Faith, on account of its supposed uncertainty. [Clement Ellis and John Fell?] London, 1674.
Vega, Lope de. *The New Art of Making Comedies.* In Allan H. Gilbert, *Literary Criticism Plato to Dryden.* New York [1940].
Vives, Juan Luis. *Vives: On Education: A Translation of the De Tradendis Disciplinis.* Translated by Foster Watson. Cambridge, 1913.

[Walker, Obadiah.] *Some Instructions concerning the Art of Oratory.* London, 1659.
———— Περιαμμα ἐπιδημιον: *Or, Vulgar Errours in Practice Censured.* London, 1659.
Ward, Edward. *The Life and Notable Adventures of that Renown'd Knight, Don Quixote De la Mancha. Merrily Translated into Hudibrastick Verse.* London, 1711.
[Ward, Tom.] *England's Reformation.* [*no title page.*]
Warner, William. *Albions England.* London, 1612.
Warton, Joseph. *The Adventurer,* Nos. 127, 133. (Augustan Reprint Society, Ser. 1, Essays on Wit No. 2, 1946.)
———— *An Essay on the Genius and Writings of Pope.* Fifth edition; London, 1806. Two volumes.
Webbe, William. *A Discourse of English Poetrie.* 1586. In G. Gregory Smith, *Elizabethan Critical Essays,* Vol. I. Oxford, 1904.
Welsted, Leonard. *A Dissertation Concerning the Perfection of the English Language, the State of Poetry, etc.* 1724. In W. H. Durham, *Critical Essays of the Eighteenth Century 1700-1725.* New Haven, 1915.
————, trans. *A Treatise on the Sublime. By Dionysius Longinus. Translated from the Greek.* Third edition; Dublin, 1727 (first published in 1712).

Wesley, Samuel. *An Epistle to a Friend Concerning Poetry.* London, 1700. (Augustan Reprint Society, Ser. 2, Essays on Poetry No. 2, 1947.)

Whately, William. *Prototypes.* . . . London, 1640.

Whitehead, William. "On Ridicule." 1743. In *The Works of the English Poets,* Vol. XVII. Edited by Alexander Chalmers. London, 1810.

Whytinton, Roberte, trans. *The thre bookes of Tullyes offyces bothe in latyne tonge & in englysshe lately translated by Roberte Whytinton poete laureate.* London (Wynkyn de Worde), 1534.

Wilkins, John. *Ecclesiastes, or, A Discourse concerning the Gift of Preaching as it fals under the rules of Art.* London, 1646.

Willet, Andrew. *Hexapla in Exodum.* . . . London, 1633 (first published in 1608).

———— *Hexapla in Genesin.* . . . London, 1608 (first published in 1605).

[Williams, John.] *Pulpit-Popery, True Popery: Being an Answer To a Book Intituled, Pulpit-Sayings: and in Vindication of the Apology for the Pulpits.* . . . London, 1688.

Williamson, George. *The Senecan Amble: A Study in Prose Form from Bacon to Collier.* London, 1951.

Wilmot, John, Earl of Rochester. *An Allusion to the Tenth Satyr of the First Book of Horace.* 1685. In J. E. Spingarn, *Critical Essays of the Seventeenth Century,* Vol. II. Oxford, 1908.

Wilson, H. S. "Gabriel Harvey's Orations on Rhetoric," *English Literary History,* XII (1945), 167-82.

Wilson, Thomas, trans. *The three Orations of Demosthenes chiefe Orator among the Grecians, in favour of the Olynthians, . . . with those his fower Orations . . . against king Philip of Macedonie.* . . . *Englished out of the Greeke by Thomas Wylson.* . . . London, 1570.

———— *Wilson's Arte of Rhetorique 1560.* Edited by G. H. Mair. Oxford, 1909. (Tudor and Stuart Library.)

Wolseley, Robert. Preface to *Valentinian, A Tragedy, As 'Tis Alter'd by the Late Earl of Rochester.* 1685. In J. E. Spingarn, *Critical Essays of the Seventeenth Century,* Vol. III. Oxford, 1909.

Wood, Anthony. *Life and Times.* Collected by Andrew Clark. Vol. II; 1664-1681. Oxford, 1892.

Worcester, David. *The Art of Satire.* Cambridge, Mass., 1940.

The World. In *The British Essayists,* Vols. XXVI-XXIX. Edited by Alexander Chalmers. London, 1817.

W.[orsley], E.[dward]. *A Discourse of Miracles Wrought in the Roman Catholick Church, or, A full refutation of Dr Stillingfleets unjust exceptions against Miracles.* . . . Antwerp, 1676.

Wotton, William. *A Defense of the Reflections upon Ancient and Modern Learning* ... *With Observations upon The Tale of a Tub.* London, 1705.

———— *Reflections upon Ancient and Modern Learning. The Second Edition* ... *With a Dissertation upon the Epistles of Phalaris, Themistocles, Socrates, Euripides; &c. and Aesop's Fables. By Dr. Bentley.* London, 1697.

[Wylkinson, John]. *The Ethiques of Aristotle* ... *now newly trãslated into English.* London, 1547.

INDEX